OCR GCSE History B

Modern World

Rachel Jones with Alex Brodkin
Ellen Carrington   Andrew Hill

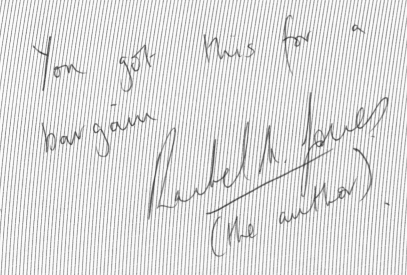

You got this for a bargain

Rachel A. Jones
(the author)

www.heinemann.co.uk
✓ Free online support
✓ Useful weblinks
✓ 24 hour online ordering

01865 888080

OCR
RECOGNISING ACHIEVEMENT

Heinemann

OCR AND HEINEMANN ARE WORKING TOGETHER TO PROVIDE BETTER SUPPORT FOR YOU

Official Publisher Partnership

Heinemann is an imprint of Pearson Education Limited, a company incorporated in England and Wales, having its registered office at Edinburgh Gate, Harlow, Essex, CM20 2JE. Registered company number: 872828

www.heinemann.co.uk

Heinemann is a registered trademark of Pearson Education Limited

Text © Pearson Education Limited 2009

First published 2009

13 12 11 10 09
10 9 8 7 6 5 4 3 2 1

British Library Cataloguing in Publication Data
A catalogue record for this book is available from the British Library

ISBN 978 0 435 510 20 6

Edited by Robin Haig
Proofread by Janice Baiton
Designed by Pearson Education Limited
Project managed and typeset by Wearset Ltd, Boldon, Tyne and Wear
Produced by Wearset Ltd, Boldon, Tyne and Wear
Original illustrations © Pearson Education 2009
Illustrated by Tek-Art, Crawley Down, West Sussex
Cover design by Pearson Education Limited
Picture research by Q2AMedia
Cover photo/illustration © Getty Images/US Air Force
Printed in the UK by Ashford Colour Press Ltd

Acknowledgements
The authors and publisher would like to thank the following individuals and organisations for permission to reproduce copyright material in the book:

p50 Tom Paxton. **p74** Tom Paxton. **p141 MR** Women Go to Work. 1920's Lifestyles and Social Trends. Gale Cengage, 1996. eNotes.com. 2006. 14 Apr, 2009.

The authors and publisher would like to thank the following individuals and organisations for permission to reproduce photographs in the book:

p20 Punch Ltd. **p25** David Low/Evening Standard on 18 February 1938/British Cartoon Archive. **p70** Khalil Bendib/Blackcommentator. **p102L** Private Collection/Archives Charmet/The Bridgeman Art Library. **p102R** Galerie Bilderwelt/Contributor/Hulton Archive/Getty Images. **p118** Mary Evans Picture Library. **p163** Kealey, E.P. (20th century)/Private Collection/Photo © Bonhams, London, UK/The Bridgeman Art Library. **p191** William Papas/The *Guardian* on 3 March 1965/British Cartoon Archive.

The authors and publisher would like to thank the following individuals and organisations for permission to reproduce photographs on the CD-ROM:

p61 David Low/Evening Standard on 5 June 1947/British Cartoon Archive. **p62** Illingworth, Leslie Gilbert/National Library of Wales, Aberystwyth/22 October 1952/British Cartoon Archive. **p101** Fotolibra.

Every effort has been made to contact copyright holders of material reproduced in this book. Any omissions will be rectified in subsequent printings if notice is given to the publishers.

Websites
There are links to relevant websites in this book. In order to ensure that the links are up to date, that the links work, and that the sites are not inadvertently linked to sites that could be considered offensive, we have made the links available on the Heinemann website at www.heinemann.co.uk/hotlinks. When you access the site, the express code is 0206T.

Contents

Introduction   iv

**Aspects of International Relations
1919–2005**

1   The inter-war years, 1919–39
Teacher notes   1–9
Worksheets   10–25
Grade Studio   26–28

2   The Cold War, 1945–75
Teacher notes   29–37
Worksheets   38–50
Grade Studio   51–56

3   A new world? 1948–2005
Teacher notes   57–63
Worksheets   64–76
Grade Studio   77–79

Studies in Depth
4   Germany, 1918–45
Teacher notes   80–89
Worksheets   90–107
Grade Studio   108–110

5   Russia, 1905–41
Teacher notes   111–116
Worksheets   117–123
Grade Studio   124–128

6   The USA, 1919–41
Teacher notes   129–135
Worksheets   136–143
Grade Studio   144–149

British Depth Study
**7   How was British society changed,
1890–1918?**
Teacher notes   150–155
Worksheets   156–167
Grade Studio   168–169

**8   How far did British society change
between 1939 and the mid-1970s?**
Teacher notes   170–177
Worksheets   178–200
Grade Studio   201

CD-ROM
Studies In Depth
1   Mao's China, c.1930–76
Teacher notes   1–8
Worksheets   9–24
Grade Studio   25–26

**5   Causes and events of the First World
War, 1890–1918**
Teacher notes   27–33
Worksheets   34–44
Grade Studio   45–48

3   End of Empire, 1919–69
Teacher notes   49–56
Worksheets   57–62
Grade Studio   63

4   The USA, 1945–75: Land of freedom?
Teacher notes   64–70
Worksheets   71–88
Grade Studio   89–91

5   Exam Café
Teacher notes   92–98
Worksheets   99–111
Lesson plans   112–116

Introduction

OCR GCSE B Modern World History is endorsed by OCR for use with the new OCR GCSE B MW specification. The course includes a Modern World History student book with ActiveBook, a Modern World History Teacher Guide and an ActiveTeach CD-ROM.

The student book

The OCR GCSE B Modern World History student book is divided into lessons. Each lesson has objectives related to the specification content and often a 'Getting Started' activity to grab students' attention straight away and continue the good practise from Key Stage 3 lessons. Throughout the chapter there are also activities that can be completed in the lesson and *Grade Studio* material.

Grade Studio is a clear and explicit focus on levels, the content becomes focussed on moving between levels and therefore the learning becomes increasingly personalised and improves students chances of achieving better grades. Grade Studio offers clears advice to help students improve their performance in exams by supporting students in developing the skills that they are required to demonstrate in Unit A971. Grade Studio is integrated throughout the student book and there are also interactive activities on the CD-ROM.

Exam Café is to be used by students when revising and preparing for exams. Exam Café is designed for use at the end of blocks of learning, it could be a tool for revision classes after school or used in revision lessons when the specification content has been delivered before examinations begin.

Exam Café helps prepare students for the final examination. Exam Café is in the student book with additional resources on the CD-ROM and guidance in the Teacher Guide. By providing students with a copy of the Exam Café CD-ROM, they will be able to access a number of useful resources which will help them organise their revision, practise exam questions, access sample mark schemes and locate extra resources to help stretch themselves. It may be advisable to spend a small amount of class time familiarising students with this resource.

The teacher guide

The OCR GCSE B Modern World History teacher guide supports the student book providing teacher notes and lesson plans to match the OCR GCSE B Modern World History specification and follow the structure of the student book. Worksheets are provided and they can be adapted by you for use in your classroom by editing the customisable worksheets on the accompanying CD-ROM.

The ActiveTeach CD-ROM

The OCR GCSE B Modern World History ActiveTeach CD-ROM provides the book on screen to be used for whole-class teaching. ActiveTeach allows you to add your own resources into the Resource Bank. The Zoom feature helps to examine sources and focus the class. The CD-ROM also includes interactive activities to be used on the whiteboard to engage your class as well as additional video and audio resources. All of the activities and additional resources are matched to the specification and the activity notes help you to prepare and deliver truly interactive lessons.

The OCR GCSE B Modern World History specification

The new OCR GCSE B Modern World History specification (J417) for first teaching in 2009 contains some key changes but also a large degree of continuity for schools who have taught specification 1937. Here we explain the content and options available for the units which are examined and an explanation of the new controlled assessment requirements.

There are three core International Relations Units, of which students must study one. The three options are:

Core Content: Unit A971 Aspects of International Relations, 1919–2005

- Part 1: The inter-war years, 1919–39

- Part 2: The Cold War, 1945–75

- Part 3: A new world? 1948–2005

There are two final examination papers, and these units are examined as part of Unit A971.

Unit A971 also requires students to answer questions on one chosen Study in Depth . The Study in Depth can be chosen from the following options:

- Depth Study 11   Germany, 1918–45
- Depth Study 12   Russia, 1905–41
- Depth Study 13   The USA, 1919–41
- Depth Study 14   Mao's China, 1930–76
- Depth Study 15   Causes and events of the First World War, 1890–1918
- Depth Study 16   End of Empire, 1939–69
- Depth Study 17   The USA, 1945–75: Land of freedom?

Both the International Relations core unit and the **Chosen Study in Depth** will require students to answer questions based on sources and 4, 6 and 10 mark questions which are entirely based on students own knowledge.

Core Content: Unit A972 British Depth Study

Unit A972 is a depth study of British society with all questions based on source material. The two options are:

- How was British Society changed, 1890–1918?
- How far did British Society change between 1939 and the mid-1970s?

Method of assessment

The assessment objectives are:

AO1   Recall, Select and Communicate
- Recall, select, use and communicate their knowledge and understanding of history.

AO2   Explanation and Analysis
Demonstrate their understanding of the past through explanation and analysis of:

- Key concepts: causation, consequence, continuity, change and significance within an historical context.

- Key features and characteristics of the periods studied and the relationships between them.

AO3   Understanding, Analysis and Evaluation
Understand, analyse and evaluate:

- A range of source material as part of an historical enquiry.

- How aspects of the past have been interpreted and represented in different ways as part of an historical enquiry.

Core Content: Unit A973 Historical Enquiry

OCR will set yearly assessment tasks which are to be completed in controlled conditions in class over a period of approximately 8 hours. OCR suggests that four hours are devoted to gathering information, making notes, planning and preparing, whilst the rest of the time is devoted to writing up the response to the task in 2000 words.

Below is some advice about the Historical Enquiry, or Controlled Assessment unit, and some suggestions for topics which could fit the requirements (topics must not be something that students are studying as part of the examined aspect of the course). There are four different options of which one must be selected and given a content specific focus by centres. The four options are:

Option 1. The Role of the Individual in History. 'Candidates will study the role of an individual in twentieth/twenty-first century history.'

Option 2. A Thematic Study in Twentieth Century History. 'Candidates will study a theme, across approximately 40 years of the twentieth/twenty-first centuries. Suitable themes include: warfare, the role of women, technology and the environment.'

Option 3. A Modern World Study. 'Candidates will study a current and major issue that is in the news during the course of study. Suitable issues include international terrorism, events in the Middle East, the environment, events in Iraq and Afghanistan.'

Option 4. A Study in Depth 'Candidates will study a society, or relations between societies/countries, in depth over a period of approximately twenty years. The chosen society should come from within the period 1850–2005.'

Each year, OCR will set new tasks relating to each of these four options. Centres decide on the content specific focus for their students.

On the OCR website (go to www.heinemann.co.uk/hotlinks, insert the express code 0206T, and click on OCR) there is a very detailed breakdown of what these options entail and clear guidance about what is required of students. Below are some of the sample assessment tasks provided by OCR and some suggestions as far as possible content is concerned:

Task 1: The Role of the Individual in History

1 How far has the importance of X been exaggerated?
   Use the sources you have researched, and your knowledge, to support and explain your answer. Your answer must show how aspects of the past have been interpreted and represented in different ways. **[50]**

   Provided students are not taking the Germany Depth Study, a possible version of this question could be:

   How far has the importance of Hitler been exaggerated in explaining the rise of the Nazis? Make sure you support your answer by using a range of sources.

   The rise of the Nazis is a key area of historiographical debate in terms of causation, and therefore this kind of question could be easily resourced with evidence for students to examine.

Task 2: A Thematic Study in Twentieth Century History

2 'X has steadily changed in the period Y.' How far do you agree with this statement?

   Use the sources you have researched, and your knowledge, to support and explain your answer. Your answer must show how aspects of the past have been interpreted and represented in different ways. [50]

   Provided students are not doing the second British Depth Study for Unit A972, a possible question could be:

   'The role of British women steadily changed in the period 1939–79.' How far do you agree with this statement? Make sure you support your answer by using a range of sources.

Task 3: A Modern World Study

3 Explain how important X has been in creating the present situation in Y.

Use the sources you have researched, and your knowledge of Y, to support and explain your answer. Your answer must show how aspects of the past have been interpreted and represented in different ways. **[50]**

Provided students are not taking International Relations Core Unit 3, a possible question could be:

Explain how important errors in American planning prior to and following the invasion of 2003 have been in creating the present situation in Iraq. Make sure you support your answer by using a range of sources.

Task 4: A Study in Depth

4 What was the most important reason why there was conflict between some groups in X during the period Y?

Use the sources you have researched, and your knowledge of X, to support and explain your answer. Your answer must show how aspects of the past have been interpreted and represented in different ways. **[50]**

Again provided students are not taking the second British Depth Study for Unit A972, a possible question could be:

What was the most important reason why there was conflict between some ethnic groups in Britain during the period 1948–72? Make sure you support your answer by using a range of sources.

Short course Controlled Assessment guidance

For the short course, students must complete a Controlled Assessment based on the content of one of the British Depth Studies for Unit A972. The sample assessment tasks from OCR are:

Task 1: How far was British society changed, 1890–1918?

This task tests Assessment Objective 1 (10 marks), 2 (15 marks), 3 (25 marks).

1 'The lives of most British people improved before the First World War but got worse during the war.' How far do you agree with this statement?

Use the sources you have researched, and your knowledge, to support and explain your answer. **[50]**

OR

Task 2: How far did British society change between 1939 and the mid-1970s?

This task tests Assessment Objective 1 (10 marks), 2 (15 marks), 3 (25 marks).

2 'In Britain between 1939 and the mid-1970s the lives of women improved more quickly than the lives of immigrants.' How far do you agree with this statement?

Use the sources you have researched, and your knowledge, to support and explain your answer. **[50]**

Mark schemes for these assessment tasks along with a lot more very useful and more detailed information can be found on the OCR website.

Centres are advised to submit their modified versions of the questions to OCR for approval.

Rationale of the OCR GCSE B Modern World History Teacher Guide

The content of the OCR GCSE B Modern World History specification course is divided into key questions, which are then subdivided into focus points. The specification structure provides the structure for the Modern World History student book and Teacher guide . The specification also provides specified content, which is reproduced under each key question. This is not an exhaustive list of everything to do with the topic, but does indicate the main areas which need to be studied.

Within the OCR GCSE B Modern World History Teacher Guide a variety of different teaching strategies are suggested, along with ideas for differentiation. The activities are all designed to closely match the requirements of the key questions and focus points. For each unit, there are ideas for starters and plenaries: all of these can be adapted to other topics and are equally relevant whatever options you select in terms of content. There are also content specific suggestions regarding how to engage student interest in each topic.

There are a number of resources provided for each topic, including worksheets to use in conjunction with the student book, additional sources and writing frames. At the end of each unit there is Grade Studio section which is specifically designed to develop examination techniques and increase students' understanding of what is required of them in the exam and how to improve their performance.

Assessment for learning

There is no replacement for constructive, specific and focussed teacher feedback. However, peer assessment can be a powerful tool for raising attainment and encouraging real assessment for learning. Examiners reports state that every year even highly able students lose large amounts of marks because they misunderstand the requirements of different types of questions. It is therefore essential to share with students the criteria by which their answers to these different types of questions will be judged. Making students familiar with mark schemes from the beginning of the course will make this much easier. Therefore this series provides a number of teacher and student-friendly mark schemes, along with model answers and peer assessment sheets, so that students can become quickly accustomed to evaluating exam answers in order to develop their own ability to meet examination criteria.

This kind of work can be very motivating for students: frustration often arises when students cannot see or understand how to progress, and giving them specific, achievable ways to move up the levels in their answers can be highly encouraging.

Even very low attainers can develop their ability to maximise the number of marks they can achieve, by focussing on things like ensuring they always receive full marks on basic, factual four mark Unit A971 questions.

GradeStudio

How to use the electronic Grade Studio activities

The Grade Studio is a unique resource designed to help improve students' answers and ultimately their grades. Its main features include:

- A **real examiner** will help you to guide your students through sample answers, marks schemes and peer and self assessment.

- An easy to use **Slider** takes the students through the levels of the marks scheme.

- Every question has sample answers for each level so these activities are suitable for **students of all abilities**.

- Each activity and sample answer can be printed out to aid preparation and to be used as you work through the activities front of class.

Available on the ActiveBook CD-ROM:

Write a sample answer

This activity is an opportunity for the student to mark their own work with the examiner's help. They can time themselves typing an answer to the set question. Or they can paste in an answer they have already written to the question. When they have finished writing, they choose the level they think they have achieved from the mark scheme. The examiner helps them to check whether they have reached this level with a series of questions. Finally the student prints out their assessed answer for the teacher to check. The answer they have written can also be saved (though without the self assessment).

This activity would work equally well front of class. You could copy and paste an existing answer into this activity and assess it on the whiteboard with the whole class.

Available on the ActiveTeach CD-ROM:

Choosing a sample answer

This activity gives a range of sample answers for each level of the mark scheme. Your students have an opportunity to pick out the best answer. They receive feedback from the examiner on the strengths and weaknesses for each sample they select.

In this activity the students can clearly see how questions are commonly misinterpreted and marks are easily lost.

Improving a sample answer

This activity is an excellent way to show students of all abilities, how to move answers to the next level in the mark scheme. You choose a level of sample answer to set your class and they will suggest improvements. You can then see how the examiner would improve the answer.

The printout for this activity allows the student to write down their own improvements in the classroom or at home. You can then work through answers on the whiteboard to see how the examiner takes the answer to the next level.

Mark a sample answer

This activity will help you and the students pull apart a sample answer with a highlighting tool. Your students will then mark the strengths and weaknesses of each section by answering a series of questions. At the end of their analysis the students can suggest the level of the sample answer.

This activity gives the students a chance to play at being the examiner and really understand the how the questions are marked.

1 International Relations Part 1: The inter-war years, 1919–39

Introduction

This topic forms the first of the three-part International Relations Core 1919–2005. Students study just **one** of these three parts, and in the exam they **must** choose their questions from just one part. If they answer questions from two different parts, one will not be marked. The content is defined through three broad key questions, developed through more specific focus points. Methodical attention to these questions and focus points should ensure students face no great surprises when they sit the examination.

Much of this supporting material concentrates on strategies to ensure students know how to approach different types of exam question, recognise the skills they are required to demonstrate and understand the best way to deploy their knowledge. The material in this section focuses on the core content, but there are other areas that it is appropriate for higher attainers in particular to study in order to deepen their understanding of the period between the two world wars.

Ideas for starters and plenaries

A FOUR-MARK QUESTION

An example is 'In what ways did the Treaty of Versailles punish Germany?' The mark scheme for this question states that students should be awarded one mark for each relevant point, with an additional mark for supporting detail. Therefore it is clearly beneficial for students to know, for example, that not only was Germany's army limited, but that it was specifically limited to 100,000 men.

Four-mark questions such as this can help to give lower attainers confidence as they can gain full marks without having to demonstrate sophisticated skills of analysis, but this is obviously dependent on acquiring an appropriate level of factual knowledge.

Something students find hard to grasp is why many considered it justified in the 1930s to appease Hitler. They see the Second World War as a black-and-white case of right against wrong,

and do not appreciate that there was actually considerable sympathy among members of the British aristocracy towards the Nazis. *The Remains of the Day* is a 1989 novel by Kazuo Ishiguro, adapted as a film (dir. James Ivory, 1993), which has a subplot concerning the Nazi sympathies of Lord Darlington, who although fictional, bears considerable similarities to genuine historical equivalents such as Lord Londonderry. The following clips from this film can be used as starters to encourage students to understand some contextual arguments used to justify appeasement and to realise that members of the British elite did have unpleasant prejudices and attitudes which also led to sympathy for Hitler:

- British anti-semitic attitudes

- attitudes towards Hitler, his actions and what Britain should do about it (from about 4 minutes into the clip)

- a meeting about what approach the rest of Europe should take towards Germany, held at the home of the (fictional) pro-Nazi Lord Darlington.

Go to www.heinemann.co.uk/hotlinks, insert the express code 0206T, and click on 'Anti-semitism', 'Attitudes to Hitler' and 'Attitudes to Germany'.

These clips should provoke discussion. Ask students to write down a list of all the reasons they hear in these clips to explain British sympathy towards Hitler and the Nazis.

Another interesting way of trying to show the effects of the Treaty of Versailles on German attitudes is the opening of the TV mini-series *Hitler: The Rise of Evil*. This shows what was happening to Hitler during and immediately after the war, and effectively portrays the anger of disaffected soldiers at the surrender and perceived betrayal of the 'November Criminals'. This is especially useful if students are also taking the Germany Depth Study option: go to www.heinemann.co.uk/hotlinks, insert the express code 0206T, and click on 'Rise of evil' (the end of this clip shows the declaration of war) and 'First World War' (this clip begins with Hitler's experiences of the First World War).

Grabbing attention

It is very important during this unit that a sense of connection to the rest of the course is maintained, and to the world-changing events that precede and follow the period. The various international events, incidents and agreements following the First World War involve big questions of morality, retribution, justice and how to run an international community. These questions are engaging for students, and can be tied in with focus points such as whether the peace treaties of 1919–23 were fair, what the motives of various leaders were, whether the League of Nations was doomed to failure, etc.

Students will (hopefully) have considerable prior knowledge of the two world wars from their studies at KS3, and may well be taking the Germany Depth Study option as part of the GCSE course. They should be regularly reminded that everything they study as part of this unit had an impact on the outbreak of the Second World War, and that they should always have in mind the interesting question of whether international relations 1919–39 made the rise of Hitler and subsequent events inevitable.

It is helpful at the start of this unit to focus on the students' knowledge regarding the First World War. Showing pictures of the devastation caused in France and Belgium can lead into a discussion and developing understanding of the possible problems that might occur after peace was declared, and the priorities that the different countries involved in the war might have. In order to fully comprehend, for example, why Clemenceau was much more vehement in his demands at Versailles than Lloyd George, students need the following contextual knowledge.

- The geographical location of the majority of fighting during the First World War.
- The type of fighting that took place, the effects of trench warfare, the damage caused, etc.
- The number of casualties from the countries involved.

STATISTICS

Statistics are often a good attention-grabber: describing the number of families who lost members during the war, or the number of British women who remained single as a result of the massive loss of young men, helps to illustrate very clearly why the British public later put pressure on David Lloyd George to press for a harsh treaty.

LOCAL EXPERIENCE

Looking at local war memorials and working out how many individuals were lost from students' own communities can also provide a shocking example of the suffering caused. Students should, of course, be reminded that this kind of suffering was replicated, sometimes on an even larger scale, in Germany and France.

Activities

It is also highly relevant (although rather difficult, given time constraints) to remind students of the causes of the First World War. This is important because students need to understand why the War Guilt clause in the Treaty of Versailles caused such anger in Germany, given the ambiguity about who was actually to blame for the outbreak of war.

KEY QUESTION 1: WERE THE PEACE TREATIES OF 1919–23 FAIR?

Specified content:

- the peace treaties of 1919–23 (Versailles, St Germain, Trianon, Sevres and Lausanne)
- the roles of individuals including Wilson, Clemenceau and Lloyd George in the peacemaking process
- the impact of the treaties on the defeated countries
- contemporary reactions to, and opinions about, the treaties.

Focus point: What were the motives and aims of the Big Three at Versailles?

Activity 1.1: Opinion line

Give students cards with the following opinions. They should discuss the views here and decide which most closely matches their own. Then they should decide where they stand on an opinion line that runs from appeasement at one end to conflict at the other.

It is the weak man who urges compromise – never the strong man.

Elbert Hubbard

An appeaser is one who feeds a crocodile – hoping it will eat him last.

Winston Churchill

Compromise is but the sacrifice of one right or good in the hope of retaining another – too often ending in the loss of both.

Tryon Edwards

Then judge the opinion of the class as a whole.

Activity 1.2: Versailles role-play

Students are divided into groups of four. They represent France, America, Germany and Britain. Each student is given a character card (see worksheets 1.1 and 1.2) that explains what their priorities are at the end of the First World War. Explain that the students must decide what is to happen to the countries involved, bearing in mind that Germany was the country that surrendered. Students must keep their character cards secret, as all the countries are instructed to ignore anything Germany says.

This task can be differentiated in that students can be given a set of questions to respond to (see worksheet 1.3), or can just come up with what they consider to be an appropriate plan of action from the information they have been given. Higher attainers or the more dramatically inclined could be given additional information on the personalities of the different leaders in order to help them get in character.

Debriefing after this task is important: students should be encouraged to reflect on how the student representing Germany felt during the discussions. This can lead into an explanation of the fact that Germany was not allowed to participate at the Versailles negotiations, and the consequent frustration and anger that Germany felt. Students can then use the character cards together with the information in the student book to fill in a table (worksheet 1.4) about the aims of each leader. In the section headed 'Guiding principles', students should comment generally on the overall attitude and priorities of each leader. In the middle column, they should record any information they can find about what the public in Britain, France and America wanted; and in the final column they should focus on recording as many specific demands as they can for each leader. Students can also be encouraged to record any areas where the leaders were willing to compromise.

Activity 1.3: Understanding what each leader wanted

WHO SAID WHAT?

As a simple way of ensuring that students understand what each leader wanted, and the (sometimes subtle, sometimes obvious) differences in their priorities, students can be given a list of statements, which they then have to match up to the correct leader (worksheet 1.5). The statements are not direct quotations, but are based on the aims and beliefs of each leader at Versailles.

GARGLING

Students then need to examine the actual terms of the treaty. They require specific factual knowledge of these terms: they may well face a four-mark question on the exam paper that asks (in one way or another) what the terms were.

A common way to help remember the terms of the Treaty of Versailles is using the acronym GARGLE. Students can use worksheet 1.6 to add the actual terms to the acronym in as much detail as possible, using page 12 in the student book. The worksheet also provides space for students to record how they think each of the 'Big Three' would feel about the terms, and the reaction they would cause in Germany.

Focus point: Why did the victors not get everything they wanted?

Focus point: What were the immediate reactions to the peace settlement?

Students can produce newspaper reports using the text and sources from the student book (pages 14–15) from the point of view of either Britain, France, America or Germany. Headlines and content can then be compared in order to illustrate how reactions to the treaty varied.

Some actual headlines from newspapers at the time of the Treaty include:

Peace signed, ends the great war. Germans depart still protesting

(USA)

THE DISGRACEFUL TREATY IS BEING SIGNED TODAY
Don't forget it!
We will never stop until we win back what we deserve

(From *Deutsche Zeitung*, a German newspaper, 28 June 1919)

he Learning Curve website provides some excellent sources to help students understand the different reactions to the treaty: go to www. heinemann.co.uk/hotlinks, insert the express code 0206T, and click on 'Treaty'.

Focus point: Could the treaties be justified at the time?

Activity 1.4: Was Harold Nicolson right?

This can lead into a debate about whether the treaties could be justified at the time and a discussion of how hindsight can alter our judgement of this issue. As a motion to present students with, Harold Nicolson's famous statement can be used:

'This house believes that Harold Nicolson was right when he stated that:

"The historian, with every justification, will come to the conclusion that we (those present at Versailles) were very stupid men. We arrived determined to get a peace of justice and wisdom. We left feeling that the terms we imposed on our enemies were neither just nor wise."'

Students can spend some time, individually or in groups, gathering evidence to support one or both sides of the argument, using the student book, sources or the internet.

You could introduce students to the concept of a formal debate, and allocate some students specific roles such as chairperson, proposer, etc. Give these students some time to prepare their speeches, then the class can conduct the debate according to the following procedure.

1 The chair opens the debate and counts all present who will be voting on the motion, and then reads it out.

2 The proposer makes a speech in favour of the motion (a time limit of two minutes could be applied).

3 The opposer gives a speech against the motion.

4 Seconders for each side give shorter speeches for and against the motion.

5 The chair then declares the debate open to the floor. Any student can speak for or against the motion for a limited time, and must put their hand up to be selected to speak by the chair.

6 After contributions from the floor, the proposer and opposer give a brief summing-up speech.

7 A vote is then held and counted by the chair.

KEY QUESTION 2: TO WHAT EXTENT WAS THE LEAGUE OF NATIONS A SUCCESS?

Specified content:

- the aims of the League, its strengths and weaknesses in structure and organisation

- successes and failures in peacekeeping during the 1920s

- disarmament

- the work of the Court of International Justice

- the International Labour Organization and the Special Commissions

- the impact of the Great Depression on the work of the League after 1929

- the failures of the League in Manchuria and Abyssinia.

Focus point: What were the aims of the League of Nations?

This focus point is another likely candidate to be the subject of a factual four-mark exam question. Students should ensure that they know at least four aims of the League and one piece of supporting information about each.

Focus point: How successful was the League of Nations in the 1920s?

Activity 1.5: Revising the work of the League of Nations in the 1920s

In exams, students often write vaguely about the reasons for the League's successes and failures (stating, for example, that the League failed due to the fact that its permanent members had a disproportionate amount of power and influence). However, they often have difficulty giving specific examples to support their arguments. This is an area where a focus on revision and the retention of factual information is important.

Worksheets 1.7 and 1.8 provide a quiz activity that can aid this revision. One student has the 'Start' card, and that student asks the first question. The student who has the answer to that on the left-hand side of their card reads it out, and then reads out the next question: this continues until all students have participated. An element of competition can be introduced by dividing the class into two sides, and higher attainers can be given more cards to manage.

This activity ensures all students are engaged and listening to each other. This particular set of questions is intended, where possible, to make clear what could be described as successes and failures for the League in the 1920s.

Another way of approaching this activity is to ask students to produce their own set of question-and-answer cards, and then test them out with the class as a whole. This can be a helpful way of revising factual content for any topic.

Focus point: How far did weaknesses in the League's organisation make failure inevitable?

Activity 1.6: What was wrong with the League of Nations?

STRUCTURE DIAGRAM

Students need to understand that, although the League did achieve some success, the structure of the organisation itself was very problematic. They can use the student book (page 27) to produce a diagram of the League's structure. This should include the *intended* role and purpose of each part of the organisation, along with an explanation of the problems often caused by the way each part of the structure functioned in reality. Higher attainers can design this diagram themselves, while lower attainers can use worksheet 1.9. Students can use worksheet 1.10 to help them divide up the relevant functions.

This question demands an evaluation of 'how far' the structure itself can be blamed for the failure of the League. The highest levels in many ten-mark exam questions require this sort of complex evaluation: it is of course difficult to say to what extent the structure was to blame, although it clearly had a part to play in the ultimate failure of the League. The answer has to be a variation on 'to some extent': whatever emphasis is placed on this factor, it is necessary for students to evaluate what part other factors played in the League's failure.

CARTOON

The fact that the USA was never a member of the League is an important issue to address. Worksheet 1.11 provides a framework to analyse a cartoon relating to America's failure to join the League, focusing on the key elements that need to be included in responses to such questions (context, surface features and hidden meaning).

Focus point: How far did the Depression make the work of the League more difficult?

Activity 1.7: Wider effects of the Depression

Students should use the diagram on page 29 of the student book and the information on increasing militarism to answer the question 'How could the Depression in America affect workers in Japan?'.

A kinaesthetic adaptation of this activity would be to use each stage of the diagram to produce cards. These could be given out to students, who are asked to position themselves so that the chain of effects is clear. They should then take it in turns to explain how each card connects to and influences the next.

Focus point: Why did the League fail over Manchuria and Abyssinia?

Activity 1.8: Storyboarding Manchuria and Abyssinia

Any question that asks students to comment on the work of the League of Nations during the 1930s will require a knowledge of events in Manchuria and Abyssinia. Especially for lower attainers, a helpful way of presenting information about these two crises is to produce a storyboard of events for one or the other (or both). Students of all abilities often find it difficult to make notes, or even to answer specific questions effectively: they have a tendency to either copy out chunks of text without really understanding the meaning of what they are reading, or provide answers/ notes that are too brief or miss out important information.

In order to address these issues, students can be told that film-makers often storyboard their movies, and they should try to think in this way when producing their work about Manchuria/ Abyssinia. Prompt them with questions such as:

- If you were making a film about this event, what scenes would you include?

- What information could be missed out?

- What are the really essential developments an audience would need to be shown in order to understand what was happening?

Students are then given a number of scenes they should include on their storyboard. They have to read through the text in the student book, and from that select the events they are going to include. They can then produce their storyboard (a piece of plain paper divided into the appropriate number of boxes will suffice), which should be completed using an illustration in each box and a brief caption underneath. Students can be given a word limit for their captions, which should again encourage them to read for meaning and summarise in their own words what is happening.

KEY QUESTION 3: WHY HAD INTERNATIONAL PEACE COLLAPSED BY 1939?

Specified content:

- the collapse of international order in the 1930s

- the increasing militarism of Germany, Italy and Japan

- Hitler's foreign policy up to 1939

- the Saar, remilitarisation of the Rhineland, Austria, Czechoslovakia and Poland

- the Nazi–Soviet Pact

- appeasement and the outbreak of war in September 1939.

Focus point: What were the long-term consequences of the peace treaties of 1919–23?

Focus point: What were the consequences of the failures of the League in the 1930s?

Activity 1.9: Understanding the causes and consequences of the failure of the League of Nations

Students often make the mistake of not being time-specific in questions that ask them about the League of Nations during a particular decade. In response to a question such as this one, students will often talk generally about problems with the League since its inception, ignoring the fact that the question is asking them to focus on *consequences* as well as causes. They therefore need to be given examples that encourage them to differentiate between the causes and consequences of the League's failures, and to differentiate between events of the 1920s and those of the 1930s.

Worksheet 1.12 contains a card sort that allows students to select information relevant to a particular question. The vast majority of

students should be able to divide these up into causes and consequences, while higher attainers can use the cards in a more sophisticated way. They can be asked to give further explanations for the 'cause' cards using connectives and analytical language. For example, the card that states 'The USA never joined the League' could be expanded with 'consequently, the League was undermined from the very beginning by the absence of a major world power'. Cards can also be expanded with specific examples; in this case, the next expansion could be 'This problem was very apparent during the crisis in Manchuria when America was willing to keep trading with Japan despite sanctions imposed by the League.'

Students can also use the cards to prioritise the causes and consequences (separately) in order of importance. They should explain, verbally or in writing (and perhaps sticking the cards down and annotating them to produce a diagram of the most important causes and consequences), why some causes and consequences were more important than others. You could look at some examples of exam questions that ask them to consider these issues (see page 28).

This type of activity can also be a great help in addressing the perennial problem of students writing everything they know about a particular topic, rather than actually answering the question. They can look at different types of question about the League, use the cards to select prompts to help them structure their answers, and identify the examples or additional information needed to support their conclusions. It would be helpful for this purpose if students have already completed some clear written work that describes the specific incidents the League was involved with, from its inception to its demise, and evaluates whether the League was successful in dealing with these incidents.

The acronym FAILURE also provides a way to remember the different reasons why the League did not succeed. Students could find examples for each letter in the student book (pages 20–36) – this could be done as a piece of extended writing, with separate paragraphs for each of the letters, or as a spider diagram. Alternatively, students could expand the letters from their own knowledge – this could be used to structure a test.

F French and British self-interest
A Absent powers (e.g. USA)
I Ineffective sanctions
L Lack of armed forces
U Unfair treaties
RE Reaching decisions too slowly

Focus point: How far was Hitler's foreign policy to blame for the outbreak of war in 1939?

Students need to understand, and have a clear factual knowledge of, the chain of events that led to the outbreak of war in September 1939. They should also reflect on where blame should be apportioned at each step. Obviously Hitler's aggressive foreign policy was to blame – but were there other factors at work as well?

Ask students to discuss the two quotes about Hitler's foreign policy (worksheet 1.13) with a partner, and challenge each other to explain their opinions. Then ask groups to pair up with another group to make a four, and to continue and expand their discussions using their own knowledge. They should consider:

• Why would such arguments be put forward about Hitler?

• Could he really have such a clear intention to fully reverse Versailles?

• What impact might the failure of the League of Nations in Manchuria and Abyssinia have had on Hitler's foreign policy?

• Discuss the view that Hitler was simply a 'pragmatic opportunist'.

Each group should then feed back to the class in a wider discussion, and form an opinion line to show their agreement or disagreement with the historical interpretations.

Activity 1.10: Steps to war

Students can use page 49 of the student book to produce a timeline of the events leading up to the outbreak of war. For each event they should explain how it could be said that either Hitler's foreign policy or another factor (or both) was

to blame. They should be encouraged to use appropriate connectives to compare different points of view.

This can be developed into a more kinaesthetic activity. One group of students is given cards with the different steps to war explained briefly, or an opinion about who was to blame for each step. Another group is given cards with one connective or connecting phrase on each. Students must work in groups to form themselves into sentences/short paragraphs using at least one connective and two separate pieces of information/opinions, preferably more. (See example at the bottom of the page.)

Focus point: Was the policy of appeasement justified?

It helps students to understand the different perspectives and arguments relating to appeasement if you prompt them to think of different scenarios in which one might or might not appease an aggressor (see lesson plan 1B). Simplistic discussions of appeasement, which might use the example of children making the choice of appeasing or standing up to bullies at school, and the pros and cons of each option, offer a way for students of all abilities to understand the meaning of the word appeasement.

Discuss with students what different responses there are to being bullied. Draw out the idea that sometimes it is (or may seem) necessary to appease a bully in order to survive. Alternatively, or in addition, discuss how this may or may not be different when countries are involved rather than individuals.

With more able students it is appropriate to consider how relevant this comparison is, and ask the question 'what makes the situation a bullied student finds him/herself in different from the position of Europe in the 1930s when faced with Hitler's aggression?' This question can begin to draw out whether there are any moral absolutes when it comes to appeasement as a concept.

Example:

In 1935, England and Germany signed the Anglo-German naval treaty.	*This allowed…*	Germany to ignore the naval restrictions of the Treaty of Versailles.	*It could be argued that…*	this was an example of selfish short-sightedness on the part of the British, who wanted to ensure their naval superiority.

It is also easy for students to jump to the conclusion that appeasement was clearly wrong because of their knowledge of what happened next. Encourage students to think about times when they might have made a decision that seemed correct at the time, but with hindsight was not.

This can lead into questions that encourage use of a skill that students sometimes find surprisingly difficult – that of thinking from the perspective of people who were actually there at the time. Source work can be used here to give arguments for and against appeasement, which were formulated at the time the policy was being pursued, specifically in relation to Hitler.

Activity 1.11: Summarising arguments for and against appeasement

Worksheet 1.14 provides students with a card sort giving the types of argument both for and against appeasement that could be used to answer questions asking whether the policy of appeasement was justified or not. Students can sort these cards into arguments for and against, which is relatively easy: words such as 'cowards' pretty much give the game away. Students often read text without really digesting it and may find note-taking difficult, so as well as sorting the cards, they must show that they have fully understood the argument by summarising it in a snappy way, as shown in the example cards which have already been completed. Higher attainers, using the text and sources in the student book, should be able to add some further arguments. For very low attainers, worksheet 1.15 provides a simple exercise in separating arguments for and against appeasement, so at least those students should be able to gain some marks on this type of question.

Provided students have sufficient knowledge from previous lessons about the policy of appeasement, show them the cartoon (worksheet 1.16) and ask them to compare it with a clip of Neville Chamberlain arriving back from Munich and proclaiming 'peace for our time'.

Another possibility would be to conduct a trial of Neville Chamberlain. When students have completed some work on arguments for and

against appeasement, they can be allocated the following roles (obviously some flexibility with numbers may be required, depending on the size of your class):

- A judge who presides over the trial, reads out the charge and gives a closing statement after a decision has been reached, giving an appropriate punishment.

- Twelve jury members (or more) who need to listen to the evidence and then decide whether Chamberlain is guilty or not.

- A prosecutor who gives a speech for the prosecution, citing specific evidence where possible.

- A defender who responds to the prosecution statement, again citing evidence.

- With a class who you feel could cope with increased complexity, some students could fill the role of witnesses who are then cross-examined by the prosecution and defence (these could include Hitler, Mussolini, etc.).

- Chamberlain himself.

You can then present students with the accusation that Chamberlain betrayed Britain by appeasing Hitler. All students could write a prosecution and/or defence statement and the most effective be selected to perform in the trial. All students not playing a role should listen to the evidence and then hold a (time-limited, managed) discussion about which side they are persuaded by. The verdict can then be given.

Students should now be introduced to the types of exam question they may have to answer in relation to appeasement. Explain they are going to look at a typical six-mark exam question where the difference between lower and higher levels is that of description as opposed to explanation (worksheet 1.17).

Focus point: How important was the Nazi–Soviet Pact?

Students should consider the advantages of the Nazi–Soviet Pact for both the USSR and Germany. They should then consider how it could be argued that the Pact was the most important cause (short-term at least) of the Second World War.

Focus point: Why did Britain and France declare war on Germany in September 1939?

Grade Studio

USING EXAM QUESTIONS, MARK SCHEMES AND PEER ASSESSMENT TO IMPROVE ATTAINMENT

Grade Studio has been designed to help both students and teachers interpret GCSE history mark schemes.

Grade Studio has a clear and explicit focus on levels. It is the point at which the teaching and practice in the student book becomes focused on moving between levels, and therefore the learning becomes increasingly personalised and improves students' chances of achieving better grades.

Exam questions in the past have asked students to describe what different leaders wanted to achieve at Versailles. These are often six-mark questions such as:

'Explain what Wilson hoped to achieve at the Paris Peace Conference.'

Students should ensure they know at least three aims for each leader, and can offer some elaboration on each. Again, these are questions which lower attainers can access and score highly on if they have sufficient factual knowledge, and if they are given plenty of practice at supporting the points that they make with further explanation.

A more complex analytical assessment of whether the different leaders actually achieved their aims can form the basis of ten-mark questions on this topic, for example:

'How far was Clemenceau satisfied with the Treaty of Versailles? Explain your answer.'

In order to score at the highest levels, students need to give two sides, commenting on both aspects with which the leader in question was satisfied, and aspects with which they were not satisfied. Again, specific reference to the terms of the Treaty is essential.

The activities in the student book and on the CD ROM should help students to improve their understanding of how to answer different types of exam question. Worksheet 1.19 contains the mark scheme for a question from the 2005 OCR exam paper, which asks students to consider three major causes of the outbreak of war in 1939. It also contains a student-friendly version of the mark scheme for use in the classroom. Lower attainers can be given a simple writing frame to help them structure a response to this question.

For example:

All three reasons contributed to the outbreak of war. Hitler's foreign policy was very aggressive. For example:

- The result of this aggression was that...

- The League of Nations was set up to promote world peace, yet it could be argued that its failure contributed to the outbreak of war because...

- Some argue that the policy of appeasement was associated with the failure of the League of Nations. The result of this policy was...

- In conclusion, I think the most important reason that war broke out in 1939 was that ..., because...

Any ten-mark question that focuses on students' understanding of causation in relation to the outbreak of the Second World War is a useful way of rounding up this unit.

1.1 Versailles character cards 1

You are **David Lloyd George**, Prime Minister of **Britain**. Your government won a massive election victory at the end of the First World War, partly by promising to 'squeeze the German lemon till the pips squeak'. The British public want you to punish Germany extremely harshly because of the suffering caused during the First World War.

You want Britain to remain Europe's number one naval power, and therefore dislike the fact that America wants all countries to have equal access to sea routes. You are keen to get rid of Germany's ships for this reason.

However, you are worried that if the Germans are treated too harshly, they may seek revenge in the future. You are also very concerned that the European economy should be allowed to recover, including the German economy: a crippled Germany would not be able to trade with Britain. This would cause British trade to be less profitable. For these reasons, you don't want to help France to keep Germany weak. You do want to maintain and possibly expand your empire.

You don't want to abandon your election promises, so you need to tread a fine line between being tough on Germany to please the public, and making sure Germany is still able to trade and isn't treated so badly that it will seek revenge in the future.

DURING THE ROLE-PLAY YOU MUST IGNORE WHATEVER THE STUDENT REPRESENTING GERMANY SAYS.

You are **Georges Clemenceau**, Prime Minister of **France**. You became leader of France in 1917, when it looked as if your country might lose the war against Germany. You rallied your people and led your country to eventual victory a year later.

Much of the fighting during the First World War took place in your country. The German army deliberately looted areas of France under its control. They destroyed mines, railways, factories and bridges as they retreated at the end of the war. This damage will cost a huge amount to repair, and will continue to have a negative effect on your country's economy.

The French public are desperate for Germany to be punished as harshly as possible. Much of north-east France has been utterly devastated. You want the German borders to be pushed right back, and you want France to be given control of several areas of German territory, including the Saar and the Rhineland. Your priorities are that Germany should pay massive amounts of compensation (reparations) to pay for the damage done to your country. You also want to ensure France will never be threatened by Germany again: for this reason you want to take as much territory off them as possible and you want their military power to be completely removed.

DURING THE ROLE-PLAY YOU MUST IGNORE WHATEVER THE STUDENT REPRESENTING GERMANY SAYS.

1.2 Versailles character cards 2

You are **Woodrow Wilson**, President of the **USA**. You are a man of strong principles, and you find it hard to accept other people's views. You kept the USA out of the war until 1917. Now it has been won, your priority is to secure a fair settlement that ensures peace in the future.

You do not think Germany should take all the blame for the First World War. You think that if Germany is helped and encouraged to rebuild, it is more likely to become a peaceful country. Your worry is that if Germany is treated too harshly, it will seek revenge in the future. You do not think France should take as much land from Germany as it wants. You think that countries should have a right to self-determination: different national groups have a right to rule themselves. You do not believe that one country should dominate important sea routes.

You do not think that Germany should be crippled by having to pay huge amounts of reparations, although you are willing to accept that they should pay something. You believe that all countries should be encouraged to disarm, not just Germany.

You want to set up an international organisation to promote world peace.

DURING THE ROLE-PLAY YOU MUST IGNORE WHATEVER THE STUDENT REPRESENTING GERMANY SAYS.

You represent **Germany**. You knew when you surrendered at the end of the First World War that you would have to pay reparations (compensation) to the countries that you were fighting against. You also knew that you would have to reduce your armed forces and surrender some territory; these are the usual consequences of defeat in war.

However, you do not believe that the First World War was entirely your fault. You are also keen that your country is allowed to recover following the loss of life and great cost that the war has caused for your country.

You do not want to hand over large amounts of territory to France: there has been a long-standing lack of trust between your countries. You particularly do not want to lose valuable areas of land such as the Saar and the Rhineland. You believe that you still need some military force to defend yourself if necessary.

1.3 Questions to consider at Versailles

Your group must discuss all the questions and then reach a joint decision, which should be recorded on this sheet.

1 What should be done about Germany's armed forces?

....

....

....

....

....

....

....

2 What should happen to Germany's overseas colonies (empire)?

....

....

....

....

....

....

....

3 Who should pay for the damage caused during the First World War?

....

....

....

....

....

....

....

4 Are there any other decisions that you think need to be made?

....

....

....

....

....

....

1.4 Aims of the leaders at Versailles

Name of leader	Guiding principles	Attitude of population at home	What they specifically wanted to achieve at Versailles
Georges Clemenceau (France)	*Clemenceau wanted to ensure that Germany could never again threaten France and was punished very harshly for its actions.*	*The majority of the French public wanted Germany to be punished as harshly as possible.*	*That Germany's military forces should be reduced to an absolute minimum.*
David Lloyd George (Britain)			
Woodrow Wilson (USA)			

1.5 Match the statements

Draw a line or lines between each statement and the leader(s) you think could have made them.

Statements	Leaders
1 Germany took huge amounts of land from Russia when it surrendered last year. We should treat them in the same way.	
2 Lloyd George is more interested in protecting Britain's trade than he is in our security.	
3 The Germans will want revenge some day if we treat them too harshly.	**Georges Clemenceau**
4 Germany was a major trading partner of ours before the war. Rebuilding Germany will actually create jobs for our workers.	
5 Unlike some of my fellow leaders, my focus is not to crush Germany or to expand my empire.	
6 It is all very well for Wilson to say he wants a fair peace. He does not have to deal with German troops on his borders.	
7 We should all reduce our armed forces if we really want peace.	
8 I need to consider what the public want, even if I have my doubts about the long-term wisdom of what they demand.	**David Lloyd George**
9 It is right that Germany should pay reparations for the damage done during the First World War.	
10 I don't think the Germans will be able to pay the reparations we are asking, but people expect me to ask for them.	
11 Several people at these discussion use words like 'justice'. I feel as if I am the only one really striving for it.	
12 Ideally, I would like to see Germany broken up into smaller states, then the threat it poses would finally be gone.	
13 Wilson is an idealist. His vision of peaceful cooperation is just a dream.	
14 We should concentrate on setting up organisations and systems to avoid war in the future, rather than looking to punish individual nations for past actions.	**Woodrow Wilson**
15 I sympathise with some of what Wilson says, but he should not try and get us to weaken our own empire by giving 'freedom' to our colonies.	
16 All nations have a right to run their own affairs: the great nations of Europe should let them do so.	

1.6 Terms of the Treaty of Versailles

	What did this term of the treaty mean?	Which member(s) of the 'Big Three' would this term please?	Potential effect on Germany
Guilt	*Germany had to publicly accept all the blame for the First World War.*	*Lloyd George and Clemenceau would be happy for Germany to admit full responsibility.*	*This clause would create great humiliation, anger and resentment in Germany. It was clearly unfair to place the entire blame for the First World War on Germany's shoulders.*
Armed forces			
Reparations			
German territory			
League of nations			

1.7 League of Nations question and answer 1

START	Q: What contested area did Sweden and Finland accept the League's decision on in 1921?
A: The Aaland Islands.	Q: Which two countries received efficient financial help from the League in the early 1920s?
A: Austria and Hungary.	Q: Vilna was the capital city of which country?
A: Lithuania.	Q: Which country occupied Vilna in 1920?
A: Poland.	Q: What did the League do about this?
A: Nothing.	Q: Why was Upper Silesia an important area?
A: The presence of lots of industry.	Q: Which countries claimed the area of Upper Silesia?
A: Poland and Germany.	Q: What did the League do about Upper Silesia?
A: It was divided between the two countries. Not everybody was happy with this, but the League's decision was accepted.	Q: Why did Mussolini, the Italian dictator, demand compensation from the Greek government in 1923?
A: Five Italian surveyors were shot when mapping the Greek–Albanian border.	Q: What did Mussolini do when he was not paid compensation?
A: He occupied Corfu in defiance of the League.	Q: What did the League do about Mussolini?
A: Put pressure on the Greek government to accept Mussolini's demands, making it seem as if powerful countries could get away with bullying less powerful ones.	Q: Which countries quarrelled over their border in 1925?

1.8 League of Nations question and answer 2

A: Greece and Bulgaria.	Q: What did the League do about this issue?
A: Put pressure on the Greeks to withdraw, which they did. However, the League did appear to treat Greece differently to the way it had treated Italy.	Q: Which country did not join the League in the 1920s, despite promoting the idea at Versailles?
A: America.	Q: Which treaty was signed without the League's involvement, bringing Germany and France closer together?
A: The Locarno Treaty	Q: What result did the Locarno Treaty have?
A: Germany was allowed into the League in 1926.	Q: What strategy could the League use to try to get countries to follow their directions?
A: Economic sanctions.	Q: Why did economic sanctions often not work?
A: Countries were unwilling to impose them because they did not want to damage their own trade.	Q: Which part of the League was responsible for encouraging countries to reduce their armed forces?
A: The Disarmament Commission. This was not very successful: a conference about disarmament did not even take place until 1932.	END

1.9 Structure of the League of Nations

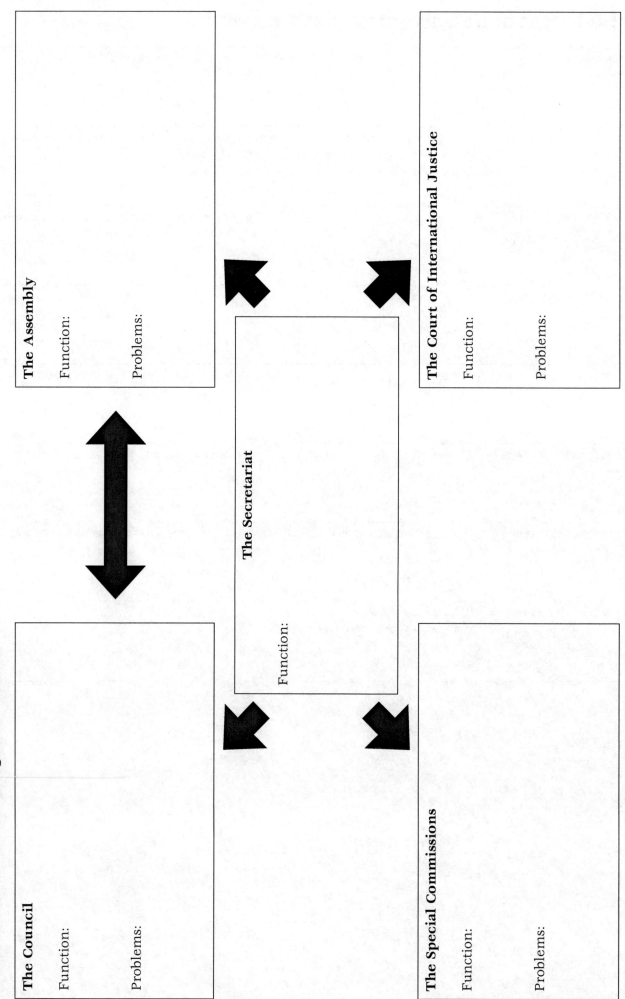

The Council

Function:

Problems:

The Assembly

Function:

Problems:

The Secretariat

Function:

The Court of International Justice

Function:

Problems:

The Special Commissions

Function:

Problems:

1.10 Structure of the League of Nations 2

Make sure you include all these bullet points in the correct place on your diagram of the League's structure:

- Settled border disputes

- Aimed to improve conditions of working people throughout the world

- Had four temporary members (for three years at a time)

- Admitted new members

- Kept records, prepared reports, etc.

- Discussed issues raised by members

- Had a range of powers:
  - moral condemnation
  - economic and financial sanctions
  - military force

- Gave legal advice to the Assembly or Council

- Like a parliament

- Supervised former German colonies now looked after by Britain or France

- A smaller group which met more frequently

- Like a civil service

- Decisions had to be unanimous

- All members sent delegates to annual meetings at the HQ in Geneva

- Helped return refugees to their original homes after the First World War

- Attempted to deal with the problem of dangerous diseases

- Agreed on finances

- Made decisions about peace-keeping

- Had four permanent members (UK, France, Italy, Japan) – each member had a veto

- Educated people about health and sanitation

- Made sure Britain and France acted on behalf of the interests of the people of the colony

1.11 'The gap in the bridge' cartoon

Surface feature:

Hidden meaning:

Surface feature:

Hidden meaning:

Surface feature:

Hidden meaning:

Surface feature:

Hidden meaning:

Surface feature:

Hidden meaning:

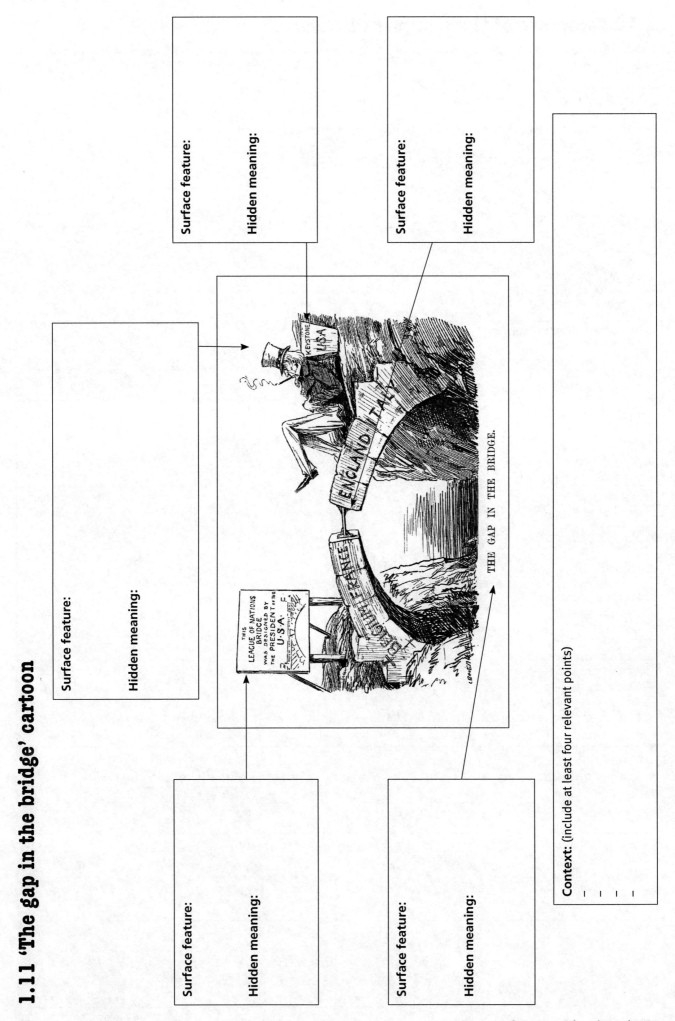

Context: (include at least four relevant points)

1.12 League of Nations card sort

The countries that had been defeated in the First World War were not invited to join the League.	France and Britain were sceptical about the League from the start and did not share Wilson's idealistic aims. Britain wanted the League to be merely a talking shop, while France wanted it to enforce the terms of the peace treaties.
America, despite the instrumental role of Wilson in promoting the League, never joined.	The Assembly of the League was too large to respond quickly to international crises.
The Council of the League was dominated by the powerful permanent members (initially Italy, Japan, France and Britain). Decisions had to be unanimous.	The Permanent Court of Justice was set up to rule on legal disputes between nations, but as countries had to agree in advance to accept the court's verdicts, many important disputes were never referred to it.
The League was never an organisation of all states, or even all the most important states.	Britain and France disagreed over the role of the League, and were often more concerned with protecting their own interests than in the success of the League.
The League had no armed forces and had to rely on sanctions to deter aggressors.	Unemployment and poverty during the Depression made governments more likely to look inwards than to address international difficulties.
Increasing militarism in some nations such as Japan, associated with problems caused by the Depression, presented the League with greater challenges during the 1930s.	During the Depression, voters in some countries were more likely to turn to extremist parties. These parties often showed an unwillingness to accept international agreements.
The Great Depression destroyed much of the goodwill the League had relied on and used to achieve some modest success in the 1920s.	During the 1920s, the League was accused of being too responsive to pressure from its most powerful members. Smaller, less powerful countries felt unfairly treated, although the League did help to resolve some situations peacefully and the Commissions improved conditions in some areas.
Japan invaded the Chinese mainland in July 1937 following the failure of the League to deal with the crisis in Manchuria. Some historians regard this as the real start of the Second World War.	On 30 June 1939, Haile Selassie made a speech in which he protested against the League's failure to defend Abyssinia against Italian aggression. Nobody took the League seriously after this and it played little part in the events immediately leading up to the Second World War.
The failures of the League encouraged nations such as Italy and Japan to believe they could get away with aggression against other nations.	Britain and France began to rearm as they realised that they might have to fight another war to deal with the dictators who had taken advantage of their weaknesses and those of the League of Nations.
The notion of collective security was destroyed as members of the League clearly would not act together firmly in the face of aggression.	Weaker nations realised that they could not look to the League for protection.
There was little progress towards disarmament during the 1920s. A conference was not set up to discuss the subject until 1932, and it was a failure.	The Mandates Commission was supposed to prepare occupied countries for eventual independence, but actually ran them as colonies. Iraq was the only mandate that was given independence in the inter-war period.

1.13 Aims of Hitler

Read the following quotes. Are Brett and Trevor-Roper right about Hitler?

Most of the aggressions, leading step by step to open war in September 1939, were the outcome of the deliberate policy of Hitler. S. Reed Brett, *European History 1900–1960* (1967)	Hitler's war aims are written large and clear in the documents of his reign… Let us take the evidence of *Mein Kampf*… the book is the expression of a political philosophy full formed. To him, from 1920 to 1945, the purpose of Nazism was always the same: it was to create an empire. Hugh Trevor-Roper, *Hitler's War Aims* (1960).

Agree   **Disagree**

$\longleftarrow\!\longrightarrow$

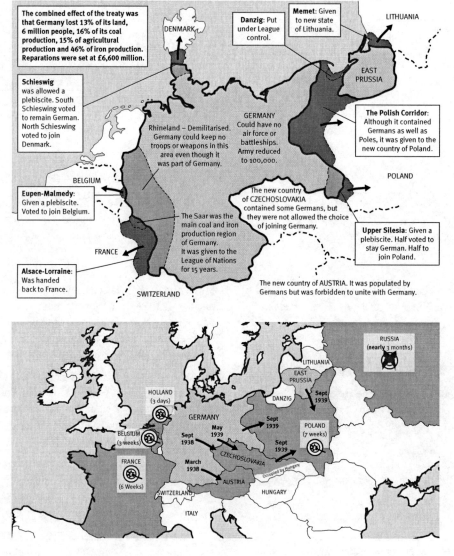

Consider the two maps of Europe.

- Which direction has Germany expanded in by 1939?

- What does that suggest about the impact of Versailles?

- Hitler said that his aim was to unite all German-speaking people in one country and restore the nation's pride. Looking ahead at his steps over the next six years, do the so-called 'steps to war' highlight a point at which his unity claim becomes untrue?

- 'Outright and straightforward imperialism' – how far do you agree with this statement?

1.14 Should Britain have given Hitler what he wanted?

Put these ideas in the correct column. Add any other arguments you can from the student book (pages 37–49).

Giving Hitler what he wanted made him think he could get away with more. This encouraged him to act aggressively.	The Treaty of Versailles was too harsh. It was right to give in to some of Hitler's demands.
Britain had to give in to Hitler. The country was not ready to fight.	Giving Hitler what he wanted was cowardly. Britain should have stood up to him earlier.
It was right to try to give Hitler what he wanted in order to avoid another war.	If Britain had stood up to Hitler and not given in to his demands, they could have beaten him. Hitler did not have the strength to fight back.

Yes! Britain should have given Hitler what he wanted.	**No!** Britain should not have given Hitler what he wanted.

1.15 Appeasement card sort

GERMANY DESERVES A FAIR DEAL	THE APPEASERS MISJUDGED HITLER
There was some sympathy for Germany: many British people believed that the Treaty of Versailles was too harsh and Hitler was only taking back what rightfully belonged to Germany. Evidence:	They mistakenly treated Hitler as a rational politician and did not realise until it was too late that they were dealing with a ruthless tyrant. The more they gave him, the more he demanded. Evidence:
Appeasement was basically cowardice and weakness. Britain and France were so afraid of another war that they allowed Germany to break international agreements without punishment. Evidence:	The appeasers were so busy trying to give Hitler what he wanted that they missed good opportunities to resist him. After the remilitarisation of the Rhineland in 1936, Hitler admitted that any sign of military action by the French would have led him to withdraw his troops immediately. Evidence:
Britain was not ready to fight. Britain's re-armament programme did not begin until 1936 and was not planned for completion until 1940. Therefore they did not feel able to intervene in areas such as the Sudetenland and risk an all-out war with Hitler before they were prepared. Evidence:	After the horrors of the First World War, it was perfectly understandable that Britain and France desired peace and did everything they could to avoid exacerbating the situation (making it worse). Evidence:

1.16 'Increasing pressure' cartoon

INCREASING PRESSURE.

What is the cartoonist's view of appeasement?
(Remember: refer to surface features, hidden meaning and context in your answers.)

....
....
....
....
....
....
....
....
....
....
....

1.17 Grade Studio: Appeasement mark schemes

TEACHER MARK SCHEME

Explain why Britain followed a policy of appeasement.   **[6 marks]**

Level 1:	General answer lacking specific contextual knowledge. e.g. 'They followed appeasement because they were weak.'	[1 mark]
Level 2:	*Identifies* **why the policy was followed but does not fully explain.** e.g. 'The Treaty of Versailles had been too harsh.' 'They wanted to avoid war.' 'They wanted to settle disputes by negotiation.' 'The aim was to keep Germany on their side.' 'To allow both countries time to prepare for war.'	[2–3 marks]
Level 3:	*Explains* **why the policy was followed.** (One explained reason 3–4 marks; two or more explained reasons 4–6 marks) e.g. 'Some British politicians thought the Treaty of Versailles was too harsh on Germany. They thought Hitler was only getting back what rightfully belonged to Germany.' 'It was right to avoid war. Memories of the First World War were still fresh and politicians were horrified at the thought of more bloodshed.' 'At the time many thought Stalin and communism to be a greater threat and many politicians saw a strong Germany as useful protection against the USSR.' 'Britain was not ready to fight Germany. Rearmament only got under way in 1936. Appeasement gave Britain the chance to re-arm.' 'Some British politicians thought the Treaty of Versailles was too harsh on Germany. They thought Hitler was only getting back what rightfully belonged to Germany. If Britain gave way to Hitler's demands he would eventually be satisfied. An example of this was the remilitarisation of the Rhineland.'	[3–6 marks]

STUDENT MARK SCHEME

Explain why Britain followed a policy of appeasement.   **[6 marks]**

Level 1:	General answer lacking specific contextual knowledge.	[1 mark]
Level 2:	Identifies why the policy was followed but does not fully explain.	[2–3 marks]
Level 3:	Explains why the policy was followed. (3–4 marks for one reason fully explained, [5–6 marks] for two or more reasons fully explained)	[5–6 marks]

1.18 Grade Studio: Appeasement writing frame

Why did Britain follow a policy of appeasement? (In other words, why did Britain give Hitler what he wanted?)

Use the FOR arguments on the worksheet to help you.

Britain followed a policy of appeasement (giving Hitler what he wanted) because most importantly, its leaders…

....
....
....
....
....
....

Another important reason why Britain appeased Hitler was…

....
....
....
....
....
....

In addition, some people believed that it was right to appease Hitler because…

....
....
....
....
....
....

Finally, another reason was that…

....
....
....
....
....
....

Try to include some connectives in each paragraph, as this makes it more likely that you are offering an explanation rather than just a description.

GradeStudio

1.19 Grade Studio: Second World War mark schemes

TEACHER MARK SCHEME

The following were all equally important reasons why war broke out in 1939:

i   Hitler's aggressive foreign policy
ii the failure of the League of Nations
iii the policy of appeasement.

Do you agree with this statement? Explain your answer referring only to **i**, **ii** and **iii**.

Target: A01. [Written communication to be assessed in this question – see examiner instructions]

Level 1:	General answer. Answers lack specific contextual knowledge. e.g. 'All these reasons contributed to an outbreak of war in 1939.'	[1–2 marks]
Level 2:	*Identifies* why these reasons contributed to the success of Hitler's foreign policy in 1939. e.g. 'Appeasement made Hitler think that he could get away with anything and no one would stand up to him; the failure of the League of Nations showed Hitler would stand up to powerful countries.' N.B. Description only **(maximum 3 marks).**	[2–4 marks]
Level 3:	*Explains* the contribution of one reason. e.g. 'The policy of appeasement contributed to the outbreak of the Second World War because it convinced Hitler that Britain and France would not stand in his way. When Hitler annexed Austria in 1938 Britain and France did nothing. This encouraged Hitler to think that he could get away with invading the Sudetenland. When Hitler demanded the Sudetenland Britain and France gave way again. This is what encouraged Hitler to invade the rest of Czechoslovakia. This took Europe closer to war; Hitler might not have gone this far had it not been for the British and French policy of appeasement.'	[3–5 marks]
Level 4:	*Explains* the contribution of more than one reason. Explains Hitler's aggressive foreign policy; the failure of the League of Nations; the policy of appeasement.	[6–8 marks]
Level 5:	Explanation of how these reasons acted together to bring about a world war in 1939, OR explanation of their comparative importance. e.g. 'Hitler was determined to make Germany great again, and he made promises to reverse the Treaty of Versailles and to create living space for the German people. This would involve an aggressive foreign policy. He saw that the League was weak because it had failed to deal with Japan and Italy. This gave Hitler freedom of action and he marched his troops into the Rhineland. This action also tested the power of Britain and France – they did nothing. The policy of appeasement highlighted their weakness and encouraged Hitler to make more territorial gains until he pushed the British too far over Poland. At this point Britain and France declared war on Germany.' (fully explained)	[9–10 marks]

STUDENT MARK SCHEME

The following were all equally important reasons why war broke out in 1939:

i   Hitler's aggressive foreign policy;
ii the failure of the League of Nations;
iii the policy of appeasement.

Do you agree with this statement? Explain your answer referring only to **i**, **ii** and **iii**.

Level 1:	General answer, lacks any specific knowledge.	[1–2 marks]
Level 2:	*Identifies* why these reasons contributed to the success of Hitler's foreign policy in 1939. Answers in this level will just be descriptive.	[2–4 marks]
Level 3:	*Explains* the contribution of one of these reasons to the outbreak of war.	[3–5 marks]
Level 4:	*Explains* the contribution of more than one of these reasons to the outbreak of war.	[6–8 marks]
Level 5:	*Explains* how all the reasons acted together to bring about the outbreak or war OR explains the comparative importance of each reason.	[9–10 marks]

2 International Relations Part 2: The Cold War, 1945–75

Introduction

This topic forms the second of the three-part International Relations Core 1919–2005. Students study just **one** of these three parts, and in the exam they **must** choose their questions from only one part. If they answer questions from two different parts, one will not be marked. The content is defined through three broad key questions, fleshed out with more specific focus points. Methodical attention to these questions and focus points should ensure students face no great surprises when they sit the examination.

Much of this supporting material concentrates on strategies to ensure students know how to approach different types of exam question, recognise the skills they are required to demonstrate, and understand the best way to deploy their knowledge. The material in this section focuses on the core content, but there are other areas that it is appropriate for higher attainers in particular to study in order to deepen their understanding of the development of the Cold War.

Ideas for starters and plenaries

A FOUR-MARK QUESTION

Students complete a four-mark Unit A971 exam question (e.g. 'Who were the Vietcong?'; worksheet 2.15) based on material covered in the previous lesson, then swap their work and award each other marks for each relevant point made. This should be used to help emphasise the importance of precise factual knowledge, and to develop exam technique. This can also be done as a plenary, particularly in a lesson that has focused on the factual content of a topic.

A SIX-MARK QUESTION – TO ENCOURAGE EXPLANATION

Six-mark Unit A971 exam questions (e.g. 'Explain why the USA became involved in Vietnam'; worksheet 2.15) can also be used as either starters or plenaries. In their responses to these types of question, students often do not explain the points they make sufficiently,

restricting their answer to description or identification. To encourage them to explain their points, a useful starter or plenary is to give students a six-mark exam question and ask them to record bullet-point responses (in the example given, this might be, for example:

- the French withdrew
- to help South Vietnam
- the domino theory.

They must then add a sentence to each bullet point in order to explain how the reason given helps to answer the question. This could be done in table format.

Example

Description/ identification	Explanation (how does this factor help to answer the question?)
The French withdrew	This led to the division of Vietnam into the Communist North and the non-Communist South.
To help South Vietnam	This meant escalating involvement, as the leader of South Vietnam was corrupt and unpopular. The Communist forces therefore had support among the South Vietnamese.
The domino theory	This idea caused the USA to believe it had to become involved in Vietnam in line with its policy of containment. The domino theory suggested that if one country in Southeast Asia fell to Communism, others would follow.

Once students are more familiar with GCSE-level work, they can dispense with the need for this type of structure, moving on to attempt the question without help and then assessing each other's work (see Peer Assessment Grids, pages 51–56).

WORD LOOPS

Word loops can be used to encourage the retention of specific factual information and an understanding of the chronology of important events – both skills that some students consistently struggle with. See worksheet 2.1 for an example that can be used as a starter (or plenary) when studying the Cuban Missile Crisis.

Each student (or pair of students) is given a slip of paper. One student will have a slip marked 'start', and they should begin reading. Students have to work out what comes next, and whoever has the relevant information on their slip of paper reads it out. This continues until all students have read their slips and thus are given an overview of the topic they are studying. Some students will need prompting/clues, and the read-through may not progress very smoothly the first time. However, students enjoy trying to perfect the exercise and ensure the read-through flows without pause.

This activity has advantages over a question-and-answer review of factual information in that it ensures all students are involved and focused. It can be easily adapted, depending on the ability of the group or individual student: higher attainers can be given more than one slip, for example.

A BIASED ACCOUNT

As a plenary, students can write a biased account of the event they have been studying that lesson. This has the added advantage of ensuring that students not only record and show they have understood historical events, but also that they understand the different perspectives that can be presented regarding those events. This could be done in different formats, such as a newspaper article, a speech by the leader of one country, etc.

HEADLINE NEWS

A briefer way to demonstrate an understanding of different perspectives, which again can be used as a starter or a plenary, is to formulate newspaper headlines about an event. This can be tied in with work on biased and persuasive language.

Example
Headlines about the Cuban Missile Crisis:

From an American perspective	From a Russian perspective
Reds on our doorstep!	Brave Cubans receive our help: American aggression must end
Kennedy holds firm, Khrushchev backs down	Khrushchev the peacemaker

LAYERS OF INFERENCE

Using a 'layers of inference' approach to sources can also prove an effective starter. This type of

task encourages students to formulate their own questions about a topic, which again stimulates curiosity. It also allows for different levels of access: lower attainers can focus on what the source actually tells them, whereas higher attainers can move on to making inferences and posing questions. Much research has focused on the necessity of acquiring the 'language of thought', meaning that it is difficult, if not impossible, to think at higher levels if you do not have the language skills and vocabulary to do so.

So in tasks such as this, it is very helpful to focus on such language, in this case the word 'infer', and to give students simple examples of how to use it before they attempt the task for the first time. Showing a photograph of someone with distinctive characteristics and asking students what they can infer about the person in the photograph from what they are wearing, what they are doing, their attitude, etc. can help them to reach an understanding of the word.

An example of layers of inference is given in worksheet 2.2. This example is also useful in helping students understand how to analyse sources in general. In the exam, they can pick up marks just from accurately describing what the source says. The first layer of the task requires them to do this. The second layer moves on to the higher-level skill of making inferences from a source, and the final layers require students to identify what the source does *not* tell them, and what other information they would need in order to understand it fully.

Many types of source can be used: the example given is of a speech by Stalin, but cartoons, headlines, extracts from songs, scenes from films or quotations from speeches could be substituted.

CARTOONS

The analysis of cartoon sources may feature on either paper. There are many websites which offer a selection of cartoons relating to the course. A good starting point for specifically British political cartoons is the British Cartoon Archive. For students, Learning Curve's Focus on Cartoons web pages provide a guide to what political cartoons are, and how to use them as evidence. Go to www.heinemann.co.uk/hotlinks, insert the express code 0206T, and click on 'British Cartoon Archive' and 'Learning Curve'.

As a plenary, students could create their own political cartoons about a particular event from a given perspective. In helping students to understand that cartoon sources have a clear purpose and message, it is a good idea to look at some examples from modern newspapers. Students can collect examples themselves, and explain to the group what issue the cartoon is commenting on and what the cartoonist is trying to say.

Grabbing attention

The Cold War provides a wealth of material that can be used to engage interest, provoke questions and stimulate debate. Initial material could include the following.

A SHORT MOVIE

Showing the film *Duck and Cover* (1952, 9 minutes), or an extract from it. This was a film produced to show American children what to do in the event of a nuclear attack, and makes for an interesting comparison with the type of educational films students will have been shown in school. Go to www.heinemann.co.uk/hotlinks, insert the express code 0206T, and click on 'Duck and Cover'.

MUSIC

There is a variety of music from the period that reveals how the paranoia, suspicion and fear of the Cold War permeated popular culture.

Examples (mostly available on YouTube) include:

- Barry McGuire – 'Eve of Destruction'
- Bob Dylan – 'With God On Our Side'
- Hedgehoppers Anonymous – 'It's Good News Week'
- Nena – '99 Red Balloons'

Music can also be used to illustrate why many in the West (particularly the rich and powerful) feared the spread of communism. Play students a recording of the Red Army Choir singing the communist/socialist anthem 'The Internationale' (www.heinemann.co.uk/hotlinks, express code 0206T, click on 'Internationale'), and provide them with the lyrics translated into English (worksheet 2.3): the stirring nature of the music, combined with the imposing presence of the Red Army and

lyrics that plainly advocate a revolutionary new order, should illustrate the point very effectively.

HEADLINES AND NEWS

Headlines from the period are an interesting starting point: if students want to find out the explanation for seemingly odd or dramatic headlines, they are more likely to engage with the topic from the beginning. Some examples include:

- 'Truman says Reds have exploded atom!'
- 'Kennedy orders blockade of Cuba as reds build nuclear bases there'
- 'The biggest bomb in the world – 50 million tons and Russia will explode it soon'

In a similar manner, stories of Cold War 'madness' can prompt students into actively wanting to find explanations for such behaviour. One example is the government investment on both sides that went into monitoring the Fischer (USA) versus Spassky (USSR) Chess World Championship match of 1972: both men had government minders and were bugged throughout. Both sides desperately wanted to win in the spirit of Cold War one-upmanship, but there were rumours that Fischer's family may have been spying for the USSR. Other rumours included the idea that the CIA and KGB had hired people they believed might have telepathic powers in order to confuse the opposing side.

MOVIES IN CONTEXT

Films from the period also provide a – sometimes subtle, sometimes extremely heavy-handed – commentary on the Cold War, and can provide insight into the conflict's enduring effect on popular culture.

For example, the Bond film *From Russia With Love* (dir. Terence Young, 1963) contains a host of Cold War KGB stereotypes. The importance of denouncing people with supposed communist leanings during the McCarthy era is made clear in films such as *Conspirator* (dir. Victor Saville, 1949) and *My Son John* (dir. Leo McCarey, 1952), which are almost comically zealous in their anti-communism. The fear of being taken over by communism found symbolic expression in several science fiction films of the 1950s and 1960s, including *Invasion of the Body Snatchers* (dir. Don Siegel, 1956). The fear of a nuclear holocaust is also a common theme, for example in *On the Beach* (dir. Stanley Kramer, 1959) and *Dr Strangelove* (dir. Stanley Kubrick, 1964).

Activities

KEY QUESTION 4: WHO WAS TO BLAME FOR THE COLD WAR?

Specified content:

- the origins of the Cold War

- the 1945 summit conferences, including the parts played by Churchill, Roosevelt, Stalin and Truman

- the breakdown of the USA–USSR alliance in 1945–46

- Soviet expansion in Eastern Europe

- the Iron Curtain

- the Truman Doctrine and the Marshall Plan

- the Berlin Blockade and its immediate consequences.

Activity 2.1: Understanding chronology

As an introductory session, introduce this key question through a card game. Randomly hand out cards with the details of the events on them so that each pupil has one, then ask them to organise themselves into a chronological line. (Chronology is a simple idea that many students fail to grasp.) Once they are in a line, students could be asked a series of questions, such as:

Who has a Western-allied action card?

Who has a Soviet-allied action card?

Are the actions military or economic?

Worksheet 2.4 provides a set of cards with details of the events of the early part of the Cold War for use with this activity. Higher attainers could make the cards themselves using the student book.

Students could organise themselves into groups: one group for Western action, one for Soviet and one for stragglers. Once in these groups, they could be given the task of investigating the actions using the internet, materials from the teacher, or the student book. They could present back to the class and make a timeline on the wall.

As an alternative, students could be asked to make their own cards giving dates and details

of the main events. Students should decide which cards could be seen as a threat from the West to the East, and *vice versa*. Care should be taken when deciding this – some cards will be retaliatory and some will constitute a fresh threat.

Throughout the following four focus points, it is helpful for students to remain aware of the overall key question, and to refer back to it each lesson.

Worksheet 2.5 provides one method that could be used to do this, and to encourage students to gather evidence in order to help them with essay-style questions on this topic. As they progress through the next few lessons, students should add to this table whenever they come across a fact or argument that could be used. They could also be encouraged to use the sources in the student book to include quotations or references to support both sides of the argument. This should provide students with a framework to answer the overall enquiry question.

Focus point: Why did the USA–USSR alliance begin to break down in 1945?

A natural and important starting point for students is to introduce (or recap, depending on options chosen within the syllabus and work done at KS3) the events of the Second World War and the shifting alliances between the USSR, USA, Great Britain and Germany. From this students should be able to suggest some pre-existing tensions between the countries.

Students must then be introduced to the individual agendas of Stalin, Roosevelt and Churchill, and the agreements that were reached at Yalta. In order to fully understand later events such as the Berlin Blockade, it is useful for students to produce an annotated map showing the decisions that were reached about the division of Germany.

Activity 2.2: Understanding different points of view at Potsdam

Students can begin by looking at the layers of inference task (worksheet 2.2). Explain that the speech was made after Potsdam, and ask students to see if they can begin to work out from the speech what might have caused disagreement. The questions they formulate during the task can be returned to at the end of the lesson to ensure they have been answered.

Students need to understand why the promising beginnings at Yalta were not translated into agreements at Potsdam.

Divide the class in half, with one half representing Stalin and the other half Truman. They should use the textbooks to make a list of priorities for their given leader. Higher attainers can be given sources about the personalities of Stalin and Truman to add depth to their responses in the next task.

Questions can then be posed to the group as a whole, such as:

- Should Germany pay reparations?

- What should happen to the nations of Eastern Europe?

Students must respond from the perspective of the leader they have been allocated. A points system can be used where groups are given one point for every valid reason that one of their members can give to support their position on the key questions at Potsdam. Students should be encouraged to challenge each other's arguments 'in character', with points awarded again for arguments that demonstrate an understanding of their point of view.

Following this, students are encouraged to reflect on questions such as:

- What was the most important cause of dispute at Potsdam?

- How did the personality of the two leaders affect the discussions?

- What were the results of the disagreements at Potsdam?

- Was either leader more to blame for the failure of negotiations?

Students must also understand the impact that news of the development of the atomic bomb had on negotiations. Using sources, students should consider what Truman's motives were when informing Stalin of the USA's work on this weapon.

Activity 2.3: Analysing sources in depth

Churchill's 'iron curtain' speech is a source that can be analysed in detail to gain a picture of the relationship between the major powers after Potsdam (see worksheet 2.6). It can also lead to a discussion of persuasive technique, and the reliability and purpose of source material. This is an issue that students often find difficult to address effectively in exams, many do not refer to the tone and language of a source even if this is highly exaggerated. It is therefore useful to spend time focusing on the provenance of different types of source whenever possible.

Before completing the analysis exercise, students will need to read through the source and note down any words or phrases they do not understand, which can then be clarified via discussion or use of the student books and/or dictionaries. An extension task for higher attainers could be to write a response to Churchill from the perspective of the USSR, challenging each point made in the 'Iron Curtain' speech in turn, and attempting to utilise similar persuasive techniques. Students can suggest further techniques and incorporate them into their writing, such as rhetorical questions, alliteration, etc.

Students should be encouraged to consider the different effects such a speech would have on the general public in Western Europe, the USSR and the USA, and how it might be presented in those countries.

Focus point: How had the USSR gained control of Eastern Europe by 1948?

Activity 2.4: Working with maps

Students could be asked to carry out research on each country in Eastern Europe, in small groups or individually. A giant map could be roughly outlined on the classroom floor using rope, and students positioned on it while they read out what happened to their country. One of them could play a satisfied Stalin watching over it all. Common themes could be drawn out about the way each country was 'voted' into communist rule, so that students gain an overall understanding of the Soviet methods of coercion. Worksheet 2.7 contains a map of Europe which students can use to annotate with their own notes about each country: this could be filled in as students who have researched a particular country feed back to the class.

Focus point: How did the USA react to Soviet expansionism?

Activity 2.5: Applying knowledge to a cartoon question

Once students have studied the Truman Doctrine and Marshall Aid, they can apply their knowledge to a cartoon exam question.

There are four main areas that students need to focus on when analysing cartoons:

- surface features
- hidden meaning
- context
- provenance/purpose.

Before students become practised at answering this type of question, it is helpful to annotate cartoon sources in order to build up different levels of analysis. Lower attainers should be reassured that even if they are unsure about the meaning of a cartoon, they can attempt to describe what they see in order to gain marks.

Focus point: Who was more to blame for the start of the Cold War, the USA or the USSR?

Activity 2.6: The USA and USSR on trial

Explain to students that the USA and the USSR are to be put on trial to find out who was to blame for the Cold War. Allocate students one of four tasks:

- USA – presenting either the case for the defence or for the prosecution
- USSR – presenting either the case for the defence or for the prosecution.

Ideally, tasks will be allocated so that a quarter of the class is addressing each one. Students should use the textbooks and the sheets on which they have been collecting information over the past few lessons. They need to prepare their case, giving as many arguments as possible. Students must use evidence, preferably including quotations from sources, to back up every argument they make.

Two (preferably confident) students can represent the USA and USSR. The four groups can then take it in turn to explain their case. They can either be given a score for the number of supported arguments they offer, or some students can form a jury, which decides whether the USA or USSR is most guilty. The students representing the USA and USSR can offer a last plea as to why they should not be found guilty. The jury members should be asked to explain why they reached the verdict that they did.

KEY QUESTION 5: WHO WAS THE WINNER IN THE CUBAN MISSILE CRISIS?

Specified content:

- the Cuban Revolution and the USA's reaction to it

- the Bay of Pigs
- the events of the crisis, including the roles of Khrushchev and Kennedy
- the resolution
- consequences of the crisis.

Focus point: How did the USA react to the Cuban Revolution?

An attention-grabbing opening to work on the Cuban Missile Crisis is to give students some examples of the methods the USA planned to use over the course of the Cold War to depose Castro. Students may have some awareness of Castro from more recent news, and could possibly suggest reasons why the USA would go to such lengths to get rid of him. The class can then return to the origins of the USA's problems with Castro: the overthrow of Batista and the subsequent Bay of Pigs fiasco.

Activity 2.7: Different perspectives

Ask students to fill in the table in worksheet 2.8 from both the American and the Cuban perspective. The answers could be used as a whole class (or at least large group) matching exercise.

Focus point: Why did Khrushchev send missiles to Cuba?

Activity 2.8: The geography of the Cold War

It is vital for this key question in particular that students have a sound grasp of the geography of the conflict. As a starter, students can be shown the photograph taken by a spy plane on 14 October 1962 (see page 74 in the student book). They should use these as a stimulus to consider the question of why Kennedy was so worried about these missiles in particular.

Students could then use the information in the student book to produce a government security report for Kennedy on the situation. Higher attainers can structure this themselves, or use headings given to them. These might include:

- What do the pictures taken over Cuba show?
- Why is what the pictures show a threat to US security?
- How might Khrushchev justify his contribution to this threat?
- What scenarios could develop from this event?

A blank map of Europe can be given to students to annotate and include in their report.

Worksheet 2.9 gives a structure for lower attainers to complete this task.

Focus point: Why did Kennedy react as he did?

Activity 2.9: Cold War decision-making

The focus point about Kennedy lends itself naturally to a decision-making exercise, where students consider the different options that were open to Kennedy and reach a conclusion about which was most appropriate. In order to do this effectively, students must understand the nature of the conflict and what priorities a Cold War leader had to consider (avoiding all-out war, propaganda, image, etc.) A starter activity for this lesson could be a simple spider diagram in which students record their ideas thus far about what was required of a Cold War leader.

Students can be given a range of options available to Kennedy. In the case of higher attainers, they could be asked to come up with their own list of possible responses. They can then use these to construct a table in which they record the advantages and disadvantages of each option and reach a conclusion regarding what they think the best decision would be for Kennedy (see worksheet 2.10). Students can then look at the events of the crisis following Kennedy's decision to blockade Cuba, and evaluate whether or not he made the correct decision.

Focus Point: Who was the winner in the Cuban Missile Crisis?

Activity 2.10: How close was the world to war?

An effective way of representing the threat level over the course of the Cuban Missile Crisis is to do so in graph format. There are various ways in which this can be done, but all should lead students to think about:

- At which points did the crisis bring the USA and USSR closest to war?

- How would the crisis be perceived by the general public?

- How did the two leaders behave during the crisis?

- How would the events of the crisis affect relations between the two countries?

One way the graph can be presented is to give students the events of the crisis on slips of paper (worksheet 2.11). Students use these to plot the threat level on the graph (worksheet 2.12; this could be copied onto A3 paper), placing a cross on the graph at the appropriate date and proximity to war, and labelling it with the relevant slip of paper. Students need to evaluate whether each step of the crisis bought the two countries closer to, or further away from, all-out war. This can form the basis for discussion about whether either leader was responsible for escalating or de-escalating the crisis, and in what ways the crisis might have had positive and/or negative results for the leadership of both countries.

Activity 2.11: Giving both sides of the argument

Taken together with an examination of the consequences of the crisis and its broader implications (see pages 77–78 in the student book), this activity will provide students with the knowledge necessary to address the focus point about who was the winner in the Cuban Missile Crisis. They can be given simple starter sentences to write up what they have discussed:

- It could be said that Kennedy emerged as the clear victor because…

- *On the other hand*, it could be argued that the USSR also made gains…

- The crisis had other long-term consequences for both countries. For example…

- *However*, some aspects of the Cold War remained unchanged, such as…

It is useful to remind students that, when addressing a question such as 'Who was the winner in the Cuban Missile Crisis?', they need to give both sides of the argument and support the points they make with evidence and specific examples. A focus on literacy skills, such as the use of connectives, can help students understand how to present two different points of view. Students can be given a list of connectives classified according to purpose, in order to help them more generally with the literacy/communication aspect of GCSE history.

For example:

Connectives that explain:
For example…
On the other hand…
Besides…
After all…
That is to say…
By contrast…

Connectives showing links between ideas:
Moreover
Therefore
However
Since
Eventually
Until
Consequently
Furthemore

Other connectives
Although
Whenever
While/whilst
Despite
When
Whereas
Wherever

Time connectives
Then
Meanwhile
Next
After
Since

Connectives to show order
First(ly)
First of all…
Finally

For this activity, students can be asked to come up with appropriate connectives to begin the sentences, and to apply the techniques to other questions. Even if they are given questions on topics they have not studied, they should be able to apply this structure, and indeed gain in confidence when they realise there are rules that can be applied to answering this type of question.

KEY QUESTION 6: WHY DID THE USA FAIL IN VIETNAM?

Specified content:

- increasing American involvement in Vietnam under Eisenhower, Kennedy and Johnson
- the main events of the war, and the tactics used by the two sides

- reasons for American withdrawal.

Focus point: Why did the USA become increasingly involved in Vietnam?

Activity 2.12: Popular music as a source of evidence

Music is a good way of engaging students, and raises interesting questions of reliability and provenance. There are many (mainly anti-war) songs about Vietnam that could be used, but the song 'Lyndon Johnson Told the Nation' by Tom Paxton contains a particularly detailed, ironic critique of Johnson's approach to the conflict (see worksheet 2.13). The song mentions several of the tactics that failed for American troops in Vietnam, and places blame for escalating the conflict firmly on Johnson's shoulders.

Students sometimes find it difficult to appreciate that popular music can be an invaluable source of historical evidence. An appropriate starter activity is to ask students what the popular music they listen to tends to be about. They will probably suggest 'love', 'relationships', etc. but with prompting they will be able to think of current songs that address more serious issues (drugs, crime, gangs, the war in Iraq). When students are then asked what this type of song could tell somebody in 100 years' time about life in the early 21st century, they begin to see that popular music can also be a source of evidence.

Worksheet 2.13 provides a framework for analysing this particular song. If it is possible to listen to the music, students should listen through once noting any terms they don't understand. Following clarification, students should listen again and begin to try to address the questions relating to each verse.

Once an understanding has been reached of what the song is trying to say, then questions of its provenance and reliability can be addressed, focusing on the purpose of the song, its audience, and what it can tell us about American public opinion in the 1960s. Appropriate questions could be:

- Why did Tom Paxton write this song?

- Is it a reliable source of evidence about the war in Vietnam?

- Could it be described as propaganda?

- What can the song tell us about American public opinion in the 1960s?

- What are the limitations of this type of source? What does it not tell us?

A lesson focusing on this song leads naturally into addressing the question of what caused the American withdrawal from Vietnam: public opinion, military failures, or both.

Focus point: What were the different ways in which the USA and the communists fought the war?

Focus point: Whose tactics were the most effective – the USA's or the communists'?

Focus point: Why did the USA withdraw from Vietnam?

Activity 2.13: Bringing together work on the war in Vietnam

Following coverage of the relevant content, worksheet 2.14 gives some model answers in response to four-, six- and ten-mark questions about the war in Vietnam. Worksheets 2.15 and 2.16 give a structure to help lower attainers attempt these questions themselves. Peer marking sheets can be used for students to assess each other's work or to mark the model answers. Model answers can also be given to students to annotate/highlight aspects of the answer that meet specific criteria. Worksheet 2.16 gives a simplified student mark scheme to aid peer assessment.

Grade Studio

USING EXAM QUESTIONS, MARK SCHEMES AND PEER ASSESSMENT TO IMPROVE ATTAINMENT

Grade Studio has been designed to help both students and teachers interpret GCSE history mark schemes.

Grade Studio has a clear and explicit focus on levels. It is the point at which the teaching and practice in the student book becomes focused on moving between levels, and therefore the learning becomes increasingly personalised and improves students' chances of achieving better grades.

The activities in the student book and on the CD-ROM should help students to improve their understanding of how to answer different types of exam question. Worksheets 2.17 and 2.18 contain some answers written at different levels in response to exam questions about the Cuban

Missile Crisis, and worksheet 2.19 contains simplified, student-friendly versions of OCR mark schemes for these questions. These resources can be used in conjunction with the peer assessment sheets in a variety of ways.

- Students can mark the questions themselves, giving both a level and a specific mark within that level. It is important that students give a reason, referring explicitly to the mark scheme, to justify the mark they have awarded. For example; 'I have given this answer a level 2 (3 marks) because it identifies four reasons why Khrushchev sent missiles to Cuba, but it doesn't explain those reasons.'

- Students will need to be given a copy of the mark scheme, and will almost certainly require model answers in order to complete this task effectively. It may be necessary to mark one or two questions together as a class, in order to make the task as constructive as possible.

- Students can annotate the model answers with criticisms and/or positive points.

- They can highlight sections of the answer that meet particular mark scheme criteria. This can be used to develop their understanding of factors such as the difference between description and explanation.

- Highlighting can also be used to identify where answers have demonstrated particular literacy-related skills, such as effective topic sentences, the use of connectives and analytical language.

- Students can attempt the questions themselves, and then use the mark scheme and peer assessment sheets to mark each other's work. Again, many students will require positive feedback and target-setting to be modelled before they attempt it.

2.1 Cuban Missile Crisis Word Loop

START	In 1959, the American-backed dictator of Cuba, a man called
Batista, was overthrown and replaced with the pro-communist Fidel Castro.	America did not want such a close neighbour to become communist, so they backed some Cuban exiles in an invasion attempt at
the Bay of Pigs. The attempt was a humiliating failure for President Kennedy.	The leader of the USSR at this time was
Khrushchev, who was pleased that the USA had been embarrassed.	He was concerned that the USA would try to
invade Cuba again, so he wanted to place missiles on the island as a deterrent.	Khrushchev also thought that it was reasonable for him to have missiles in Cuba as the USA had missiles in
Turkey, which was close to the USSR.	On 14 October 1962, a US spy plane took pictures of
missile sites on Cuba.	This was the beginning of a two-week crisis, which many people suggest took the world as close as it has ever been to all-out
nuclear war.	Kennedy had to decide what to do about the missiles. Some of his advisors, known as the hawks, encouraged him to use force immediately. However, Kennedy decided to
blockade Cuba to stop Soviet ships getting in.	This was dangerous as stopping a Soviet ship was technically
an act of war.	120,000 US soldiers gathered on
the Florida coast, which suggested to Khruschev and Castro that the Americans were about to invade.	Khrushchev sent Kennedy a letter on 26 October which offered
to remove the missiles if Kennedy promised not to invade Cuba.	The next day, Kennedy received another letter which still offered to remove the missiles, but this time with the extra condition that
the USA should remove its missiles from Turkey.	After a day of tension, Kennedy
accepted Khrushchev's offer, but only if the deal was kept secret.	Following the crisis, Cuba remained
a communist country and Fidel Castro continued to survive American attempts to get rid of him.	Both the USA and USSR said they were keen to avoid such a situation recurring and set up
a telephone link between the two leaders. Many historians suggest that the crisis helped to thaw Cold War relations between the USA and the USSR.	FINISH

2.2 Layers of inference

What questions do I need to ask?

What does this source **NOT** tell me?

What can I **INFER** from this source?

What does this source **DEFINITELY** tell me?

The following circumstances should not be forgotten. The Germans made their invasion of the USSR through Finland, Poland, Rumania, Bulgaria and Hungary. The Germans were able to make their invasion through these countries because, at the time, governments hostile to the Soviet Union existed in these countries …And so what can there be surprising about the fact that the Soviet Union, anxious for its future safety, is trying to see to it that governments loyal in their attitude to the Soviet Union should exist in these countries?
(Stalin, in response to a speech by Churchill, 1946).

2.3 The Internationale

The Internationale

Arise ye workers from your slumbers
Arise ye prisoners of want
For reason in revolt now thunders
And at last ends the age of cant.
Away with all your superstitions
Servile masses arise, arise
We'll change henceforth the old tradition
And spurn the dust to win the prize.

So comrades, come rally
And the last fight let us face
The Internationale unites the human race.
So comrades, come rally
And the last fight let us face
The Internationale unites the human race.

No more deluded by reaction
On tyrants only we'll make war
The soldiers too will take strike action
They'll break ranks and fight no more
And if those cannibals keep trying
To sacrifice us to their pride
They soon shall hear the bullets flying
We'll shoot the generals on our own side.

No saviour from on high delivers
No faith have we in prince or peer
Our own right hand the chains must shiver
Chains of hatred, greed and fear
E'er the thieves will give up their booty
And give to all a happier lot.
Each at the forge must do their duty
And we'll strike while the iron is hot.

2.4 Cold War timeline

February 1945 = Yalta Conference attended by Churchill, Roosevelt and Stalin. They discussed what to do with Germany after the war (divide it into four), how the Soviet Union would join the fight against Japan 90 days after the defeat of Germany, and what to do with Poland.	*April 1945* = Roosevelt died and was replaced by Harry Truman. Truman had a much less trusting attitude towards the Soviet Union.
July 1945 = Potsdam Conference attended by Churchill (replaced by Clement Attlee halfway through), Truman and Stalin. They discussed the detail of the occupation and reconstruction of Germany and other nations, and warned Japan to surrender.	*1945* = Annexation of Baltic States. Latvia, Lithuania and Estonia were occupied by the Soviet Union during the war, the Soviet Union saw no reason to release them once it was over.
1944–46 = Bulgaria became a satellite state of the Soviet Union, with rigged elections and the abolition of the monarchy ensuring communist-dominated government.	*1945* = Yugoslavia, a communist country, started with a good relationship with the Soviet Union but this deteriorated and its leader, Tito, turned to the West for aid.
1945–47 = Romania became a satellite state of the Soviet Union, with a forced appointment of a communist prime minister and the abolition of the monarchy ensuring communist-dominated government.	*1945–47* = Hungary became a satellite state of the Soviet Union, with rigged elections and a total ban on all other political parties, ensuring communist-dominated government.
January 1947 = Rigged elections in Poland saw the 'London Poles' ousted and replaced by communists, ensuring communist-dominated government.	*1946–48* = A communist-led seizure of power followed by rigged elections ensured a communist-dominated government.
February 1947 = The Truman Doctrine. America was prepared to give help to any country under threat from communism.	*June 1947* = The Marshall Plan. Truman decided that the USA should use its wealth to provide economic aid to Europe.
September 1947 = The Soviet Union formed the Communist Information Bureau (Cominform) to strengthen ties between communist countries.	*June 1948* = Berlin Blockade and start of airlift to get supplies to residents of West Berlin (Blockade called off May 1949).
January 1949 = Stalin announced the formation of the Council for Mutual Economic Aid (Comecon) to rival the Marshall Plan.	*April 1949* = The North Atlantic Treaty Organization was formed as a military alliance of European and North American countries.
May 1949 = The British, American and French zones of Germany were formally united in the Federal Republic of Germany (West Germany).	*October 1949* = The Soviet-controlled part of Germany formally became a separate state called the German Democratic Republic (East Germany).
1949 = Greek Civil War between a Western-backed government and communists ended with the government victorious. Stalin kept his promise to the West not to get involved.	*1949* = Soviet scientists developed an atomic bomb.
1949 = China becomes a communist country.	*1955* = West Germany became a member of NATO.
1955 = The Warsaw Pact formed as a military alliance of communist states.	

2.5 Who was to blame for the Cold War?

Country	To blame	Not to blame
USSR	It could be argued that the USSR was to blame for the Cold War because… Source references/quotations:	It could be argued that the USSR was not to blame for the Cold War because… Source references/quotations:
USA	It could be argued that the USA was to blame for the Cold War because… Source references/quotations:	It could be argued that the USA was not to blame for the Cold War because… Source references/quotations:

2.6 Churchill's 'Iron Curtain' speech

Why does Churchill then go on to emphasise his admiration of the Russian people and their leader?

What picture does Churchill bring to mind in his opening sentence?

What impression does Churchill give of the USSR in this paragraph?

Why do you think Churchill chose the phrase 'iron curtain'?

What does he claim is happening behind the 'iron curtain'?

What does Churchill suggest the USSR's intentions are for the future?

What sort of leader do you think Churchill wants his listeners to see him as?

What does Churchill accuse the 'Russian-dominated Polish government' of doing? What adjectives does he use to describe their actions?

What negative developments does Churchill describe in the Soviet-dominated countries of Eastern Europe?

A shadow has fallen upon the scenes so lately lighted by the Allied victory. Nobody knows what Soviet Russia and its Communist international organization intends to do in the immediate future, or what are the limits, if any, to their expansive...tendencies.

I have a strong admiration and regard for the valiant Russian people and for my wartime comrade Marshal Stalin. We understand the Russian need to be secure on her western frontiers from any German aggression...It is my duty, however, to place before you certain facts about the present position in Europe – I am sure I do not wish to, but it is my duty, I feel, to present them to you.

From Stettin in the Baltic to Trieste in the Adriatic, an iron curtain has descended across the Continent. Behind that line lie all the capitals of the ancient states of central and eastern Europe...all these famous cities and the populations around them lie in the Soviet sphere and all are subject...not only to Soviet influence but to a very high and increasing measure of control from Moscow. The Russian-dominated Polish government has been encouraged to make enormous and wrongful in-roads upon Germany, and mass expulsions of millions of Germans on a scale grievous and undreamed of are now taking place.

The Communist parties, which were very small in all these Eastern states of Europe, have been raised to pre-eminence and power far beyond their numbers and are seeking everywhere to obtain totalitarian control. Police governments are prevailing in nearly every case, and so far, except in Czechoslovakia, there is no true democracy. Turkey and Persia are both profoundly alarmed and disturbed at the claims which are made upon them and at the pressure being exerted by the Moscow government. An attempt is being made by the Russians in Berlin to build up a [kind of] Communist Party in their zone of occupied Germany by showing special favours to groups of Communist German leaders.

2.7 Europe in 1948

The USSR

Romania

Bulgaria

Poland

The USSR

POLAND

CZECHOSLOVAKIA

HUNGARY

ROMANIA

BULGARIA

THE GDR

ALBANIA

GDR

Czechoslovakia

Hungary

Albania

2.8 Different perspectives

Action	Whose perspective?	Outcome
Cubans win independence from Spain (1898)	Cuban	Initially positive because of American investment in Cuban industry.
	American	Positive because, although USA has to spend money in Cuba to help its industrial development, USA benefits from trade and influence with Cuba.
Military takeover of Cuba by American-backed Batista	Cuban	
	American	
Initial 1959 Cuban Revolution led by Fidel Castro	Cuban	
	American	
US trade ban on Cuban goods	Cuban	
	American	
Cuban trade agreement with Soviet Union	Cuban	
	American	
Invasion by 'Cuban exiles' at the Bay of Pigs	Cuban	
	American	
Cuban nationalisation of industries	Cuban	
	American	

2.9 Report on Cuba

TOP SECRET

> ## Report to the government of the United States on the situation in Cuba
> ## 14 September 1962

Cuba has been a problem for the USA since 1959 because...

Today, the situation in Cuba has become even more serious. A spy plane took a picture which showed...

Although we live in dangerous times, this is particularly worrying because...

Khrushchev may say that he has the right to use Cuba as a missile base because...

We cannot allow this to happen, however. If we allow him to use Cuba, the consequences could be that...

There are several different scenarios that could develop. For example...

I have included a map with this report which helps to explain...

2.10 Decision-making: President Kennedy

Decision	Advantages	Disadvantages
Launch another ground invasion of Cuba using infantry soldiers.		Last time this was attempted it resulted in humiliation for Kennedy. Could involve a considerable loss of American lives. Could initiate a war with Cuba and/or the USSR; makes Kennedy appear the aggressor.
Bomb the missile sites.		
Place a ring of ships around Cuba in order to stop any vessels from the USSR getting in or out.		
Try and negotiate with Khrushchev to remove the missiles without confrontation.		
Appeal to the United Nations (international peace-keeping organisation) for help.		
Do not get involved: keep an eye on the situation but allow the missile sites to remain for the time being.	Avoids confrontation. Avoids the risk of immediately escalating the situation.	
I think the best thing for Kennedy to do would be…		
I think that this would be the best decision because…		
I believe that the worst option for Kennedy would be to…		
because…		

2.11 Cuba graph labels

14 October A spy plane takes pictures of missile sites in Cuba.	**16–20 October** Kennedy and his advisors argue about what to do. Some want immediate action, others are more cautious.
21 October Kennedy decides to blockade Cuba, telling his brother Robert that the plan is 'one hell of a gamble'.	**22 October** Kennedy appears on US television to inform the public of what is happening. Khrushchev tells his advisers that he thinks Kennedy will invade Cuba, and promises to respond if he does.
23 October Soviet ships carrying missiles approach Cuba. There is some panic among the American people, and Khrushchev announces that the blockade is unjustified.	**24 October** US armed forces are put on Defcon 2, the highest alert level during the whole Cold War. Soviet ships stop before the blockade but do not turn round.
25 October A Soviet ship carrying oil is allowed by the USA to pass through the blockade.	**26 October** With 120,000 US troops gathered near the Florida coast, Kennedy gets a letter from Khrushchev promising to remove the missiles if he promises not to invade Cuba.
27 October A US spy plane is shot down over Cuba. Khrushchev sends a second letter, this time saying he will remove the missiles from Cuba only if the USA removes theirs from Turkey.	**27 October** Kennedy admits that Khrushchev's request is fair and agrees to it, provided the deal is kept secret. Khrushchev then announces that the USSR will remove its missiles from Cuba.

2.12 Cuba graph: level of threat in 1962

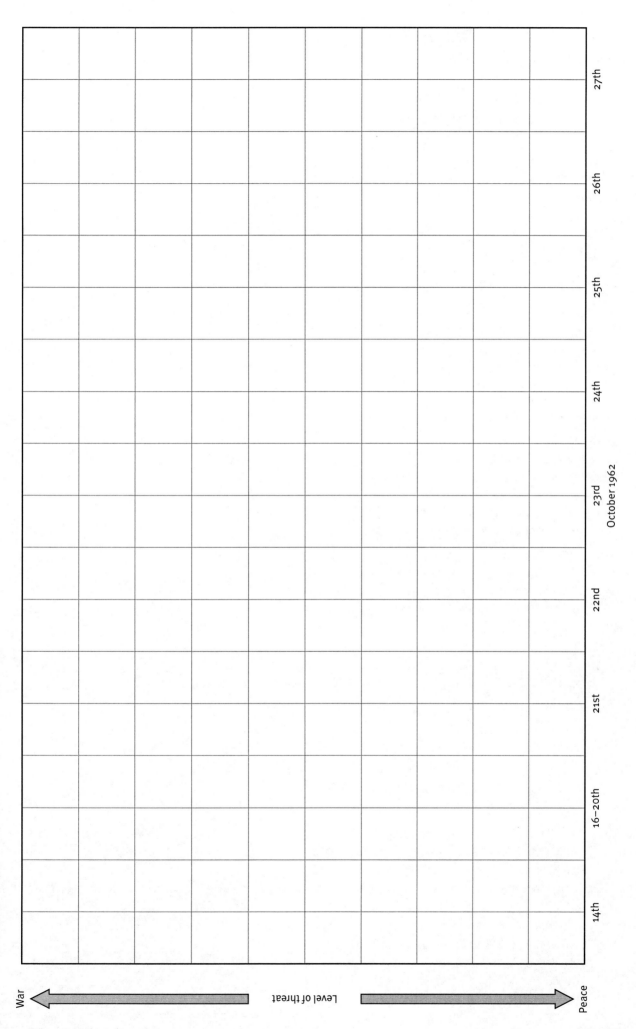

Level of threat

War ← → Peace

14th   16–20th   21st   22nd   23rd   24th   25th   26th   27th

October 1962

2.13 Lyndon Johnson Told the Nation

Words and Music by Tom Paxton

I got a letter from L. B. J.
It said this is your lucky day.
It's time to put your khaki trousers on.
Though it may seem very queer
We've got no jobs to give you here
So we are sending you to Vietnam

> Does the writer of the song really mean it was his 'lucky day'? What technique is he using here?
>
> What does Tom Paxton suggest the real reason for sending troops to Vietnam might be?

Chorus:

Lyndon Johnson told the nation,
'Have no fear of escalation.
I am trying everyone to please.
Though it isn't really war,
We're sending fifty thousand more,
To help save Vietnam from Vietnamese.'

> What does escalation mean?
>
> What does the final sentence of the chorus suggest?

I jumped off the old troop ship,
And sank in mud up to my hips.
I cussed until the captain called me down.
Never mind how hard it's raining,
Think of all the ground we're gaining,
Just don't take one step outside of town.

> What problem facing the American soldiers does Paxton highlight in this verse?

Every night the local gentry,
Sneak out past the sleeping sentry.
They go to join the old VC.
In their nightly little dramas,
They put on their black pajamas,
And come lobbing mortar shells at me.

> What problem facing the American soldiers does Paxton highlight in this verse?

We go round in helicopters,
Like a bunch of big grasshoppers,
Searching for the Viet Cong in vain.
They left a note that they had gone.
They had to get down to Saigon,
Their government positions to maintain.

> What problem facing the American soldiers does Paxton highlight in this verse?

Well here I sit in this rice paddy,
Wondering about Big Daddy,
And I know that Lyndon loves me so.
Yet how sadly I remember,
Way back yonder in November,
When he said I'd never have to go.

> What opinion do you think Tom Paxton has of Lyndon Johnson?

Questions:

1 How does Tom Paxton use irony in this song?
2 What is his real opinion of the war in Vietnam?
3 In what ways is this source useful to a historian studying American public opinion towards the war?
4 Does this source support or contradict your own knowledge about the war in Vietnam?
5 How reliable is this as a source of evidence?
6 Is there any other information you would need in order to fully assess the reliability of this source?
7 What questions would you like to ask the writer of this song?

2.14 Grade Studio: Vietnam sample answers

a Who were the Vietcong? **[4 marks]**

> The Vietcong were communist fighters in Vietnam. They wanted to overthrow the leader of South Vietnam, Ngo Dinh Diem. Many peasants in South Vietnam supported the Vietcong and this, together with the effective guerrilla tactics they used against the Americans, made them hard to defeat.

b Explain why the USA became involved in Vietnam. **[6 marks]**

> American involvement in Vietnam began when they tried to help the French regain control over the country following the Second World War as they did not want it to fall under the control of the communist Ho Chi Minh. When this attempt failed, America transferred its support to Ngo Dinh Diem, the anti-communist leader of South Vietnam. As Diem's regime was corrupt and unpopular, it required increasing amounts of American involvement to prevent the whole country becoming communist.
>
> Underpinning the USA's approach to Vietnam and another reason for their involvement was the 'domino theory'. This idea influenced American foreign policy because it suggested that if one country in South East Asia fell to communism, the rest would follow. America obviously wanted to avoid this situation, and in the context of the Cold War believed that it was their role to stop it.

c Which was more important in bringing about the USA's failure in Vietnam: the military tactics of the North Vietnamese or public opinion in the USA?
Explain your answer **[10 marks]**

> The war in Vietnam was clearly a failure from the perspective of the USA. The reasons for that failure include both the military tactics of the North Vietnamese and the pressures of public opinion within the USA.
>
> The North Vietnamese used military tactics which were very effective against the American army. They knew the terrain in which they were operating much better than the American soldiers did, which enabled them to conduct very effective surprise attacks and then disappear quickly. They avoided open combat, where the Americans would have been able to utilise their superior equipment more effectively, and used a complex system of underground tunnels to escape the threat of American bombs.
>
> Public opinion also affected the actions of the USA in Vietnam. As early as 1968 the new president, Richard Nixon, was looking for a way to reduce and eventually end US involvement in the country. This was partly because it was clear that many Americans were becoming increasingly unhappy with the war, and a large, high-profile peace movement had developed to voice their dissatisfaction via demonstrations, protests and the media.
>
> Overall, I believe that the two factors are very closely connected; but the tactics of the Vietcong were the most important in bringing about American failure in Vietnam. They are connected because the tactics of the Vietcong caused the Americans to resort to such strategies as 'search and destroy', which in turn led to atrocities such as the events at Mai Lai and a consequent fall in American support for the war. Despite this, many Americans continued to support the war, suggesting that if the tactics of the Vietcong had not proved so difficult to tackle, America may well have succeeded.

2.15 Grade Studio: Vietnam writing frame 1

a Who were the Vietcong? **[4 marks]**

You MUST make FOUR relevant points

The Vietcong were:

– ....

– ....

– ....

– ....

b Explain why the USA became involved in Vietnam. **[6 marks]**

You should aim to give two or three relevant reasons why the USA became involved in Vietnam, backed up with a further explanation. Use these starter sentences to help:

America first became involved in Vietnam when...

....

....

....

This made the USA concerned because...

....

....

....

A second reason for US involvement in Vietnam was...

....

....

....

This was also significant because...

....

....

....

Another reason for involvement was...

....

....

....

This reason encouraged the US government to become involved because...

....

....

....

2.16 Grade Studio: Vietnam writing frame 2 and mark scheme

c Which was more important in bringing about the USA's failure in Vietnam; the military tactics of the North Vietnamese or public opinion in the USA? Explain your answer. **[10 marks]**

This question needs to be broken down into paragraphs. A suggested structure is given, along with some possible topic sentences and content you may want to include.

1 Brief introduction, referring to the question.

2 How could it be said that the military tactics of the North Vietnamese contributed to the USA's failure?

Topic sentence: The North Vietnamese used military tactics which were very effective against the American army.

Content:
Nature of guerrilla warfare (tunnels, surprise attacks, disappearing into peasant villages, etc.)
Why the USA was unable to counter North Vietnamese tactics (examples of US failures)
What effect this had on the war in general (e.g. unpopularity of American tactics with Vietnamese people, lost support)

3 How could it be said that public opinion brought about the USA's failure in Vietnam?

Topic sentence: Public opinion also affected the actions of the USA in Vietnam. This was because...

Content:
Impact of television
Reporting of events such as Mai Lai
Protests in the USA
Changing attitudes in 1960s America
Pressure on US government

4 Conclusion: what is your opinion?

Topic sentence: Overall, I believe that...

Remember! Always give reasons and/or evidence to support your conclusions.

STUDENT MARK SCHEME

a Who were the Vietcong? **[4 marks]**
One mark for each relevant point, or two marks for a relevant point which is then explained.

b Explain why the USA became involved in Vietnam. **[6 marks]**

Level 1:	General answer without specific details.	[1 mark]
Level 2:	*Identifies* or *describes* reasons why America became involved in Vietnam without explanations.	[2–3 marks]
Level 3:	*Explains* reasons why America became involved in Vietnam (more explained reasons = more marks).	[3–6 marks]

c Which was more important in bringing about the USA's failure in Vietnam: the military tactics of the Vietcong or public opinion in the USA? Explain your answer. **[10 marks]**

Level 1:	General answer without specific details.	[1–2 marks]
Level 2:	*Identifies* or *describes* reasons why one factor led to US failure. **OR**	[2–3 marks]
	Identifies or *describes* at least one reason for *each* factor (public opinion AND military tactics).	[2–4 marks]
Level 3:	*Explains* why one of these reasons (military tactics OR public opinion) led to US failure.	[4–6 marks]
Level 4:	*Explains* why both reasons led to US failure (gives both sides of the argument).	[6–9 marks]
Level 5:	*Explains* with evaluation which was more important and why.	[9–10 marks]

2.17 Grade Studio: Cuba sample answers 1

a What happened in the Bay of Pigs invasion of 1961?   **[4 marks]**

Answer A

Kennedy did not like the new leader of Cuba, Fidel Castro. He tried to get rid of Castro but then he found out that nuclear weapons were on Cuba. This almost led to war between the USA and the USSR, as the USSR supported Castro.

Answer B

In 1959, Fidel Castro overthrew the American-backed dictator Batista and became the new leader of Cuba. This was unpopular with the USA, as Castro was strongly pro-Communist. President Kennedy was worried about having a Communist country so close to America and consequently he tried to overthrow Castro at the Bay of Pigs.

Answer C

In 1961, President Kennedy supplied arms and transport to 1400 Cuban exiles who had fled the country after the pro-Communist Fidel Castro became leader in 1959. When the exiles landed at the Bay of Pigs they were met by 20,000 well-armed Cuban soldiers. They were defeated, and the invasion was a humiliating disaster for Kennedy.

---

b Explain why Khrushchev sent missiles to Cuba in 1962.   **[6 marks]**

Answer A

There were several reasons why Khrushchev sent missiles to Cuba in 1962. Most importantly he wanted to win the arms race. Another reason is that he wanted to help Fidel Castro, the leader of Cuba who had overthrown Batista in the Cuban Revolution of 1959.

Answer B

Khrushchev thought he could use the missiles to bargain with Kennedy. His idea was that if Kennedy insisted he remove the missiles from Cuba, then he could put pressure on Kennedy to remove the USA's missiles from Turkey, where they posed a threat to the USSR.

Answer C

Cold War tensions meant that Khrushchev could use missiles on Cuba as an issue to test the inexperienced Kennedy and see how strong the USA really was. He believed he could do this at the same time as helping Castro, a fellow Communist leader, who feared another US attack after the Bay of Pigs. In addition to this, Khrushchev was concerned to keep up with the USA in terms of the arms race: placing missiles on Cuba made it less likely that the USA would launch a 'first strike' against the USSR in the future.

2.18 Grade Studio: Cuba sample answers 2

c 'The Cuban Missile Crisis was never a threat to world peace.'
  How far do you agree with this statement? Explain your answer.   **[10 marks]**

Answer A

The Cuban Missile Crisis was a big threat to world peace. The Cold War was all about looking like a strong leader so neither Khrushchev nor Kennedy wanted to back down. Lots of people were telling them to go to war and to make sure that they came out as the winner. The Cuban Missile Crisis brought the USA and USSR very close to war because both leaders were willing to fight and did not want to be the first one to back down.

Answer B

At the time, many people around the world perceived the Cuban Missile Crisis to be a major threat to world peace. However, examining the facts of the crisis would suggest that the statement is actually correct, and the world was not really very close to war at all.

Cuba had reason to fear an American invasion, and Khrushchev wanted to help prevent such an event: it could be argued in this way that the missiles were for defensive purposes. Not only that, but Khrushchev ignored advice from Castro to make the first strike and instead wrote a letter to Kennedy.

Kennedy also showed a willingness to compromise and a reluctance to start an all-out war. He bought time in delaying his reply to Khrushchev's first letter in the hope that the Russians would back down, thus avoiding the need for further conflict. Furthermore, he agreed to quietly withdraw the USA's missiles from Turkey in order to reach a mutually acceptable agreement with Khrushchev.

Both leaders showed throughout the crisis that they wanted to negotiate and would make concessions if necessary to avoid war, and I therefore agree with the statement that 'The Cuban Missile Crisis was never a threat to world peace.'

Answer C

There is evidence to support the statement that 'The Cuban Missile Crisis was never a threat to world peace'. Kennedy and Khrushchev both showed a willingness to compromise during the crisis, which would suggest that both were keen to avoid war. Soviet ships did not try to break through the American blockade, and indeed Khrushchev promised to take the missiles away if America said that it would not invade Cuba. Kennedy was not excessively aggressive during the crisis, for example allowing a non-missile carrying Russian ship to pass through the blockade. He also suggested that the USA would be willing to remove missiles from Turkey, which gave Khrushchev an incentive to back down further and ultimately defuse the crisis.

However, events could have taken a very different path. There were people on both sides pushing for an escalation of the conflict. Castro encouraged Khrushchev to make the 'first strike' against the USA, and with 120,000 US troops near the Florida coast the threat of invasion could have provoked a reaction from Khrushchev. Some US military advisors urged Kennedy to order an immediate air-strike following Khrushchev's first communication. More than one forceful ultimatum was given to the Russians and it would be hard to argue that there was no threat to world peace on 27 October, when Cuban forces shot down a US spy plane and Khrushchev made additional demands in a second letter to Kennedy.

The consequences of the crisis also suggest there was a belief in both countries that the world had been close to disaster. A telephone hotline was set up, for example, which allowed the leaders of the USA and USSR to speak directly.

In conclusion, I believe that there are arguments to be made in support of the statement. Both leaders clearly did not want to initiate an escalation of the Cold War, and both showed a willingness to make some concessions. However, Kennedy was forceful in his demands that the missiles be removed, and if Khrushchev had listened to Castro's advice, it does seem that the USA would have responded with force. Therefore it cannot be said with absolute certainty that the Cuban Missile Crisis was never a threat to world peace.

2.19 Grade Studio: Cuba mark scheme

STUDENT MARK SCHEME

a What happened in the Bay of Pigs invasion of 1961?   **[4 marks]**

One mark for each relevant point OR two marks for a relevant point which is then explained.

b Explain why Khrushchev sent missiles to Cuba in 1962.   **[6 marks]**

Level 1:	General answer without specific details.	[1 mark]
Level 2:	*Identifies* and/or *describes* reasons why Khrushchev sent missiles to Cuba with no explanation (more reasons = more marks).	
Level 3:	*Explains* reason(s) why Khrushchev sent missiles.	

One explained reason 3–4 marks; two or more explained reasons 5–6 marks.

c 'The Cuban Missile Crisis was never a threat to world peace.' How far do you agree with this statement? Explain your answer.   **[10 marks]**

Level 1:	General answer lacking any details.	[1–2 marks]
Level 2:	*Identifies* and/or *describes* arguments that could be used to agree or disagree with the statement in the question (more relevant points = more marks).	[2–4 marks]
Level 3:	*Explains* agreement OR disagreement with the statement in the question.	[3–6 marks]
Level 4:	*Explains* agreement AND disagreement with the statement (giving both sides of the argument).	[6–9 marks]
Level 5:	*Explains* with evaluation of 'how far' you agree with the statement.	[9–10 marks]

3 International Relations Part 3: A new world? 1948-2005

Introduction

This topic forms the third of the three-part International Relations Core 1919–2005. Students study just **one** of these three parts, and in the exam they **must** choose their questions from only one part. If they answer questions from two different parts, one will not be marked. The content is defined through three broad key questions, developed through more specific focus points. Methodical attention to these questions and focus points should ensure students face no great surprises when they sit the examination.

Much of this supporting material concentrates on strategies to ensure students know how to approach different types of exam question, recognise the skills they are required to demonstrate, and understand the best way to deploy their knowledge. The material in this section focuses on the core content, but there are other areas that it is appropriate for higher attainers in particular to study in order to deepen their understanding.

Ideas for starters and plenaries

TALK IT THROUGH

Class discussions are in many ways a useful method of checking understanding and ensuring lesson objectives have been met and learning outcomes have been reached. One problem may be that some students are very reluctant to participate, due to either disengagement or a lack of confidence.

One method of encouraging all students to participate in effective discussions is to use a 'discussion carousel' as part of lesson activities or as a plenary. All students form two large, concentric circles and sit facing a partner. Each pair is then given a card with a question on it, and asked to have a conversation about it for a certain amount of time (2–3 minutes is probably ideal). Each student should have a chance to speak (you can let students know when half the time has passed). When the time is over, students in the outer circle move round until you tell them to stop, and then sit down with another partner. Before the new pair begin discussing the

question, each student should summarise their previous partner's opinion. It is very helpful for students to articulate their ideas verbally in this way, and hopefully this task should ensure that they encounter different responses and perspectives in relation to different questions.

CARD GAME

Students work in groups of two to four. They receive a set of cards with a different keyword on each one. Students decide the order for their group, and the first student selects a card, which must be kept secret. The other members of the group question them in order to try to identify the keyword. The student who has the card can only answer 'yes' or 'no'. The group should try to identify the keyword as quickly as possible: the number of questions asked can be limited, or you can place a time limit on each turn.

STEPPING STONES

The idea of 'stepping stones' can be used as a plenary. This works particularly well in lessons that have focused on causation. Several pieces of A4 paper represent the stepping stones, which should be laid out on the floor in order. On each is a key term, event or personality that connects to the previous and next stepping stones. Ask for volunteers who think they can get from one end of the stepping stones to the other, and ask them to stand on the first piece of A4 paper. They can only move to the second stone if they can explain how it is connected to the one they are standing on. If you (and the rest of the class) are satisfied with their explanation, then they can be allowed to move on, and so on until they reach the last stone. A very simple example including the explanations students could give is shown on page 58.

Grabbing attention

The topic of International Relations 1948–2005 should present no problems in terms of engaging student interest. It covers events that have taken place, and continue to take place, during students' own lifetimes. Students may have relatives who have served in Iraq – or they may themselves have relatives who live in Iraq.

Stepping stones	Connections
Rákosi	
↓	*Was an unpopular Hungarian leader who was replaced by Imre Nagy*
Imre Nagy	
↓	*Nagy introduced several reforms, including free elections*
Reforms	
↓	*Nagy also took Hungary out of the Warsaw Pact*
Warsaw Pact	
↓	*This led Khrushchev to believe that events were part of an anti-Soviet plot; he therefore sent in Soviet troops and tanks*
Soviet response	

Even those who are not directly affected often display both curiosity about the war, and frustration that they don't really feel they know what is going on there, or why events happened as they did. They display many misconceptions about both Iraq and terrorism. Students – even successful history students – sometimes don't apply the lessons they have learned about the reliability, provenance and purpose of source material to the modern media, accepting what they read and hear in today's news as the whole truth. This topic again provides an excellent opportunity to look at modern coverage of the Iraq War, events in the Middle East and terrorism through the eyes of a historian, and to encourage students to question the sources of information that are available to them.

FOOTAGE

In terms of the first section of this unit, showing students footage of the Berlin Wall coming down in 1989 can be a good initial stimulus (for example the BBC's archived report, or fascinating reportage of 'the opening of the Wall at Berlin Bornholmer Strasse 1989'; go to www.heinemann.co.uk/hotlinks, insert the express code 0206T, and click on 'Berlin Wall BBC' and 'Berlin Wall opening').

As far as the war in Iraq is concerned, Rageh Omar's gushing coverage of the arrival of American and British troops in Baghdad in 2003 can be an interesting way to begin (go to www.heinemann.co.uk/hotlinks, insert the express code 0206T, and click on 'Rageh Omar').

Students can be questioned about what impression the coverage gives, whether such enthusiasm has been justified in the years that have followed, and how we would regard such source material in terms of reliability, bias etc. The war in Iraq has provoked such strong feelings from a range of perspectives that another useful way to begin the topic is to show students a variety of source material across the range of opinions about the war in Iraq and begin to draw out the key issues from those sources.

Activities

KEY QUESTION 7: HOW SECURE WAS THE USSR'S CONTROL OVER EASTERN EUROPE, 1948–c.1989?

Specified content:

- the nature of Soviet control in Eastern Europe from 1948

- the Hungarian Uprising of 1956 and the Soviet reaction

- the building of the Berlin Wall in 1961

- the 'Prague Spring' of 1968 and the Soviet reaction

- 'Solidarity' in Poland

- Gorbachev's policies and other factors leading to the collapse of Soviet control in Eastern Europe, including the fall of the Berlin Wall.

Focus point: Why was there opposition to Soviet control in Hungary in 1956 and Czechoslovakia in 1968, and how did the USSR react to this opposition?

Focus point: How similar were events in Hungary in 1956 and in Czechoslovakia in 1968?

Activity 3.1: Comparing Hungary and Czechoslovakia

Worksheet 3.1 provides a table that students can use to compare the events of 1956 in Hungary with the events of 1968 in Czechoslovakia. They should use the student book (pages 98–105) to complete the table with the causes, events and consequences of the uprisings.

A task in the student book (page 100) asks students to divide and organise the Soviet response to events in Hungary: students should be encouraged to list brief bullet points of the key facts from the text on page 99 in the student book. It is important that they do this in the style of the examples, rather than just copy chunks of text into the table, in order to show they have understood the information. When the table is complete, students can draw lines to show connections between causes, events and consequences that were similar in both cases. They can then use pages 102–103 of the student book, where the similarities of both events are described, to check that the information in their table tallies with the information in the book.

To assist with this task, worksheet 3.2 contains a writing frame for lower attainers to use in order to write a letter protesting against the events in Hungary. This can help to consolidate knowledge of the events of 1956.

Activity 3.2: Understanding the impact of the Berlin Wall

One way of getting students' attention and helping them to begin to understand the impact of the Berlin Wall is to give them a map of their home town. Ask them to mark any significant places to them on the map. This could include where they live, where they go to school, where they like to go with their friends, where friends and family live, local shops, where their parents work, etc. Then ask them to draw a line through the middle of the town (this does not need to be exact, so long as the town is roughly split in two). Then ask students what effect it would have on them if, overnight, a wall was built along the line they have drawn, with armed soldiers guarding it to make sure they could not cross. Students will then begin to be able to see all the effects such a division would have on the population of a city or town: these could include being cut off from relatives, having to find different employment, being unable to see friends in the other half of town, etc.

Focus Point: How important was Solidarity?

Activity 3.3: Analysing a cartoon about Solidarity

The student book (page 105) contains a copy of the question which students should answer to help them analyse this cartoon. They should focus on the content of the cartoon (its surface features), comment on the hidden meaning of those features, and also make some relevant points about the context of the cartoon. Even very low attainers can be encouraged when they realise that they can pick up some marks just by discussing the basic content of the cartoon.

Using the CCCJ (content, comment, context, judgement) model help students remember what they need to include in their responses to cartoon questions. They should also be encouraged to comment on the overall message of the cartoon.

Focus Point: How far was Gorbachev responsible for the collapse of the Soviet Empire?

Activity 3.4: The end of the Soviet Empire

Worksheet 3.3 gives a set of six cards, each with a different reason for the collapse of the Soviet Empire in Eastern Europe. These cards could be photocopied onto large pieces of paper in order to do this as a whole class activity, or copied as they are if you want students to work in small groups on this task. Using the cards, students should add a short paragraph underneath each heading (using pages 110–13 in the student book) to explain how it could be argued that each factor helped bring about the end of the Soviet Empire. See the table on page 60 for examples.

When students have completed the cards, they should begin to think about how significant each factor was in bringing about the end of the Soviet Empire. They should position the cards on a significance line:

| Least significant ——————————— Most significant |

This could be done on a piece of paper, or across the classroom with students holding the relevant card. Students should be able to explain why they have positioned the cards in this way. Give them sentences/examples to help, such as:

> 'I think social problems in the Soviet Empire were more significant than the war in Afghanistan because many people in Eastern Europe were not particularly affected by the war, but they were becoming increasingly angry about their standard of living. The citizens of various parts of the Soviet Empire would not have been so willing to participate in the (mostly) peaceful revolutions of 1989 if their standard of living had been better, or they were less aware of it.'

There is not a right or wrong response to this task, but students will need to practise explaining the relative importance of different factors, as this is something they generally find difficult but is necessary to achieve higher levels in the final examination.

Factor	It could be argued that this helped bring about the end of the Soviet Empire because…
Domestic policies including *perestroika* and *glasnost*	These policies led to less government control over both the economy and the media. Some embarrassing facts were revealed about the history of the USSR, which caused disillusionment with the regime.
The end of the Brezhnev doctrine	Many groups within the Eastern European countries realised that Gorbachev would not send in Soviet tanks, which led to demonstrations against communist governments throughout Eastern Europe. Over the next few months, the communists were ousted from power in Poland, Hungary, Bulgaria, Romania and East Germany. This would eventually result in the fall of the Berlin Wall in 1989.
The war in Afghanistan	This was a war that angered the Muslim world, which was a problem for the Soviet Empire as there were large Muslim populations living within its borders. Gorbachev's withdrawal of troops indicated that Russia was conceding that they were not in a position to use force to interfere in the affairs of other countries.
Weakness in the Soviet economy	Compared with the USA, the Soviet economy was backward – factories and mines were decrepit and out of date. In addition, there were increasing environmental problems, such as pollution, the Chernobyl nuclear power plant explosion of 1986 and the drying up of the Aral Sea. Gorbachev had no choice but to reform the Soviet economy. The USSR could no longer afford the arms race.
Social problems in Eastern Europe and the USSR	Many people in Eastern Europe were much poorer than even the poorest people in the capitalist West. In addition to the unrest over food shortages, crime, alcoholism and drugs were out of control in Soviet towns. Yet awareness grew of the disparities in living standards, with West German television (illegally) available, and Finnish television available in Estonia, for example.
Unpopularity of Gorbachev's reforms with hardliners in the Communist Party	Hardliners attempted a coup in 1991. Although Gorbachev survived the attempt, his authority was undermined and he was replaced by Boris Yeltsin, who became President of the Russian Federation.

KEY QUESTION 8: HOW EFFECTIVE HAS TERRORISM BEEN SINCE 1969?

Specified content:

- the Provisional IRA 1969–98, from the emergence of the Provisional IRA to the Good Friday Agreement
- the Palestine Liberation Organisation 1969–93, from Yasser Arafat becoming Chairman to the Oslo Accords
- al-Qaeda mid-1980s to 2004, from the resistance against the Soviet invasion of Afghanistan to the American 'War on Terror' since 9/11.

Candidates will not be required to have a detailed knowledge of the history of these three groups, but will need to have knowledge of the main events and developments relating to them.

Focus point: What is terrorism, and why do people become terrorists?

Focus point: Why is terrorism generally condemned?

Activity 3.5: What constitutes terrorism?

Obviously terrorism is to be condemned, but students need to understand that there is a very hazy moral difference between terrorist actions and the actions of some states. What, after all, is more morally reprehensible – a suicide bomber killing civilians on a busy shopping street, or the USA supplying weapons and money to right-wing guerrillas in Central America, who deliberately target civilians?

Worksheets 3.4 and 3.5 provide scenarios from across the globe to illustrate how it is sometimes rather more complicated to decide who the terrorists are than some governments/media might suggest. Students should consider each scenario, and record or discuss answers to the questions at the bottom of the worksheet. It is important that students consider the third question carefully: they do not have a great deal of information on each scenario, and as historians they need to consider what other evidence or information they might need to evaluate the situation fully. Students can then be questioned as to why some states are permitted to behave in ways that they themselves condemn when practised by other nations or groups, and how they use propaganda – and sometimes outright lies – to justify their actions.

Focus point: How different are terrorist groups in their membership, aims, motives and methods?

Activity 3.6: Similarities and differences between terrorist groups

Worksheet 3.6 gives a table for use with pages 120–25 of the student book. Students should use it to record the key features of the main terrorist groups they are asked to examine. They should then highlight the similarities and key differences between the groups.

Activity 3.7: Comparative exam questions

This focus point invites comparisons between different terrorist groups. Worksheet 3.14 contains student and teacher mark schemes for a question which asks students to compare the methods of different groups. This could easily be adapted to questions that invite different comparisons between either the aims of terrorist groups, their leaderships, or how governments have responded to them.

Focus point: How important are the leaders of terrorist groups?

Focus point: How have governments reacted to terrorism?

Focus point: How effective have terrorist groups been?

Activity 3.8: Drawing together work on terrorism

In order to address these focus points, students can be allocated one specific terrorist event or campaign from the content they have studied. Explain to students that the piece of work they are going to produce as a class will help them answer questions relating to any of the three previous focus points in particular, but will also assist with any comparative questions about the nature and effectiveness of terrorist actions. Allocate each pair of students a specific terrorist action/campaign from the content they have studied (e.g. 9/11, the killing of Lord Mountbatten by the IRA). Give students a large piece of paper and four different-coloured pens. They should write the name of the event clearly at the top of the paper, and research (using the student book and/or additional resources/the internet) the answers to each of the following questions.

a What event(s) took place?

b In what way was the leadership of the terrorist group involved in the event(s)?

c What action did government(s) take in response to this event?

d How could it be said that the terrorist actions were effective/ineffective?

Students should then summarise the information they have found out on their large sheet of paper, using a different colour for each question. In order to encourage students to communicate only the highly relevant aspects of their research, they could be limited to no more than 50 words for each question. The large pieces of paper can then be stuck on the wall in a chronological timeline. This work could then be used to help begin to formulate answers to all three focus points, pointing out common themes and things that are very different when comparing the events, governmental responses, role of leadership, and effectiveness of terrorist groups and their actions.

KEY QUESTION 9: WHAT IS THE SIGNIFICANCE OF THE IRAQ WAR?

Specified content:

- the debate over weapons of mass destruction, Saddam Hussein's human rights record, claims about his links with al-Qaeda, 9/11, spreading democracy, Iraq's oil
- the roles of the UN, Bush and Blair
- opposition to the invasion in Britain and in other parts of the world
- the main events of the invasion
- the post-invasion condition of Iraq – breakdown in law and order, the insurgency, the methods used by the Americans and British against the insurgency
- everyday life for the Iraqi people; human rights abuses
- the elections of 2005 and setting up the Transitional Government
- the international consequences of the Iraq War.

Focus point: Why did the multinational force invade Iraq in 2003?

Activity 3.9: Analysing political cartoons

Worksheet 3.7 shows a cartoon with a clear perspective on the war in Iraq. This is useful in terms of explaining to students how the message of any cartoon can be read.

Students should record on the worksheet the surface features, hidden meanings of those features, and relevant points about context. They can use these notes to form the basis of an answer to an exam-style question relating to the cartoon, for example 'What message is the cartoonist trying to convey about the causes of the war in Iraq?'

Activity 3.10: Public reasons for the war in Iraq

Bush's State of the Union Address from 2002 gives the public line on the war in Iraq. Worksheet 3.8 provides a framework for students to analyse the source in detail, focusing on the type of language used and the persuasive techniques contained within the source. Students should be encouraged to reflect on the purpose of the source: the President is not just presenting information in a neutral fashion, but is trying to encourage support for the intended actions of the USA.

Students can use this source as one of several: worksheet 3.9 contains other sources giving different reasons to explain why the war in Iraq began. Students can gather evidence from these sources in a table, collecting different reasons along with reflections on the relative reliability of the different materials.

Activity 3.11: Analysing a variety of source material

Focus point: How was the invasion completed so quickly?

Focus point: Why was there opposition in many countries to the invasion?

Activity 3.12: Using popular music

There are many anti-war songs which can be used for various purposes and in particular can help provide some ideas in relation to this focus point: they can be used as initial stimulus material, analysed as sources in detail, or examined to see what reasons they give for opposition to the war. Some mainstream artists have recorded anti-war songs, such as Pink ('Dear Mr President') and George Michael ('Shoot the Dog'): go to www.heinemann.co.uk/hotlinks, insert the express code 0206T, and click on 'Pink' and 'George Michael') – as have some songwriters who may be less familiar to students.

Tom Paxton wrote a famous anti-Vietnam song called 'Lyndon Johnson Told the Nation', the lyrics to which are included in Unit 2 (page 50 of this teacher's guide). He rewrote the song recently as a comment on the situation in Iraq (see worksheet 3.11). Students could use these to begin to consider why comparisons are made between the situation in Iraq and that in Vietnam, and how that can help to explain opposition to the war. They should also consider the other reasons Paxton gives which explain this opposition.

Activity 3.13: Anti-war protestors

Worksheet 3.10 contains some material from an American anti-war organisation. Students should look at this and consider all the different reasons it gives for opposition to the war in Iraq. They could also consider the purpose of this material, remembering it is intended to shift opinion about the war. How well supported do they think the statements on the sheet are, and what other evidence would they need to decide whether the fact sheet is accurate?

An interesting comparison can be made between American and British anti-war materials: the Stop the War Coalition has quite a collection of samples from Britain on its website, which students can look at to see if they can find similarities and differences. Picture sources can also provide an interesting starting point when considering reasons for opposition to the war: pictures of the huge protests in several major cities in 2003, for example, will contain shots of many different banners and slogans, which students can use as prompts to try to work out different reasons for opposition.

Focus point: What were the consequences of the invasion inside Iraq and internationally?

One of the consequences of the war in Iraq which might not immediately spring to mind is the politicisation of some young people: the outbreak of war saw an unprecedented response from school students in different areas of the country.

You could refer to an article from the *Guardian* that considers the implications of this politicisation and whether such involvement should be actively encouraged in schools: go to www.heinemann.co.uk/hotlinks, insert the express code 0206T, and click on 'Guardian'.

This can give students a consequence of the Iraq war to talk about in an exam question – but should also lead them to consider whether the political action described in the article touched their school (perhaps being encouraged to ask older students/relatives), and what they think of the students involved and their actions. Students could also put forward their opinions on what approach they think schools should take when it comes to dealing with controversial current and recent historical events. All this discussion can lead back to their own History GCSE and how/whether their studies have affected their view of the world.

More obvious consequences are humanitarian and military. The following sources provide different perspectives on the consequences of the war and, as they contain some difficult material, are an ideal way to stretch higher attainers. Students can look at each of the resources (worksheets 3.12 and 3.13 provide hard copy of two of the documents; others are online, see below) and address each of the following questions:

a What does the source suggest are the main consequences of the war in Iraq?

b What other information would you need access to, in order to evaluate the source fully?

c Does the source raise any questions?

d How reliable do you think the source is?

Students could work in groups on this as the materials are lengthy and include links/videos (for example, Barack Obama talking about his plans with regard to Iraq), which could be used to extend the activity by looking at further evidence. They could then present back to the group using the questions to structure their feedback.

SOURCES

- an Amnesty International report on the humanitarian situation in Iraq

- Barack Obama's campaign website on Iraq

- a 2008 press release from the White House

(go to www.heinemann.co.uk/hotlinks, insert the express code 0206T, and click on 'Amnesty', 'Obama' and 'White House').

Grade Studio

USING EXAM QUESTIONS, MARK SCHEMES AND PEER ASSESSMENT TO IMPROVE ATTAINMENT

Grade Studio has been designed to help both students and teachers interpret GCSE history mark schemes.

Grade Studio has a clear and explicit focus on levels. It is the point at which the teaching and practice in the student book becomes focused on moving between levels, and therefore the learning becomes increasingly personalised and improves students' chances of achieving better grades.

The activities in the student book and on the CD-ROM should help students to improve their understanding of how to answer different types of exam question.

Worksheet 3.15 provides a student and teacher mark scheme. This can be used to help students structure a question that ties together all the work they have done on the causes of the war in Iraq. Worksheet 3.16 contains two sample answers in response to this question. Answer A reaches level 3 because it doesn't describe but explains other reasons for the war, but it cannot be placed higher than level 3 because it does not explain how it could be said that oil was a reason for the war. Answer B reaches level 5 because it explains both oil and other reasons, and evaluates 'how far' oil was the most important reason.

3.1 Comparing Hungary and Czechoslovakia

	Hungary 1956	Czechoslovakia 1968
Causes of opposition to the Soviet regime	– Hungary was traditionally a strongly Catholic country. Under Soviet control religion was banned.	
Events that took place as a result of this opposition (including key personalities)	– Imre Nagy replaced the more hardline and unpopular Rakosi as leader of Hungary.	
Soviet response to opposition/ uprisings	– Tanks were sent in and around 4000 Hungarians were killed during the fighting.	

3.2 Events in Hungary

Dear Prime Minister,

Understandably, the people of Hungary have been unhappy for some time with the way their country has been governed. This is because...
(now explain as many reasons as you can why the people of Hungary were unhappy; remember, don't just make a list, but explain your points fully, using persuasive language if possible.)

....

....

....

....

....

....

They decided to take action, which involved...
(explain what happened in Hungary in opposition to Soviet control)

....

....

....

....

....

....

The response of the Soviet Union has been shockingly brutal...
(explain what the USSR did to suppress opposition in Hungary)

....

....

....

....

....

....

I believe the government of Britain must make our feelings known about these events. We could...
(finally, suggest what you think Britain should do in response to the events in Hungary)

....

....

....

....

....

Yours truly,

....

3.3 End of the Soviet Empire

Domestic policies including Perestroika and Glasnost
It could be argued that this helped to bring about the end of the Soviet Empire because…

The war in Afghanistan
It could be argued that this helped to bring about the end of the Soviet Empire because…

Social problems in Eastern Europe and the USSR
It could be argued that this helped to bring about the end of the Soviet Empire because…

The end of the Brezhnev Doctrine
It could be argued that this helped to bring about the end of the Soviet Empire because…

Weakness in the Soviet economy
It could be argued that this helped to bring about the end of the Soviet Empire because…

Unpopularity of Gorbachev's reforms with hardliners in the Communist Party
It could be argued that this helped to bring about the end of the Soviet Empire because…

3.4 Terrorism scenarios 1

SCENARIO A

The government of Country A is very unhappy with the government of Country B, whose leaders came to power in a revolution that threw out the former Country B dictator. Country A decides to do everything in its power to overthrow the new leaders of Country B. It begins funding a guerrilla army that attacks Country B from another country next door. Country A also builds army bases in the next-door country and allows the guerrilla army to use its bases. Country A supplies almost all of the weapons and supplies of the guerrilla army fighting Country B. The guerrillas generally try to avoid fighting Country B's army. Instead, they attack clinics, schools, cooperative farms. Sometimes they mine the roads. Many, many civilians are killed and maimed by the Country A-supported guerrillas. Consistently, the guerrillas raid Country B and then retreat to the country next door, where Country A has military bases.

SCENARIO B

Country A is considered by many to be one of the most repressive countries in the world, especially if you are not white. Only whites can vote, only whites can travel freely, only whites can live where they like. Most whites live comfortably, even luxuriously. Conditions for people who are not white are some of the worst in the world. Country A imprisons people who campaign for change. Torture is widespread. Over the years, there have been numerous massacres of non-white country A civilians – sometimes of young children. The main organisations working for change in country A have asked the world not to invest money in country A and not to have economic or cultural relations with the country until it commits itself to change. Nonetheless, many countries continue to do business with country A. One in particular, country B, has allowed its corporations to increase their investments in country A from $150 million to $2.5 billion – all this during a period of tremendous violence and discrimination.

SCENARIO C

Farmers from country A are angry at their own government and at a corporation from country B. The government of country A has allowed the corporation to plant 'test' crops of genetically engineered cotton. The genetically engineered crops produce their own pesticide. Many farmers in country A worry that the genetically engineered crops will pollute their crops – as has happened many times in other countries – and will lead to a breed of super-pests that will be immune to chemical pesticides and also to the organic pest control methods many poor farmers use. Without growing and selling cotton, the farmers have no way to feed their families. Farmers from country A also believe that the corporation does not really care about them because they only care about their own profits. Farmers from country A further point out that the corporation has not told farmers that the 'tests' on their land may be risky, and could pollute their non-genetically engineered cotton crops

Farmers from country A have announced that they will burn to the ground all the genetically engineered cotton crops. They hope to drive the corporation out of country A. The farmers have also threatened that they may destroy the offices of the corporation.

For each scenario, you need to decide:

a Which, if any, of these activities should be considered 'terrorism' according to your definition?

b Who are the terrorists?

c What more would you need to know to be more sure of your answer?

3.5 Terrorism scenarios 2

SCENARIO D

Led by country A, the United Nations waged a war against country B because it illegally invaded another nearby country. After country B's army was defeated and removed from the country it had invaded, country A pushed for sanctions against country B, until country B could prove that it was not engaged in a programme to produce 'weapons of mass destruction' like nuclear bombs or poison gas. The sanctions meant that country B was hardly allowed to buy or sell anything from other countries. Country B cannot get spare parts to repair water purification plants damaged by bombing during the war. It cannot get medicines and spare parts for medical equipment. Country B claims that it has allowed inspections from the United Nations, but country A says that it has not. According to the United Nations perhaps a half a million children have died as a result of the sanctions. Documents from country A show that it knew civilians in country B were dying as a result of water-borne diseases. When asked in a television interview about the reports of massive numbers of civilian deaths – perhaps as many as a million people over several years – a high government official from country A said: 'It's worth it'.

SCENARIO E

Simultaneously, the embassies of country A in two other countries were bombed. In one country, 213 people were killed and over 1000 injured; in the other, 11 people were killed and at least 70 injured. In retaliation, about three weeks later, country A launched missiles at the capital city of country B, destroying a pharmaceutical factory and injuring at least ten people, and killing one. Country A claimed that this factory was manufacturing chemicals that could be used to make VX nerve gas – although it offered no substantial proof of this claim. Country A also claimed that a prominent individual who they linked to the embassy bombings was connected with the pharmaceutical factory, although they provided no evidence of this claim, either. Country B pointed out that two years earlier they expelled the prominent individual, and vigorously denied that the pharmaceutical plant was producing nerve gas agents. They said that this was an important factory, producing 70 per cent of the medicines needed by the people of country B – including vital medicines to treat malaria and tuberculosis. They allowed journalists and other diplomats to visit the factory to verify that no chemical weapons were being produced there. Journalists and others who visited the factory agreed that the destroyed factory appeared to be producing only medicines. It is not known how many people may have died in country B for lack of the medicines that were being produced in that factory. Country A blocked the United Nations from launching the investigation demanded by country B.

SCENARIO F

Soldiers from country A surround a refugee camp made up of people from country B. The refugee camp is crowded and the people there are extremely poor. Most of the people in the refugee camp hate the army of country A, believing that it has invaded country B, has taken all the best land and resources for itself, and treats people from country B very poorly. Young men in the refugee camp sometimes fire guns at the soldiers. According to an eyewitness, a reporter from *The New York Times*, soldiers from country A use loudspeakers to call insults into the refugee camp – in the language of country B. They dare young boys from country B – sometimes as young as 10 or 11 – to come out near the electric fence that separates the refugee camp from a relatively wealthy settlement of citizens from country A. When the boys and young men go near the fence to throw stones or yell at the soldiers, the soldiers fire on the boys with live ammunition using silencers, often killing or maiming the boys. *The New York Times* reporter was horrified by what he had witnessed. He wrote: 'Children have been shot in other conflicts I have covered – death squads gunned them down in El Salvador and Guatemala, mothers with infants were lined up and massacred in Algeria, and Serb snipers put children in their sights and watched them crumple onto the pavement in Sarajevo – but I have never before watched soldiers entice children like mice into a trap and murder them for sport.' The government of country A knows about the behaviour of its soldiers and does nothing to stop them. Two additional facts: every year, country A is given enormous amounts of money and military equipment by country C, which is aware of how these are used by country A. Some extreme individuals and groups from country B have used suicide bombers to attack civilians from country A.

For each scenario, you need to decide:

a Which, if any, of these activities should be considered 'terrorism' according to your definition?

b Who are the terrorists?

c What more would you need to know to be more sure of your answer?

3.6 Comparing terorist groups

	Provisional IRA	PLO	Al-Qaeda
Background			
Aims			
Membership			
Tactics			

3.7 War in Iraq cartoon

Surface feature:

Hidden meaning:

Surface feature:

Hidden meaning:

Surface feature:

Hidden meaning:

Surface feature:

Hidden meaning:

Surface feature:

Hidden meaning:

Surface feature:

Hidden meaning:

Context:

Overall message of the cartoon:

3.8 George Bush's State of the Union Address

Make a list of all the things Iraq is accused of in this paragraph:

What does Bush mean by the phrase 'axis of evil' and why does he use it?

What does the phrase suggest?

What does the word 'flaunt' suggest?

Iraq continues to *flaunt* its hostility toward America and to support terror. The Iraqi regime has plotted to develop anthrax, and nerve gas, and nuclear weapons for over a decade. This is a regime that has already used poison gas to murder thousands of its own citizens – leaving the *bodies of mothers huddled over their dead children*. This is a regime that agreed to international inspections – then kicked out the inspectors. This is a regime that has something to hide from the *civilised world.*

States like these, and their terrorist allies, constitute an *axis of evil*, arming to threaten the peace of the world. By seeking weapons of mass destruction, these regimes pose a grave and growing danger. They could provide these arms to terrorists, giving them the means to match their hatred. They could attack our allies or attempt to blackmail the United States. In any of these cases, the *price of indifference would be catastrophic.*

George Bush, *State of the Union Address* (29 January 2002)

Why do you think Bush uses this particular image?

Why do you think he uses the phrase 'civilised world'? What does this suggest about Iraq?

Questions to think about:
1 Do you think this source provides convincing arguments to justify attacking Iraq?
2 Do you think this is a reliable source? Why/why not?
3 What questions could this source help you to answer? In other words, how useful is this source, and what is it useful for?

3.9 War in Iraq sources

Let me say a word about what you call the new strategy of pre-emption. There's nothing new about pre-emption. If you know that you are about to be attacked, it is certainly sensible if you can act first and avoid that attack to do so. I don't think anybody would dispute that. So then the question is how imminent must the attack be to justify the pre-emptive response. Here, we need to think more carefully about the concept of imminence. In 1981, the Israelis, after a long and, I gather, heated cabinet debate, decided to destroy the reactor that Chirac had sent to Osirak, not because it was about to produce nuclear weapons. It wasn't. It was about to produce plutonium and it was under IAEA safeguards so the Iraqis would have had to siphon off small, undetectable quantities of plutonium and it would have taken them time to build a nuclear weapon based on what they would get from the Osirak reactor. But, nevertheless, the Israelis decided to strike some years in advance of the production of the nuclear weapon that they were concerned about.

Now, why did they do that? They did it because the Iraqis were about to load fuel into the reactor and once they did so, they would not have had an opportunity to use an air strike without doing a lot of unintended damage around the facility, because radioactive material would have been released into the atmosphere. So from an Israeli point of view, what was imminent and what had to be acted against in a pre-emptive manner was not the ultimate emergence of the threat but an event that would lead inexorably to the ultimate emergence of the threat. They had to deal with a threshold that once crossed, they would no longer have the military option that could be effective at that moment.

Richard Perle, speech in New York on Iraq (13 February 2003)

He doesn't want to make glib comparisons with the 1930s, but suggests that despite many obvious differences, there are some similarities. One is that 'although with hindsight the decision that this was a real threat we had to confront was obvious, at the time it wasn't so obvious'.

'A majority of decent and well-meaning people said there was no need to confront Hitler and that those who did were war-mongers. When people decided not to confront fascism, they were doing the popular thing, they were doing it for good reasons, and they were good people ... but they made the wrong decision.'

Hitler's appeasers, he suggests, were also saying, like today's anti-war protesters: 'Well look, this is ridiculous. OK, this is a long way from us, why on earth should we be involved in it.' Yet, history had proved them wrong, and clearly, in this case too, Mr Blair believes history will judge him right.

Tony Blair, interviewed by Jackie Ashley of the *Guardian* (February 2003)

It's no surprise that so many multinationals are lunging for Iraq's untapped market. It's not just that the reconstruction will be worth as much as $100bn; it's also that 'free trade' by less violent means hasn't been going that well lately. More and more developing countries are rejecting privatisation, while the Free Trade Area of the Americas, Bush's top trade priority, is wildly unpopular across Latin America. World Trade Organisation talks on intellectual property, agriculture and services have all got bogged down amid accusations that the US and Europe have yet to make good on past promises.

So what is a recessionary, growth-addicted superpower to do? How about upgrading from Free Trade Lite, which wrestles market access through backroom bullying at the WTO, to Free Trade Supercharged, which seizes new markets on the battlefields of pre-emptive wars? After all, negotiations with sovereign countries can be hard. Far easier to just tear up the country, occupy it, then rebuild it the way you want. Bush hasn't abandoned free trade, as some have claimed, he just has a new doctrine: 'Bomb before you buy'.

Naomi Klein, *The Nation* (14 April 2003)

3.10 Iraq War – fact sheet

From an American organisation that states: 'We are a nonprofit, nonpartisan, and nonviolent site formed in opposition to the Bush Administration's pre-emptive military strike on Iraq and attack on civil liberties at home. We provide tools to grassroots organizers working to elect new government.'

1 The 9–11 tragedy was used to go to war with a country that had nothing to do with the bombing!
Osama Bin Ladin and his followers (the Al Qaeda) from Afghanistan were the group who caused the bombings – not Iraq. The media preyed upon Americans' lack of knowledge of Mideast geography and stacked news reports together so that every time 9/11 was mentioned, Iraq was associated with it.

2 War on Arab nations was planned prior to Bush's election.
In 1997, a group of 18 men wrote a paper called PNAC (Project for the New American Century) announcing their plan to go to war on the whole Middle East. Ten are now leaders in the Bush administration, among them: Cheney, Rumsfeld, Wolfowitz, Armitage, Bolton, Khalilzad, and Perle.

3 The American *people* went to war to free a country. American *leaders* went to war for greed.
Saddam was a terrible dictator, but the U.S. helped him build weapons... until he refused our plans to build a pipeline in his country and switched from the U.S. dollar to Euros. Politicians manipulated the nobility of the American spirit.

4 The administration intends to go to war with many other countries, one by one.
Rumsfeld said only days after the fall of Baghdad that terrorism is a 'network' (meaning the U.S. doesn't have to respect any nation's borders) and will call any country 'terrorist' that it wants to bully: Syria, Iran, Sudan, Egypt, Jordan and Yemen. The strategy is to make each country in turn look dangerous, until the U.S. dominates the Mideast.

5 War on the Middle East will increase terrorism, not fight it.
What you don't see on the news is that the rest of the world now views us as the evil empire. Former allies no longer support us. American embassies are attacked. Our aggression results in a vicious circle: we intimidate nations, then have to bankrupt our economy to protect our borders... against people we think we may have scared into retaliation.

6 What you see on the news is strictly controlled by the administration.
Before reporters were 'embedded,' they had to convince the government they would report only the military's point of view. Journalists know they will be fired if they criticize the United States. All U.S. television is owned by only six media mega-corporations, who favor the war. You were not allowed to see or hear the details of civilian casualties because you might feel empathy for the Iraqi people.

7 The budget allots billions to military spending while cutting back on social programs.
Halliburton, Bechtel... companies who paid for Bush's election will make fortunes rebuilding Iraq; of Bush's 30 defense contractors, 9 have ties to companies that have already won $76 billion in defense contracts. They get rich while 1 in 3 Americans is uninsured, 1 of 4 homeless has a job, and it takes 2½ full-time jobs at minimum wage in some cities to rent a 1-bedroom apartment.

8 Recent tax cuts will make the poor of this nation much, much poorer.
The current estimated tax bill to each person in this country to pay for the war is an average of $2,000. If you earn less than $50,000 you should worry. The bottom 40% (almost half!) of wage earners has already lost 80% of their wealth during the last round of tax cuts.

3.11 George W. told the nation

By Tom Paxton

I got a letter from old George W.,
It said, 'Son, I hate to trouble ya,
But this war of mine is going bad.
It's time for me to roll the dice;
I know you've already been there twice,
But I am sending you back to Baghdad.'

Chorus:
Hey! George W. told the nation,
'This is not an escalation;
This is just a surge toward victory.
Just to win my little war,
I'm sending 20,000 more,
To help me save Iraq from Iraqis.'

And, so, I made it to Iraq
In time for one more sneak attack,
And to my old battalion I was sent.
We drive around in our Humvees,
Listening to The Black-Eyed Peas
And speaking fondly of the president. (To Chorus)

Celebrities all come to see us,
Grateful they don't have to be us,
Politicians show their best face card.
Where is Bubba? Where's our leader?
Where's our favorite lip reader?
AWOL from the Texas National Guard

If you're hunkered in Fallujah
Wondering who it was who screwed ya,
Wondering what became of 'Shock and Awe!'

You are feeling semi-certain
It has to do with Halliburton,
Dick Cheney's why you drew that fatal straw.

3.12 Barack Obama on Iraq

The Problem

Inadequate Security and Political Progress in Iraq: Since the surge began, more than 1000 American troops have died, and despite the improved security situation, the Iraqi government has not stepped forward to lead the Iraqi people and to reach the genuine political accommodation that was the stated purpose of the surge. Our troops have heroically helped reduce civilian casualties in Iraq to early 2006 levels. This is a testament to our military's hard work, improved counterinsurgency tactics, and enormous sacrifice by our troops and military families. It is also a consequence of the decision of many Sunnis to turn against al Qaeda in Iraq, and a lull in Shia militia activity. But the absence of genuine political accommodation in Iraq is a direct result of President Bush's failure to hold the Iraqi government accountable.

Strains on the Military: More than 1.75 million servicemen and women have served in Iraq or Afghanistan; more than 620,000 troops have completed multiple deployments. Military members have endured multiple deployments taxing both them and their families. Additionally, military equipment is wearing out at nine times the normal rate after years of constant use in Iraq's harsh environment. As Army Chief of Staff General George Casey said in March, 'Today's Army is out of balance. The current demand for our forces in Iraq and Afghanistan exceeds the sustainable supply and limits our ability to provide ready forces for other contingencies.'

Resurgent Al Qaeda in Afghanistan: The decision to invade Iraq diverted resources from the war in Afghanistan, making it harder for us to kill or capture Osama Bin Laden and others involved in the 9/11 attacks. Nearly seven years later, the Taliban has reemerged in southern Afghanistan while Al Qaeda has used the space provided by the Iraq war to regroup, train and plan for another attack on the United States. 2007 was the most violent year in Afghanistan since the invasion in 2001. The scale of our deployments in Iraq continues to set back our ability to finish the fight in Afghanistan, producing unacceptable strategic risks.

A New Strategy Needed: The Iraq war has lasted longer than World War I, World War II, and the Civil War. More than 4000 Americans have died. More than 60,000 have been injured and wounded. The United States may spend $2.7 trillion on this war and its aftermath, yet we are less safe around the globe and more divided at home. With determined ingenuity and at great personal cost, American troops have found the right tactics to contain the violence in Iraq, but we still have the wrong strategy to press Iraqis to take responsibility at home, and restore America's security and standing in the world.

Source: Barack Obama website

3.13 President Bush discussing Iraq, 2008

THE PRESIDENT: Good morning. Fifteen months ago, I announced the surge. And this week, General Petraeus and Ambassador Crocker gave Congress a detailed report on the results.

The immediate goal of the surge was to bring down the sectarian violence that threatened to overwhelm the government in Baghdad, restore basic security to Iraqi communities, and drive the terrorists out of their safe havens. As General Petraeus told Congress, American and Iraqi forces have made significant progress in all these areas. While there is more to be done, sectarian violence is down dramatically. Civilian deaths and military deaths are also down. Many neighborhoods once controlled by al Qaeda have been liberated. And cooperation from Iraqis is stronger than ever – more tips from residents, more Iraqis joining their security forces, and a growing movement against al Qaeda called the "Sons of Iraq."

Improvements in security have helped clear the way for political and economic developments described by Ambassador Crocker. These gains receive less media coverage, but they are vital to Iraq's future. At the local level, businesses are re-opening and provincial councils are meeting. At the national level, there's much work ahead, but the Iraqi government has passed a budget and three major 'benchmark' laws. The national government is sharing oil revenues with the provinces. And many economic indicators in Iraq – from oil production to inflation – are now pointed in the right direction.

All our efforts are aimed at a clear goal: a free Iraq that can protect its people, support itself economically, and take charge of its own political affairs. No one wants to achieve this goal more than the Iraqis themselves. Those who say that the way to encourage further progress is to back off and force the Iraqis to fend for themselves are simply wrong. The Iraqis are a proud people who understand the enormity of the challenges they face and are anxious to meet them. But they know that they still need our help until they can stand by themselves. Our job in the period ahead is to stand with the Iraqi government as it makes tough choices and makes the transition to responsibility for its own security and its own destiny.

On the political front, Iraq has seen bottom-up progress – as tribes and other groups in the provinces who fought terror are now turning to rebuilding local political structures and taking charge of their own affairs. Progress in the provinces is leading to progress in Baghdad, as Iraqi leaders increasingly act together and they share power, and they forge compromises on behalf of the nation. Upcoming elections will consolidate this progress. They'll provide a way for Iraqis to settle disputes through the political process instead of through violence. Iraqis plan to hold provincial elections later this year, and these elections will be followed by national elections in 2009.

A stable, successful, independent Iraq is in the strategic interests of Arab nations. And all who want peace in the Middle East should support a stable, democratic Iraq. And we will urge all nations to increase their support this year.

Some in Washington argue that the war costs too much money. There's no doubt that the costs of this war have been high. But during other major conflicts in our history, the relative cost has been even higher. Think about the Cold War. During the Truman and Eisenhower administrations, our defense budget rose as high as 13 percent of our total economy. Even during the Reagan administration, when our economy expanded significantly, the defense budget still accounted for about 6 percent of GDP. Our citizens recognized that the imperative of stopping Soviet expansion justified this expense. Today, we face an enemy that is not only expansionist in its aims, but has actually attacked our homeland – and intends to do so again. Yet our defense budget accounts for just over 4 percent of our economy – less than our commitment at any point during the four decades of the Cold War. This is still a large amount of money, but it is modest – a modest fraction of our nation's wealth – and it pales when compared to the cost of another terrorist attack on our people.

We should be able to agree that this is a burden worth bearing. And we should be able to agree that our national interest requires the success of our mission in Iraq.

Source: adapted from the White House website

GradeStudio

3.14 Grade Studio: Terrorism mark schemes

TEACHER MARK SCHEME

'Many terrorist groups use the same methods.' How far do you agree with this statement. Explain your answer. **[10 marks]**

Target: AO1 and AO2

Level 0:	No evidence submitted or response does not address the question.	[0 marks]
Level 1:	General answer lacking specific contextual knowledge. e.g. 'They all use different methods. Some use methods that others do not.'	[1–2 marks]
Level 2:	Identifies or describes methods – but no attempt to say if shared between groups OR Identifies shared or different methods (must be identified with particular groups). e.g. 'Some Palestinian groups use suicide bombers but the IRA do not.'	[1–4 marks]
Level 3:	Explains similarities or differences – must be specific and related to particular groups. e.g. 'Some Palestinian terrorists believe that it is a good thing to die for a good cause. They believe that they will become martyrs and go to paradise if they die fighting the enemies of their religion. This has led to some becoming suicide bombers and being used by to kill people in Israel. Hamas has used this tactic against Jewish settlers in the Gaza Strip. The IRA have not used suicide bombers because they do not have the same religious beliefs. But some of them have gone on hunger strike like Bobby Sands when they have been in prison. He died of his hunger strike. So there are some similarities but they are not the same.'	[4–6 marks]
Level 4:	Explains similarities and differences – must be specific and related to particular groups.	[6–9 marks]
Level 5:	Explains with evaluation of 'how far'.	[10 marks]

STUDENT MARK SCHEME

'Many terrorist groups use the same methods.' How far do you agree with this statement. Explain your answer. **[10 marks]**

Level 1:	General answer which does not show specific knowledge.	[1–2 marks]
Level 2:	*Identifies/describes* similarities or differences but does not compare groups OR *identifies* some shared or different methods.	[1–4 marks]
Level 3:	*Explains* similarities *or* differences (must refer to particular groups).	[4–6 marks]
Level 4:	*Explains* similarities *and* differences (must refer to particular groups).	[6–9 marks]
Level 5:	Same as level 4, but also evaluates how far the groups are similar/different.	[10 marks]

3.15 Grade Studio: Iraq War mark schemes

TEACHER MARK SCHEME

'The most important reason why the multi-national force invaded was the oil in Iraq.' How far do you agree with this statement? Explain your answer. **[10 marks]**

Level 0:	No evidence submitted or response does not address the question.	[0 marks]
Level 1:	**General answer lacking specific contextual knowledge.** e.g. 'There were lots of reasons for the invasion and the oil was not one of the most important.'	[1–2 marks]
Level 2:	**Identifies or describes other reasons.** e.g. 'weapons of mass destruction', 'bringing democracy to Iraq', 'Bush and Blair', '9/11', 'wrong intelligence', 'regime change'	[2–4 marks]
Level 3:	**Explains oil as a reason OR explains other reasons.** e.g. 'The most important reason why Iraq was invaded was that Bush wanted to get rid of Saddam Hussein. He had been causing a lot of trouble for America. The Americans were worried that he was building up nuclear weapons and germ warfare and that he could threaten the rest of the world with these. They were also worried by the fact that he had committed lots of human rights abuses in his own country like the treatment of all opponents. No political parties were allowed and opponents were tortured. Whole communities were wiped out. Britain and America decided on 'regime change'. Also if the government in Iraq was friendlier to the West this would help a lot.'	[4–6 marks]
Level 4:	**Explains oil AND other reasons.**	[6–9 marks]
Level 5:	**Explains with evaluation of 'most important'.**	[9–10 marks]

STUDENT MARK SCHEME

'The most important reason why the multi-national force invaded was the oil in Iraq.' How far do you agree with this statement? Explain your answer. **[10 marks]**

Level 1:	General answer which does not show specific knowledge.	[1–2 marks]
Level 2:	Identifies or describes (lists) other reasons for the invasion.	[2–4 marks]
Level 3:	Explains why oil was a reason for the invasion OR explains other reasons for the invasion.	[4–6 marks]
Level 4:	Explains oil AND other reasons for the invasion.	[6–9 marks]
Level 5:	Same as level 4, but evaluates what the most important reason for the invasion was.	[10 marks]

3.16 Grade Studio: Iraq War sample answers

'The most important reason why the multinational force invaded was the oil in Iraq.' How far do you agree with this statement? Explain your answer. **[10 marks]**

Answer A

Oil was not the main reason why the multinational force invaded Iraq. Intelligence reports suggested that Saddam Hussein may have been building weapons of mass destruction. Western governments felt that he must not be allowed to do this as he was an unstable dictator who might use them against the West or his own people. Just allowing Saddam Hussein to have one nuclear warhead could result in great destruction.

In addition to this, some politicians also said that Iraq had connections with Al-Qaeda. In the aftermath of 9/11, America wanted to bring to justice the terrorists and those who had helped them, and felt that by invading Iraq they would be contributing to the war against terror.

A final reason why the invasion of Iraq took place was to protect Iraqi citizens: Saddam Hussein was a cruel dictator who had been responsible for persecuting the Kurds and other groups within Iraq. By removing him from power, the American government believed they would improve human rights in the region.

Answer B

Many reasons were given in public to explain why the invasion of Iraq by a multinational task force was necessary. It was claimed that Saddam Hussein was building weapons of mass destruction (WMD) and must be stopped in order to ensure the safety of the global community. It was also argued that he was a vicious dictator who treated his own people badly and supported terrorism.

However, it now seems that intelligence reports were not definitive with regard to WMD: in fact, none have been found in post-invasion Iraq. It also cannot be argued that the most important reason was Saddam Hussein's human rights abuses: after all, there are other dictators in existence whose human rights abuses are worse and yet their countries have not been invaded. No proven links have been made between Iraq and the events of 9/11. So there must be another motivating factor, and that seems clearly to have been the strategic importance of controlling Iraq's oil reserves. American (and other Western) companies have made huge amounts of money from the 'reconstruction' of Iraq and have benefited from access to the oil in the region. Some of President Bush's closest advisors and friends have made money themselves from the invasion. This seems to suggest that oil is the most important explanation for the invasion of Iraq.

---

4 Study in Depth: Germany, 1918–45

Introduction

This topic forms the first of seven studies in depth in Unit A971. The content begins with the effects of the Treaty of Versailles on Germany: if students have studied International Relations Core Unit 1, then they should already have an awareness of the terms of the treaty and its consequences. Students then examine how and why Germany recovered somewhat during the 1920s, what role Hitler and the Nazis played during this period, the impact of the Wall Street Crash and the Great Depression, and the subsequent appointment of Hitler as Chancellor. The study then focuses on what it was like to live in Nazi Germany, considering key historical questions such as how much opposition to the regime existed and what form it took. Of all the depth studies, this is probably the one about which students will have the most prior knowledge from their work at KS3. This unit is tested as part of Unit A971: there will be one compulsory source-based question and a choice of two four-, six- and ten-mark three-part questions.

Much of this supporting material concentrates on different ways of delivering what can be very challenging areas of content, such as the nature, causes and effects of hyperinflation in 1923. There is also an explicit focus on the skills required to do well in examinations, including ways of encouraging the retention of relevant factual knowledge and how to answer different types of exam question.

Ideas for starters and plenaries

WHAT NOT TO SAY

As a revision exercise, students can play a game where they are given a series of topics which they then describe to their partner without using certain key words. Their partner has to guess which topic they are describing. Worksheet 4.1 provides some examples for this depth study. If the sheet is cut in half, the first student describes four topics, as does the second student – they can take it in turns.

This task may need to be adapted depending on the ability of your group and the detail in which they have studied certain topics: it is easy to make this task either more challenging, by

adding more words that cannot be used, or easier by reducing the number of words that are not allowed.

STEPPING INTO THE PAST

An effective way of trying to encourage students to empathise with particular groups or individuals is introducing the idea of 'stepping into' a picture. For example, if you are trying to teach about the appeal of Nazi youth organisations, then you could play a film clip of the Hitler Youth marching in a Nazi rally. Freeze the clip at an appropriate point, and ask students to imagine they are stepping into the picture, perhaps taking the place of someone of their own age in the audience. Ask them to describe, in as much detail as possible, what they can see and hear. They can then move on to think about how the sights and sounds might make them feel, and what their response might be. This can be used to draw out the idea of why young people were often attracted to Nazi youth organisations. Some suggestion of clips you could use include:

- a scene from the film *Cabaret*, which captures perfectly a fervent, emotional demonstration of Hitler Youth sentiment – although this sentiment might not have been shared by all members of the organisation, it certainly played a part for many

- a clip of real Hitler Youth members.

For these clips go to www.heinemann.co.uk/hotlinks, insert the express code 0206T, and click on 'Cabaret' or 'Hitler Youth'.

Another example might be to show students a picture of Cologne's Edelweiss Pirates, again asking them to position themselves in the picture, describe what they can see and hear, and what effect it might have on them (drawing out the effectiveness of terror as a form of control). Alternatively, the film *Edelweiss Pirates* (dir. Niko von Glasow, 2004) is based on their story, and is available on DVD with subtitles.

JIGSAW

A good way of encouraging students to engage in examining a picture source closely and trying to interpret all its features is to give them one piece at a time. This can be used for a political cartoon or a photograph. Students can be given a blank piece of A4 paper (or a piece of A4 paper with a grid drawn out for them) to place the 'jigsaw' pieces in the correct position as they receive them. As the pieces are given out, students should note down (or discuss) what they can see, what they think it might mean, and what they think the image might be showing. Careful prompt questions should ensure that not too much is given away, but that students are kept on the right track.

For example, a detailed photograph of a Nazi rally, cut into pieces, showing lots of different types of people, facial expressions, groups, etc., could lead to a wide-ranging and general discussion about the nature of the society in question.

Grabbing attention

THE MOVIES

This topic provides a wealth of material to engage interest from the start. Hitler is possibly the most recognisable historical figure of all time, and explaining to students that this topic is about how he became leader of Germany and what he did in that role stimulates interest in itself.

The BBC series *The Nazis: A Warning From History* (available on DVD) is an excellent resource for the whole topic: it ties in very closely with several of the focus points and can be a useful revision tool. Through extensive interviews with those who lived through and even participated in the Nazi regime, it gives a sense of the diversity of German opinion, and makes it clear that there was by no means uniformity in terms of compliance with or support for Hitler's leadership. Students often have many preconceptions about German attitudes, and such material is useful when challenging this. The opening of the first programme could be used as a starter for the whole topic: students can be questioned about what it tells them, what they know already or can infer from what they see, and what the images and music used suggest.

Leni Riefenstahl's propaganda work can also make for an arresting start to the topic. Students can be shown a clip from *Triumph of the Will* (1935; available on DVD) and asked to reflect on questions such as:

- What does the film suggest to us about the Nazi regime?
- What impression does it give of Germany?
- How does this fit in with what you know about Germany between the wars?

(Levels of knowledge will vary depending on the International Relations options taken).

A scene from a film such as *Schindler's List* (dir. Steven Spielberg, 1993) could also be used to provoke interest and encourage students to predict what it might take for a society to reach a point where it was possible for such large-scale atrocities to occur (ideas might include a dictatorial leader, problems within society that lead to scapegoating certain groups, the use of terror to control opposition). Obviously this question needs treating with sensitivity. Students can return to their predictions later in the topic to see if they were accurate.

CULTURE AND SOCIETY

All these examples of initial stimulus material can be used to ensure that the Weimar Republic and the events of the 1920s are always examined with causation in mind: the types of question often posed in examinations require students to see the topic as a coherent, related whole.

General discussions about the nature of different types of society (liberal, dictatorship, etc.) and what might make different societies follow different paths are also an interesting way to start.

SYNOPTIC LEARNING

Students can then be encouraged to recall what they already know about the First World War and the situation in Europe between the wars. It is helpful for students to learn more synoptically than they often do – if they study International Relations Part 1: the inter-war years 1919–39, then they should regularly reflect on the connections between that topic and the Germany Depth Study where relevant.

TODAY'S MEDIA

As a homework task, students could be asked to look carefully over the course of several weeks at any newspapers or TV magazines they have at home, and record how many mentions of Hitler or Nazi Germany there are in the news and TV schedules. This again brings home to students how Hitler and his regime continue to loom large in national and international consciousness.

Activities

This depth study poses four key questions, which are then subdivided into focus points. The following activities are designed to address a key question or focus point, or to communicate an area of the specified content. There are also activities designed specifically to assist in developing exam technique.

KEY QUESTION 1: WAS THE WEIMAR REPUBLIC DOOMED FROM THE START?

Specified content:

- the Revolution of 1918–19 and the establishment of the Republic
- the Versailles settlement and German reactions to it
- the Weimar Constitution
- the political disorder of 1920–23
- economic distress and hyperinflation
- the occupation of the Ruhr
- the Stresemann era – recovery at home and abroad
- underlying weaknesses of the Republic
- cultural achievements of the Weimar period.

Focus point: How did Germany emerge from defeat in the First World War?

Activity 4.1: Gathering evidence about the success and failures of the Weimar Republic

Here students require a sound, specific, factual knowledge of the Weimar period and an overview of its chronology. Even at KS4, some students find it hard to grasp the chronology of events or the timescale of different developments. It is helpful to encourage students to reflect on this key question from the beginning of the unit, rather than bringing it in when the content has been covered. The worksheets provide two different ways for students to record information that will help them answer the key question: 'Was the Weimar Republic doomed from the start?'

Worksheet 4.2 is a table in which higher attainers can record key points and information

from sources that they will use to support their answer to the key question. Once collected, these can be written up at the end of these focus points. Give students five minutes at the end of each of the following lessons to record any relevant information in their table, preferably including direct references to sources. In the first column, students should record the event or period they have examined during the lesson. These titles could be given to students, or they can decide what to call each event themselves.

For lower attainers, worksheet 4.3 gives a visual timeline of events for them to fill in. They should reflect on whether or not each one indicates that the Weimar Republic was doomed. They should try to fill in both sides of the argument wherever possible, although sometimes, in a clear-cut case, it is appropriate to just fill in one side.

Focus point: What was the economic and political impact of the Treaty of Versailles on the Weimar Republic?

Activity 4.2: Cartoon analysis in stages

In 1919, a British newspaper published an amazingly prescient political cartoon which predicted another war in 1940 as a result of the terms of the Treaty of Versailles (see page 19 of the student book). This cartoon can be used either as a starter for this whole topic, or after some discussion has taken place about the background to Germany immediately after the First World War and what students already know about the Treaty of Versailles.

An option would be to provide a large copy of the cartoon, which can be cut up into pieces to distribute to students one at a time. As the pieces are given out, students should note down what they see, what it might mean, and what they think the cartoon might be about, building up the jigsaw as they go along. It would be helpful if students have seen pictures of the 'Big Four' at Versailles (including Orlando, the Italian Prime Minister, who appears in this cartoon). Other useful prompting information that can be passed on when appropriate is that Clemenceau's nickname was 'The Tiger', and the meaning of the phrase 'cannon fodder'. Students' (educated) guesswork can lead into useful discussions of a general nature about the period and context.

With this source, hopefully understanding will gradually dawn on students as they put the picture back together and realise the importance of looking at all the small details of a cartoon source. Students are often surprised (and impressed) by Will Dyson's foresight. This can lead into a discussion of what the cartoon suggests about the impact of the Treaty of Versailles on Germany, and an examination of the events of 1918–23.

Activity 4.3: The ideological spectrum

Depending on the ability of the class, it may be helpful to do some work on the nature of German democracy prior to the First World War and to discuss the problems that a new democracy may encounter. Students must also understand the pressures that were placed on the new Weimar government from both sides of the ideological spectrum. Worksheet 4.4 provides a diagram for students to record information about the main groups in opposition to the Weimar government and the key problems it faced.

Worksheet 4.5 gives an extract of a speech by Hitler to the Reichstag in 1933, which makes detailed reference to the Treaty of Versailles and the perceived effect it had. Students can analyse this speech, focusing on the points in bold, with a view to developing an understanding of the long-term effects of the Treaty and how Hitler's views fitted in with those held by some groups in Germany immediately after the Treaty was signed.

Activity 4.4: Explaining hyperinflation

Hyperinflation is a difficult concept to explain to students. They do not need to get bogged down in complex economic theory, but they do need to understand what it was, and what effect it had on the German people. Worksheet 4.6 uses an activity by Ian Dawson to illustrate the impact of hyperinflation.

Discuss the meaning of the word inflation. Ask students what they hear adults complaining about – they will probably mention increasing prices, the cost of living, etc. Ask them why these things loom so large in the minds of the population now.

Use the student book (pages 155–56) to introduce the hyperinflation crisis. Explain (or ask students to write down) the chain of

events that led to hyperinflation in 1923. Then tell students they are going to participate in an activity to illustrate the effect hyperinflation had on ordinary German families and businesses. It may be helpful to have examined the events in the Ruhr during the previous lesson.

For the activity, you will need to find a number of willing volunteers among teaching staff and support staff around school to act as shopkeepers. Each shopkeeper needs a copy of the minute-by-minute price guide (worksheet 4.7). Provide explanations as you go along, particularly about the average loss of value.

Once they have carried out the calculations and arrived at 672,222.2 marks an hour, demonstrate to the class how these figures might have affected ordinary Germans.

In each minute, the currency devalues, on average, at 11,203.7 marks per minute. At the start of the lesson a box of chocolates cost 10 German marks, and a much-needed board marker cost 2 German marks.

The task of one individual in each group is to purchase you a board marker. Give each group a 2 million mark note, and the location of somewhere in school where the items can be purchased. If they have enough change, they can buy a box of chocolates as well.

Send the chosen pupils to make their purchases. Ask the students who have stayed in the room what they expect the shoppers to return with. Will they have enough money to make their purchases? What could they do if they don't have enough money? What problems would there be for these shoppers if this situation was actually the family's weekly food shop?

Your volunteer shopkeepers should barter with students if they don't have enough money, and should not hand over the chocolates unless they are satisfied with the value of the goods offered by the students. For example, they might hand over the chocolates in return for a student's pen, coat, bag, trainers, etc.

Given the usual amount of time it takes for a class to arrive at your room, your introduction, the maths exercise and the time it takes the group to get to the location of the shopkeeper, it's more than likely they will not have enough money to make the purchase.

When the group return, discuss the implications of the shopping trip they've just been on. They had 2 million marks to buy something that would have cost 12 marks only 20 or so minutes earlier. Ask them to explain what they had to do to purchase everything they wanted.

How would this affect Germans who were trying to buy food, pay rent or hire essential equipment?

How would it affect businesses wanting to order raw materials, workers collecting their wages or politicians trying to plan for future improvements?

What might be the political impact of hyperinflation? Who would people blame – their own government or would they connect hyperinflation with events abroad, e.g. the Treaty of Versailles?

For homework, students should write up what they have learned during the practical activity and from the student book (pages 153–56). They should include the events that led to hyperinflation; how hyperinflation affected ordinary Germans; and who ordinary Germans blamed (anger towards Weimar politicians, but also the architects of the Treaty of Versailles and the French invasion of the Ruhr, and the fact that the Munich Putsch happened in 1923).

Ask students what they think could be done to solve the crisis and what they think its long-term impact might be. This can lead into thinking about the next lesson, which should focus on what Stresemann did to alleviate the problems in Weimar Germany and the beginning of its recovery (not losing sight of the fact that some problems did remain).

Students can complete an exam question relating to hyperinflation and the events of 1923 in general. Worksheet 4.18 contains questions and mark schemes which could be used.

Focus point: To what extent did the Republic recover after 1923?

Activity 4.5: Learning how to describe and explain

The Weimar Republic had numerous successes between 1924 and 1929. A question from OCR's sample assessment materials asks students to 'Explain why the period from 1924 to 1929 was successful for the Weimar Republic' (6 marks).

This gives an opportunity to work with students to develop their ability to explain rather than describe, which is essential in order to achieve high marks on these 6-mark questions.

One way of doing this is to ask a student to give one success of the republic using only ten words. This should limit them to simple description. Another student should then be asked to give another ten words of further description. Explain that students are still only describing the success. Ask a third student to give an appropriate connective or opening of a new sentence, which could help develop the answer into an explanation. A fourth student should complete the sentence, again using no more than ten words. This should encourage students to keep their answers completely relevant to the question. For example:

- In 1925 Stresemann signed the Locarno Treaties...

- ... guaranteeing that Germany would not change its western borders.

- Consequently:

- Germany was accepted into the League of Nations in 1926.

Worksheet 4.20 gives a mark scheme for this question.

Focus point: What were the achievements of the Weimar period?

Activity 4.6: Researching Weimar Germany's culture

This focus point gives an ideal opportunity (time and ICT facilities permitting) for students to research the various cultural achievements of the Weimar period. Worksheet 4.8 gives some suggested areas for research and some examples within each area: students can be allocated topics to research or allowed to choose one they are most interested in. Students can use the internet, but should be given specific websites to look at in order to make the most efficient use of their time. They should ensure the information they record is summarised in easily understandable and brief points so that they can feed their information back to the class. Students should concentrate throughout their research and give feedback on:

- What was different/new about Weimar culture?

- What were the achievements of different individuals working within Weimar Germany?

- What was it about Weimar culture that Hitler and other traditionalists disliked?

Students should remember that the Weimar government was not out of the woods, despite the achievements of the period – for example, apparent economic recovery was heavily reliant on foreign loans.

They should consider how German traditionalists might respond to the cultural achievements that have been described, looking at the notion of 'decadent' culture and tying this in later with Hitler's ideological perspectives on culture.

KEY QUESTION 2: WHY WAS HITLER ABLE TO DOMINATE GERMANY BY 1933?

Specified content:

- the early years of the Nazi Party

- Nazi ideas and methods

- the Munich Putsch

- the role of Hitler and other Nazi leaders and the change of tactics after the Putsch

- the impact of the Depression on Germany

- the political, economic and social crisis of 1930–33

- reasons for growing support for the Nazis and the election results 1928–33

- how Hitler became Chancellor in 1933

- the Reichstag fire, Hitler's use of emergency powers, the Enabling Act of 1933.

Focus point: What did the Nazi Party stand for in the 1920s?

Activity 4.7: The 25-point programme

Ask students to look at the 25 points in worksheet 4.9. Match the four Germans to the points of the programme that might appeal to them. There may be more than one point for each person.

What other sections of society might have gained or lost from the 25 points of the German Workers' Party?

Activity 4.8: Hitler's defence

One way of getting students to understand the basic principles of the Nazi Party during the 1920s is to prepare a statement to be given by

Hitler (or his legal representative) at his trial, explaining why he organised and participated in the Munich Putsch. Some possible suggestions for how to structure the statement could include:

- the weaknesses of the Weimar constitution

- the terms of the Treaty of Versailles

- the needs of the German people

- what is wrong with German society

- how the Nazi Party would address these problems

- why Hitler felt he should not be found guilty of treason.

Worksheet 4.10 gives a writing frame for lower attainers to help them with this task. Completing the statement could also involve some examination of Hitler's rhetoric and the techniques he used to get his message across. This brings in a focus on speech as a form of propaganda, and some literacy work on different styles of writing/speaking, purpose and audience.

Focus point: Why did the Nazis have little success before 1930?

Activity 4.9: Why would anybody vote for Hitler?

Students often find it hard to separate their perceptions of Hitler, knowing what they know about events such as the Holocaust, from perceptions of Hitler in 1933 in Germany. They therefore find it difficult to understand how anybody could vote for such a man, particularly given what they perceive as his very odd manner and rhetorical technique. This is another example where specific examples of individual experiences can encourage empathy. Students can be given characters from the year 1928:

- a factory worker whose friends vote communist

- an ex-soldier who has found it hard to get a job after the First World War

- a poor farmer

- a wealthy factory-owner who has done well under the Weimar government

- a traditional German woman with strong Catholic beliefs, who lost money during the hyperinflation crisis but whose husband has a good job in a big firm

- a small shopkeeper who suffered under hyperinflation but is now making a good profit

- a schoolteacher who is worried about the poverty some of his/her students live in and frightened of the attitudes displayed by the Hitler Youth.

These characters should be fleshed out with other realistic biographical details (attitude towards Jewish people, family, etc.) Students can then be given a list of the main political parties in Germany in 1928, what they stood for and what they proposed to do in government. They can then write down for each character which political party they think would have appealed to them most, and why. Hopefully, they should realise that only certain groups would have responded particularly positively to the Nazi message in the 1920s.

After they have studied the impact of the Wall Street Crash and the ensuing depression, students can return to these characters and suggest what would have changed for them. They should look again at the choice of political parties, and explain why more of their characters might now turn to the Nazis.

Focus point: Why was Hitler able to become Chancellor by 1933?

Students need to understand all the reasons why the Nazis had significant support among the German public in the early 1930s, and the part that this played in bringing Hitler to power. However, they must also understand the other factors that were at work, particularly the scheming of the 'old guard' including Hindenburg and von Papen. Students can be divided into two groups, one to write a statement accusing these individuals of being to blame for Hitler's seizure of power, and one to write a short defence of their actions. Students can then decide how much responsibility they believe the 'old guard' had for Hitler becoming Chancellor in 1933.

Focus point: How did Hitler consolidate his power in 1933?

Activity 4.10: Investigating the Reichstag fire

The Reichstag fire is an important example of how Hitler used events to his advantage in order to gain control of Germany. This can be presented as a detective-style task in order to engage interest: show students a picture of the burning Reichstag building as a starter, and question them on what the picture shows and what they think may have happened. Worksheet 4.11 gives some sources of evidence supporting one of three theories:

- the fire was started by an isolated individual (the Communist van der Lubbe)

- it was part of a Communist plot

- it was started by the Nazis themselves.

Students should use the sources and their knowledge of the period to decide which theory they think is correct. Alternatively, confident students could be prepared to take on the role of key individuals (van der Lubbe, Goebbels, a Communist party activist, etc.) and answer questions from students on who caused the fire. This activity should be used to develop students' understanding of the fact that whoever caused the fire, Hitler and the Nazis used it effectively to secure their stranglehold on the government of Germany. It can also be used to work on their skills of assessing the provenance, usefulness and reliability of source material.

KEY QUESTION 3(A): THE NAZI REGIME: HOW EFFECTIVELY DID THE NAZIS CONTROL GERMANY, 1933–45?

Specified content:

- the nature of Nazi rule in Germany
- the Night of the Long Knives
- the death of Hindenburg
- removal of opposition, methods of control and repression, and the roles of the SS and the Gestapo
- use of culture, propaganda and the mass media
- opposition to Nazi rule – the Communists, church leaders, passive resistance, youth groups, growing opposition during the war, including from within the army
- persecution of the Jews and the Final Solution
- persecution of other minorities.

Focus point: How much opposition was there to the Nazi regime?

Activity 4.11: Different types of opposition

Students need to consider the different types of opposition that existed towards the Nazi regime.

This can begin with a general discussion about how they themselves might go about opposing something they disagree with, or how people express opposition in modern British society. Students can then be introduced to these terms:

- resistance – implies open opposition aimed at destroying the target of the opposition

- dissent – low-level opposition that expresses disagreement or a lack of involvement in required activities

- conformity – going along with things.

Students can then look at different examples and sources that describe a variety of attitudes towards the regime, and decide which category they fit into.

Focus point: How effectively did the Nazis deal with their political opponents?

Focus point: How did the Nazis use culture, propaganda and the mass media to control the people?

Activity 4.12: Researching the Berlin Olympics

The Berlin Olympics provide an interesting case study that encapsulates many of the key issues surrounding life in Nazi Germany, propaganda, control and the persecution of minorities. This is an ideal topic for students to research and produce some extended writing or a presentation.

Students could be given the question 'What can the Berlin Olympics tell us about life in Nazi Germany?' and the following subheadings to research online, where there is a large amount of material available:

- race hygiene

- sport as military training

- Nazi control of the Olympics

- exclusion of Jews and persecution of athletes

- Nazi propaganda and nationalism

- opening of the games

- black athletes and Jewish athletes.

Students can either research all issues as individuals, or work in groups to look at specific aspects of the games and give feedback to the class.

Activity 4.13: Analysing examples of propaganda

Another activity relating to propaganda is to show students a series of images and/or film clips and, for each one, ask them to consider the following questions:

- Who is the propaganda targeted at? Who are the intended audience?

- What message is the propaganda intended to convey?

- What techniques are being employed in this piece of propaganda?

These images are most effective if shown at full size and in full colour, which is possible if you have access to a whiteboard and the internet: there are huge amounts of examples of Nazi propaganda easily accessible online.

- The German Propaganda Archive has an excellent selection of Nazi propaganda posters that make it easy to show students the different techniques used and groups/issues targeted.

- The BBC History website also has useful examples.

Go to www.heinemann.co.uk/hotlinks, insert the express code 0206T, and click on 'Posters' or 'Propaganda Gallery'.

If this is not possible, there are examples in the student book (pages 175, 184 and 186). Worksheet 4.12 contains examples of a variety of propaganda to show students how to analyse these sources of evidence, along with some examples for them to complete. There are also sources with questions that ask students to reflect on the principles behind Nazi propaganda. This can be done as a self-contained homework task or in class.

Focus point: Why did the Nazis persecute certain groups in German society?

Useful citizenship links can be made in this section. Students can be encouraged to reflect on groups that suffer persecution today, and on the idea of scapegoating or blaming particular groups for all the problems in society in order to create the kind of negative cohesion that Hitler utilised. This needs to be handled sensitively, but attention can be drawn to the attitudes of various elements of the press and certain political groups in Britain today towards refugees and asylum-seekers, the lies that are told about them, and how this is generally accepted and repeated among large sections of the population. This can involve an examination of the language used in such situations and the similarities in terms of issues: the idea of certain groups 'flooding' a country, 'taking over' and receiving benefits that the 'real' people of the country are denied. Students can then think about what it takes to move from this kind of generalised prejudice to the state-sanctioned persecution that took place in Nazi Germany. Obviously this does not involve suggesting that there are direct comparisons – rather that many societies over time have found it expedient to make scapegoats of minorities within the country. This must include an examination of the specific nature of anti-semitism in Germany over time, and how this was utilised and changed in some senses by Hitler, along with the reasons why such unthinkable atrocities were committed and allowed to continue. Students should also consider Hitler's overall racial ideology and why this resulted in the persecution of homosexuals, gypsies, the disabled, etc.

Students can look at some further examples of propaganda here, focusing on the idea of negative cohesion and how propaganda targeted against particular groups helped Hitler to gain support.

KEY QUESTION 3(B): THE NAZI REGIME: WHAT WAS IT LIKE TO LIVE IN NAZI GERMANY?

Specified content

- the Hitler Youth and the League of German Maidens
- the aims and development of Nazi policies towards women and the family
- the effectiveness of German economic policies
- rearmament
- the impact of the Second World War on the lives of the German people
- conversion to a war economy.

Focus point: What was the purpose of the Hitler Youth?

Activity 4.14: Education as social control

One way of getting students to think about Nazi educational policies is to give them a large, blank school timetable. Ask them to record all the subjects they study in the relevant sections of the timetable, and then to cross out all the subjects they don't think they would have studied in Nazi Germany (for example, boys would get rid of food technology). These subjects can be replaced

with subjects that students don't study now but might have done under the Nazi regime. Then ask students to briefly record in the relevant sections how they think each subject that has remained the same would be taught differently in Nazi Germany. They could reflect, for example, on the types of history they currently study, the purpose of their history lessons, how they are (hopefully) encouraged to question source material, what sort of questions it is acceptable to ask, and so on. They could then think about how history might be taught differently under the Nazi regime, which can lead into a productive discussion about how education can be used as a form of social control. Any subject can provide a useful discussion point, even those that do not have such an immediately apparent capacity for ideological manipulation: show students some questions from Nazi mathematics books to make the point. Students should consider what different purposes education can serve, what purpose it served for Hitler, and what purpose it serves in modern Britain.

Students can then be questioned about other influences outside school that affect their opinions, how they spend their spare time, etc. The topic of the Hitler Youth and the League of German Maidens can then be introduced.

Focus point: How successful were Nazi policies towards women and the family?

Activity 4.15: Stretching gifted and talented students

This activity is adapted from the work of Alison Kitson, which was designed to make evidential work more meaningful for AS and A2 students. It is also accessible to GCSE students, although the difficulty of the text, the amount of reading required and the challenging concepts involved mean that this activity as it stands is appropriate for very high attainers at GCSE level. There is no reason, however, why the concept behind the activity could not be adapted for lower attainers with much reduced source material.

Unless you have a double lesson, this activity is designed to cover two sessions. Students should be introduced to the key question 'How successful were Nazi policies towards women?' at the start of the two lessons, and should continually be encouraged to refer back to it, particularly at the beginning and end of each lesson. Alternatively, this lesson could be completed in one session if work has already been completed on Nazi policies towards women and the reading of the accounts is set as homework before the lesson.

The accounts of the four women used in this activity all come from a book called *Frauen* by Alison Owings, written in the 1990s. The text requires a good understanding of the context of Nazi Germany and therefore this lesson should only be attempted when a considerable amount of work has been completed on resistance, dissent and conformity, and students have already examined topics such as Nazi attitudes and policies towards young people. Students could reflect on the provenance of the book itself as a source of evidence and any problems with the accounts contained within it.

First, ask students what different attitudes exist in society today about the role of women. How and why do people hold different attitudes about this issue? Are there generational differences? Explain to students that they are going to examine the Nazi view of and policies towards women and look at some case studies to see if all women complied with these policies.

Then show students examples of sources and propaganda relating to the Nazi regime's view of the role of women. Question them about what the sources can tell us about how the Nazis believed women should behave, how these ideas fitted in with Nazi ideology in general, and what practical reasons Hitler had for promoting the role of women as mothers and the nuclear family.

- Using the student book, ask students to make a list of actual policies the Nazis put in place relating to women. Ensure that they have a sound grasp of the chronology of these policies (this could be completed during the previous lesson).

- Students should be divided into groups of four. Each student in the group is given a different woman to read about (see worksheets 4.13–4.16), and they then answer the questions on worksheet 4.17.

Focus point: Were most people better off under Nazi rule?

Focus point: How did the coming of war change life in Germany?

Students can complete a simple timeline with the events of the Second World War on one side,

and how each event affected people at home in Germany on the other, using the student book (pages 181–88).

Grade Studio

USING EXAM QUESTIONS, MARK SCHEMES AND PEER ASSESSMENT TO IMPROVE ATTAINMENT

Grade Studio has been designed to help both students and teachers interpret GCSE history mark schemes.

Grade Studio has a clear and explicit focus on levels. It is the point at which the teaching and practice in the student book becomes focused on moving between levels, and therefore the learning becomes increasingly personalised and improves students' chances of achieving better grades.

The activities in the student book and on the CD-ROM should help students to improve their understanding of how to answer different types of exam question.

Worksheets 4.19 and 4.20 provide a four- and six-mark question about Weimar Germany with sample answers and a mark scheme. Students need to understand how to approach four-, six- and ten-mark questions, and this should help them to develop a sharper focus when responding to such questions.

For the four-mark question, when marking the model answers, they are looking for either four relevant factual points or two developed points for full marks.

For the four-mark question, answer A should receive full marks. Answer B talks about problems with the constitution rather than its actual features, and so can only be awarded one mark.

Answer A to the six-mark question describes rather than explains successes and then discusses problems which is not required, and therefore should be awarded three marks. Answer B secures full marks by explaining three successes. Students need to understand that while they need to give a balanced argument in a ten-mark question, in this six-mark question they only need to write about successes during that specific period.

4.1 Revision game

Player 1

Topic: The Treaty of Versailles

You cannot use the words:
Treaty
Versailles
Woodrow Wilson
Georges Clemenceau
David Lloyd George
Germany
First World War

Topic: The invasion of the Ruhr

You cannot use the words:
Ruhr
France
Invasion
Industrial
Reparations

Topic: The Night of the Long Knives

You cannot use the words:
Night of the Long Knives
Ernst Röhm
Stormtroopers
SA
Murder

Topic: The Enabling Act

You cannot use the words:
Enabling Act
Law
Power
Dictator(ship)
Hitler
Totalitarian

Player 2

Topic: Hyperinflation

You cannot use the words:
Stresemann
Money
Worthless
Savings
Bank notes
Currency
Hyperinflation
Inflation

Topic: Propaganda

You cannot use the words:
Propaganda
Goebbels
Radio
Cinema
Posters
Films
Leni Riefenstahl
Ministry of Enlightenment and Propaganda

Topic: The Reichstag Fire

You cannot use the words:
Reichstag
Fire
Arson
Van der Lubbe
Parliament building
Communist plot

Topic: Kristallnacht

You cannot use the words:
Kristallnacht
Night of Broken Glass
Shops
Jews/Jewish
Synagogues
Anti-Semitic

4.2 Evaluating the Weimar Republic 1

Focus of lesson	Information suggesting that the Weimar Republic was doomed	Information suggesting that the Weimar Republic was not doomed	Evidence from sources

4.3 Evaluating the Weimar Republic 2

Doomed?	Was the Weimar Republic doomed from the start?	Not doomed?

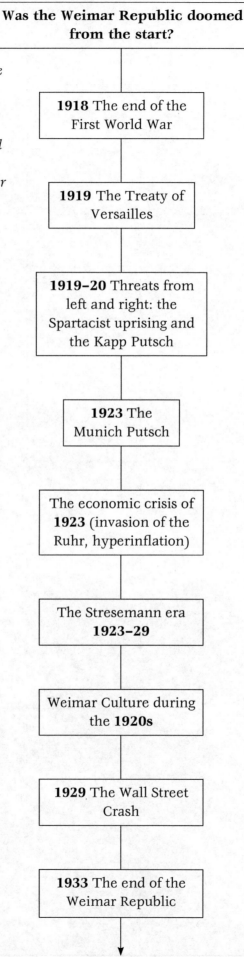

– Ebert seen as a traitor from the beginning for signing the armistice ('The November Criminals').

– Much hostility between left and right in Germany.

– Constitution of the new Weimar Republic had several weaknesses, e.g. likelihood of coalition governments.

1918 The end of the First World War

1919 The Treaty of Versailles

1919–20 Threats from left and right: the Spartacist uprising and the Kapp Putsch

There were continued tensions between left and right and both groups still wanted Germany to be ruled in a very different way to the Weimar Republic.

The army refused to fire on the Freikorps during the Kapp Putsch. This was a bad sign for the government.

1923 The Munich Putsch

Both the Spartacist uprising and the Kapp Putsch were defeated. Workers went on strike to prevent Kapp from taking over, showing support for the Weimar Republic among ordinary German people.

The economic crisis of **1923** (invasion of the Ruhr, hyperinflation)

The Stresemann era **1923–29**

Weimar Culture during the **1920s**

1929 The Wall Street Crash

1933 The end of the Weimar Republic

4.4 Threats facing the Weimar Republic

On the right of the political spectrum, the Freikorps are another threat. They are an organisation which…

They are opposed to your government because…

I believe they present a clear danger because…

Mr Ebert, I believe that the main problems facing your new government are…

1

2

3

4

5

On the left of the political spectrum, the Communists (Spartacists) are a threat. They are an organisation which…

They are opposed to your government because…

I believe they present a clear danger because…

4.5 Hitler's Reichstag speech

The protection of the frontiers of the Reich and thereby of the lives of our people and the existence of our business is now in the hands of the Reichswehr, which, in accordance with the terms imposed upon us by the *Treaty of Versailles*, is to be regarded as the only really disarmed army in the world. In spite of its *enforced smallness and entirely insufficient armament*, the German people may regard their Reichswehr with proud satisfaction. This little instrument of our national self-defence has come into being under the most difficult conditions. The spirit imbuing it is that of our best military traditions. The German nation has thus fulfilled with painful conscientiousness the *obligations imposed upon it by the peace treaty*; indeed, even the replacement of ships for our fleet then sanctioned has, I may perhaps be allowed to say, unfortunately, only been carried out to a small extent.

For the overcoming of the *economic catastrophe* three things are necessary:

1 Absolutely authoritative leadership in internal affairs, in order to create confidence in the stability of conditions.

2 The securing of peace by the great nations for a long time to come, with a view to restoring the confidence of the nations in each other.

3 The final victory of the principles of common sense in the organisation and conduct of business, and also a general *release from reparations and impossible liabilities for debts and interest*.

Adolf Hitler speaking to the German Reichstag, 23 March 1933

4.6 Hyperinflation

Organise yourselves into groups of three or four.

PART I: CALCULATIONS FROM THE WHOLESALE PRICE INDEX

The chart below shows the Wholesale Price Index for Germany in the early 1920s. The starting point for the index is the outbreak of the First World War, with an index score of 1 assigned to that date.

Date	Index
July 1922	100.6
Jan 1923	2785.0
July 1923	194,000.0
Nov 1923	726,000,000,000.0

1 Discuss with your group what these numbers actually mean. How would these figures affect ordinary people in their everyday lives?
2 The chart covers a 15-month period. Work out, on average, how quickly the German mark was losing its value at this time.

In theory, something that cost 100 marks in July 1922 would, at the height of the hyperinflation crisis in 1923, cost 726,000,000,000.

3 Divide 726,000,000,000 by 100 to make the sums easier. Now divide that number by 15. This provides you with an average loss of value, or increase in wholesale price, in each month covered by the chart. Discuss what this means.
4 How would these figures change on a daily basis?
5 Take your figure for an average month – which should be 484,000,000. What is that each day? Divide by 30 to get an average. Again, discuss what this figure means – 16,133,333.33 per day.
6 What might this mean to ordinary Germans, banks or businesses?
7 Now consider how these figures would affect ordinary people in 'real' terms and in 'real' time. Calculate the hourly rate of devaluation (divide by 24).
8 How would 672,222.2 marks an hour affect the daily lives of ordinary Germans?

PART II: GO SHOPPING

Your teacher will now ask you to go shopping.

PART III: QUESTIONS

1 How would this affect Germans who were trying to buy food, pay rent or hire essential equipment?
2 How would it affect businesses wanting to order raw materials, workers collecting their wages, or politicians trying to plan for future improvements?
3 What might be the political impact of hyperinflation? Would people blame their own government – or would they connect hyperinflation with events abroad (such as the Treaty of Versailles)?

4.7 Hyperinflation 2

Wholesale price index for Germany in the early 1920s.

The following is a minute by minute price guide:

Minutes of lesson transpired	Cost of marker and chocolates
0	12.0
1	134,444.4
2	268,888.8
3	403,333.2
4	537,777.6
5	672,222.0
6	806,666.4
7	941,110.8
8	1,075,555.2
9	1,209,999.6
10	1,344,444.0
11	1,478,888.4
12	1,613,332.8
13	1,747,777.2
14	1,882,221.6
15	2,016,666.0
16	2,151,110.4
17	2,285,554.8
18	2,419,999.2
19	2,554,443.6
20	2,688,888.0

4.8 Weimar Republic research

Art
- Ernst Barlach – sculptor
- Max Beckmann – painter, printmaker
- Otto Dix – painter
- George Grosz – painter
- John Heartfield – photomontage artist
- Käthe Kollwitz – printmaker, sculptor, artist
- Paul Klee – painter
- Hannah Höch – photomontage artist

Architecture
- Walter Gropius – architect, founder of the Bauhaus
- Ernst May – architect
- Erich Mendelsohn – architect

Literature
- Bertolt Brecht – playwright
- Christopher Isherwood – novelist
- Heinrich Mann – novelist
- Klaus Mann – novelist
- Anna Seghers – novelist
- Kurt Tucholsky – satirist

Music
- Alban Berg – composer
- Paul Hindemith – composer
- Otto Klemperer – conductor and composer
- Arnold Schoenberg – composer
- Anton Webern – composer
- Kurt Weill – composer

Theatre and film
- Marlene Dietrich – actress
- Carl Froelich – director
- Greta Garbo – actress
- Fritz Lang – filmmaker
- Ernst Lubitsch – film director
- Max Reinhardt – theatre producer
- Lotte Reiniger – pioneering animator
- Hans Richter – filmmaker, actor, writer

4.9 The 25 points of the German Workers' Party

- Herr Schmidt: a German-born citizen who fought bravely in the First World War
- Herr Meyer: a poor, illiterate German-born citizen with four children.
- Frau Müller: a teacher with liberal political leanings
- Frau Brun: a retired housewife and small shopkeeper

THE 25 POINTS OF THE GERMAN WORKERS' PARTY

1 We demand the union of all Germans in a Greater Germany on the basis of the right of national self-determination.

2 We demand equality of rights for the German people in their dealings with other nations, and the revocation of the peace treaties of Versailles and Saint-Germain.

3 We demand land and territory (colonies) to feed our people and to settle our surplus population.

4 Only members of the nation may be citizens of the State. Only those of German blood, whatever be their creed, may be members of the nation. Accordingly, no Jew may be a member of the nation.

5 Non-citizens may live in Germany only as guests and must be subject to laws for aliens.

6 The right to vote on the State's government and legislation shall be enjoyed by the citizens of the State alone. We demand therefore that all official appointments, of whatever kind, whether in the Reich, in the states or in the smaller localities, shall be held by none but citizens.
   We oppose the corrupting parliamentary custom of filling posts merely in accordance with party considerations, and without reference to character or abilities.

7 We demand that the State shall make it its primary duty to provide a livelihood for its citizens. If it should prove impossible to feed the entire population, foreign nationals (non-citizens) must be deported from the Reich.

8 All non-German immigration must be prevented. We demand that all non-Germans who entered Germany after 2 August 1914 shall be required to leave the Reich forthwith.

9 All citizens shall have equal rights and duties.

10 It must be the first duty of every citizen to perform physical or mental work. The activities of the individual must not clash with the general interest, but must proceed within the framework of the community and be for the general good.

We demand therefore:

11 The abolition of incomes unearned by work.
   The breaking of the slavery of interest.

12 In view of the enormous sacrifices of life and property demanded of a nation by any war, personal enrichment from war must be regarded as a crime against the nation. We demand therefore the ruthless confiscation of all war profits.

13 We demand the nationalisation of all businesses which have been formed into corporations (trusts).

14 We demand profit-sharing in large industrial enterprises.

15 We demand the extensive development of insurance for old age.

16 We demand the creation and maintenance of a healthy middle class, the immediate communalising of big department stores, and their lease at a cheap rate to small traders, and that the utmost consideration shall be shown to all small traders in the placing of State and municipal orders.

17 We demand a land reform suitable to our national requirements, the passing of a law for the expropriation of land for communal purposes without compensation; the abolition of ground rent, and the prohibition of all speculation in land.

18 We demand the ruthless prosecution of those whose activities are injurious to the common interest. Common criminals, usurers, profiteers, etc., must be punished with death, whatever their creed or race.

19 We demand that Roman Law, which serves a materialistic world order, be replaced by a German common law.

20 The State must consider a thorough reconstruction of our national system of education (with the aim of opening up to every able and hard-working German the possibility of higher education and of thus obtaining advancement). The curricula of all educational establishments must be brought into line with the requirements of practical life. The aim of the school must be to give the pupil, beginning with the first sign of intelligence, a grasp of the nation and the State (through the study of civic affairs). We demand the education of gifted children of poor parents, whatever their class or occupation, at the expense of the State.

21 The State must ensure that the nation's health standards are raised by protecting mothers and infants, by prohibiting child labour, by promoting physical strength through legislation providing for compulsory gymnastics and sports, and by the extensive support of clubs engaged in the physical training of youth.

22 We demand the abolition of the mercenary army and the foundation of a people's army.

23 We demand legal warfare on deliberate political mendacity and its dissemination in the press. To facilitate the creation of a German national press we demand:

a that all editors of, and contributors to newspapers appearing in the German language must be members of the nation;

b that no non-German newspapers may appear without the express permission of the State. They must not be printed in the German language;

c that non-Germans shall be prohibited by law from participating financially in or influencing German newspapers, and that the penalty for contravening such a law shall be the suppression of any such newspaper, and the immediate deportation of the non-Germans involved.

The publishing of papers which are not conducive to the national welfare must be forbidden. We demand the legal prosecution of all those tendencies in art and literature which corrupt our national life, and the suppression of cultural events which violate this demand.

24 We demand freedom for all religious denominations in the State, provided they do not threaten its existence or offend the moral feelings of the German race.

The Party, as such, stands for positive Christianity, but does not commit itself to any particular denomination. It combats the Jewish-materialistic spirit within and without us, and is convinced that our nation can achieve permanent health only from within on the basis of the principle: The common interest before self-interest.

25 To put the whole of this programme into effect, we demand the creation of a strong central state power for the Reich; the unconditional authority of the political central Parliament over the entire Reich and its organisations; and the formation of Corporations based on estate and occupation for the purpose of carrying out the general legislation passed by the Reich in the various German states.

The leaders of the Party promise to work ruthlessly – if need be to sacrifice their very lives – to translate this programme into action.

4.10 Hitler's defence

I admit that I tried to overthrow this government, but I did it with good reason. The German people are suffering under its leadership. For example… *(give some examples of recent problems in Germany)*

....

....

....

....

Not only are we suffering now, our leaders are those same men who accepted the terms of the Treaty of Versailles. This has meant that… *(mention how the Treaty has affected Germany, and what Hitler and his supporters thought of those people who signed it)*

....

....

....

....

German society under the Weimar government is corrupt and decadent. For example… *(give some examples of Weimar culture that Hitler disapproved of and mention his beliefs about the role of the Jews)*

....

....

....

....

I believe that the kind of society we want is one where… *(explain Hitler's beliefs about traditional values)*

....

....

....

....

As leader of Germany, I would… *(think about Hitler's 25 points)*

....

....

....

....

I do not believe that this court should find me guilty of treason because…

....

....

....

....

4.11 Reichstag fire sources

SOURCE A

At nine, the Fuhrer came to supper. We had a little music and talked. Suddenly the telephone rang. The Reichstag is burning! I thought the news was pure fantasy and, at first, did not inform the Fuhrer. After a few more calls, I was able to confirm that the terrible news was true... There could be no doubt that the Communists had made a final attempt to seize power by creating an atmosphere of panic and terror.

From Joseph Goebbels: *My Part in Germany's Fight*.

SOURCE B

I was a member of the Communist Party until 1929... In Holland, I read that the Nazis had come to power in Germany. In my opinion, something had to be done in protest against this system... I did not wish to harm ordinary people... As to the question of whether I acted alone, I declare emphatically that this was the case. No one at all helped me.

From Marinus van der Lubbe's statement to the police in 1933.

SOURCE C

The voluntary confession of van der Lubbe prevented me from thinking that he needed any helpers. Why should not a single match be enough? But this specialist had used a whole knapsack full of inflammable material. He had been so active that he had laid several dozen fires... I reported on the results of the first interrogations of van der Lubbe – that in my opinion he was a maniac.

From an account by Rudolf Diels, head of the Prussian police.

SOURCE D

I needed no pretext to strike against the Communists. Their debts were so heavy, their crimes so tremendous, that without any further prompting I was determined to begin the most ruthless war of extermination against them with all the instruments of power at my command... as I testified at the Reichstag Fire trial, the fire, which forced me to take measures so rapidly, was actually extremely awkward for me, since it compelled me to act faster than I had intended and to strike before I had made all my thorough preparations.

From Hermann Göring, *The Building of a Nation*, 1934.

SOURCE E

Göring, Himmler and Frick... were talking together. Göring was giving details of the Reichstag fire, the secret of which was still being carefully guarded. I myself had unhesitatingly ascribed it to arson on the part of persons under Communist influence. It was not until I heard this conversation that I discovered that the National Socialist leadership was solely responsible, and that Hitler knew of the plan and approved of it... The complacency with which this close circle... discussed the deed was shattering. Gratified laughter, cynical jokes, boasting... Goring described how 'his boys' had entered the Reichstag building by a subterranean passage from the President's palace...

From Herman Rauschning, *The Voice of Destruction*. Rauschning was a former Nazi who quarrelled with Hitler, fleeing to Switzerland and then America where he became a vocal critic of the Nazi regime.

4.12 Nazi propaganda

'Germans buy German goods.'

A recruiting poster used in the Netherlands which encourages young men to fight Bolshevism (communism)

Comment on purpose, message and audience:

....

....

....

Comment on purpose, message and audience:

....

....

....

The masses find it difficult to understand politics, their intelligence is small. Therefore all effective propaganda must be limited to a very few points. The masses will remember only the simplest ideas repeated a thousand times over. If I approach the masses with reasoned arguments, they will not understand me. In the mass meeting, their reasoning power is paralysed. What I say is like an order given under hypnosis. (Hitler)

The entire German news and propaganda policy must now be devoted exclusively to re-establishing and increasing the power of resistance, the war effort and fighting morale both at the front and at home. To achieve this aim all resources must be harnessed to produce a direct and indirect impact on readers and audiences. Anything which can be detrimental to this aim or runs counter to it, even only passively, can have no place in press or radio in these decisive days of our fateful struggle. Anything which contributes to the achievement of this great purpose should be expressly promoted and henceforth be a central feature of our newscasting. (Goebbels)

Read these quotations from Hitler and Goebbels and comment on what they tell you about the principles behind Nazi propaganda:

....

....

....

4.13 Frau Margarete Fischer

Born in the North German port of Bremen in 1918, Margarete Fischer was brought up by her mother and grandmother. She had one brother. She was hugely influenced by a teacher who 'embodied the ideals of National Socialism in such a way that I'd still say, if National Socialism had really been how this woman believed it and embodied it something completely different would have come out of it. She showed us by example what community is, what sacrifice for others is. She never thought of herself. She always lived and worked for others. Exemplary!'

'I looked exactly the way Hitler wanted German women to look. Blonde with braids, and tall and slim and lively.'

She only started to have doubts about Nazism after Kristallnacht. Her family was not political and this was exacerbated by not having a father at home (her parents were divorced), because it was the father who often represented a link to the political sphere. Her brother joined the Hitler Youth but Frau Fischer did not 'because I rejected the autocratic form'. But after training to be a primary school teacher, she did help the BDM (League of German Maidens) in its training. This was so successful that she was offered a leadership position which she refused. She did subsequently work for the NSV (National Socialist People's Welfare Organisation). It sent her off to train for two years to teach children's health care and gymnastics.

Meanwhile the war began. 'I wept uncontrollably... It was at this point that the inner resistance began... the war freed me far and away from National Socialism thought possession.'

In 1941 Margarete Fischer married Fritz Fischer. He was away at war much of the time. Meanwhile, Frau Fischer pursued her career, which was advanced by the Nazi regime. In 1942 she was promoted by the NSV to a 'key position' as head of teacher training for children's health care and gymnastics in all the primary schools in the Hanover and Brunswick area. She was very, very busy – with little time to really reflect or think about politics. She refused to join the Nazi Party, however, largely because she disliked Hitler's closest advisors. 'Himmler we all found monstrous. I never wanted to identify with them. Perhaps still with Hitler. He seemed to us somehow still driven by idealism.'

'We did not comprehend until '45 what really stood behind it.' One heard rumours, but 'one suppressed it.' She listened to foreign broadcasts (a forbidden act) when she could, but it was difficult because most radios only received Nazi transmissions. In any case, she did not always believe the content of foreign broadcasts – 'To us, a lot of it seemed very improbable and also coloured. At that time perhaps we also didn't want to believe it all.'

She did not know any Jews but still firmly believes they are a different race with very particular characteristics. She despised their persecution, however.

She emphasises that although war was distressing, the Third Reich as a whole had many happy moments. 'The mood, the spirit of the times was certainly positive. In the thirties, things went uphill.' She says it's easy for people to say now they were 100% against Nazism but that most people tried to 'adapt themselves' and almost all had some positive experiences. After the war, when she was reunited with the teacher who had influenced her so much, they both wept with the disappointment of it all.

Frau Fischer believes that the Third Reich made a crucial contribution to female emancipation. 'That all really happened in spite of Hitler's wanting the woman to stay with the saucepan.' Membership of the BDM, for example, provided many opportunities for career development. And war meant women had to be self-sufficient and independent. It was difficult to make readjustments when the men returned from the front.

4.14 Frau Ellen Frey

Born in 1915. She was always very patriotic, even before Hitler.

'Hitler understood how to fascinate women… he did right for us young people… He said 'Volk und Vaterland' and 'we must bring our people together' and what he had for slogans, that somehow had value for young people, to fight for something, let's say. Just for Volk and Fatherland and what is really German again.'

She spent a lot of time with the BDM and became a youth leader. She knew Jews were not allowed to join. She agrees that there was a difference between the Jews she knew personally and those that one heard about – 'Ja, that's exactly right. Everyone had his 'house Jew' as one put it then…'

It was a disappointment when a friend's father left the Nazi Party after the Putsch against Röhm in 1934. It was possible to leave the party then without reprisals. She herself left the BDM when she refused to take on more responsibility – 'and nothing happened.'

'I grew up in a circle that was for National Socialism.' Her father joined the Nazi Party for the good of his business. Her mother always voted the way her father did. They all believed that Kristallnacht was instigated by the 'common' members of the SA – did not believe it came from above.

Ellen Frey's first husband was a member of the SA. Her mother-in-law was a fervent Nazi, but she herself was a 'human being to whom it doesn't matter'. She met her husband when she was 17 and he was 23. Hitler made the marriage possible because her first husband finally got a job when Hitler came to power. Her husband was pro-Hitler from the start. But was she?

'And me, too, ja. I didn't hear anything bad about him.' Despite the fact that he became 'crazy' during the war, she was against the assassination attempt in 1944.

She has three children, but her husband never returned from the war. When he was alive and on leave, they didn't really talk about politics.

'You know, in the war, when things with the Jews probably also were going on, we had so many problems ourselves. To keep our heads above water, that one had enough to eat, to get everything the children needed. One really had so many problems.'

Frau Frey's second husband had been a member of the SS.

So – was she disappointed or angry with Hitler by the end of the war?

'Nein, nein. That's the funny thing, Not one of my children understands it. They always say, you lost your husband, and I loved my husband very much, my first one. We had a terrific marriage. I was not disappointed. It is such a peculiar phenomenon, I don't comprehend it myself. We did love our Fuhrer, really! It was true. And when that's inside you as a young person, it doesn't leave quickly… When I see him today, it's always a wonder that it was not possible to see through this human being. It can't be possible that everything was all lies and all false, because we definitely did not want to harm anyone. No foreigner and no Jew.'

4.15 Frau Erna Dubnack

Born in 1909 in Berlin. Has never lived anywhere else. A true worker – a life-time of low-paying, physically demanding jobs. Now receives a pension.

'Besides being a Berliner and a worker, Frau Dubnack belongs to a rarer category. In the vocabulary of post-Holocaust consciousness, she is a 'righteous Gentile'; a non-Jew who during the Third Reich saved a Jewish life. Implicit in such righteousness is not having acted for any material gain. Also implicit is having acted at the risk to one's own life. Righteous Gentiles typically provided food or shelter for varying amounts of time, depending on circumstances. Erna Dubnack provided a woman named Hildegard Naumann with both food and shelter for over two years.'

To shelter a Jew was dangerous enough – but was especially so between 1943 and 1945.

She met her Jewish friend in 1935 on the shore of a Berlin lake. Both were 26. She was there with her husband-to-be and a crowd of others. Frau Naumann was there alone and looked lonely – and very Jewish. Erna Dubnack felt sorry for her and they struck up a friendship. Hildegard Naumann was well educated and had had a job in a library, but the Nazis had removed her from her post. Thereafter she did menial types of work.

Erna Dubnack got a job at Siemens – and was uncomfortable about admitting this. She excused it on the grounds that she needed a job because she was poor. Her parents were not pro-Hitler at all and voted for the SPD (socialists).

Hildegard Naumann got to know Erna Dubnack's family and friends. The friendship began about a month before the Nazis passed the Nuremberg race laws. They had to be 'careful'. But they still managed to go on a cycling holiday together.

Erna Dubnack got married and had one son, Peter. After his birth, she wanted to leave her job at Siemens, 'but the Nazis ordered women to keep working unless they had two young children'. When war broke out, Herr Dubnack was drafted immediately.

Both Frau Dubnack and Hildegard Naumann knew of the deportations of Jews, although they did not know of gas chambers. After Hildegard Naumann's sister was taken, she moved in with Frau Dubnack in January 1943. Hildegard Naumann's mother killed herself with poison.

The situation was highly dangerous for Frau Dubnack and her son. But she was busy working and caring for her son. 'I didn't have so much time to reflect'. Peter never knew that Hildegard Naumann actually lived with them – it was kept hidden from him.

At one point she was bombed and had to move to a new apartment where the neighbours included a member of the SS. 'One trusted nobody'. She fed Hildegard Naumann throughout, despite only having her own rations.

They all survived the war, though the ending of the war brought its own difficulties, including Russian soldiers who raped Frau Dubnack's sister. Less than a year after the war ended, Hildegard Naumann was killed in a car accident, probably on her way to see her long-time boyfriend, a German soldier just back from the war. She was buried in Berlin's Jewish cemetery. 'For a long time, I could not cope with it.'

We know about Frau Dubnack's bravery because she was eventually persuaded to register what she had done after appeals by the new German government.

'I registered for the sake of Berlin…That Berliners were not all so bad. Because it wasn't the case that it all came from Berlin. We weren't all so very much for Hitler.'

4.16 Frau Wilhelmine Haferkamp

Seventy-six years old when interviewed, living alone in a small apartment over a furniture store in Würselen, outside Aachen, West Germany. Husband dead, and one child also. Has nine other children, five of whom live in the USA.

Born in 1911 in Oberhausen. Father and two brothers all train conductors. In 1919, sent to Holland briefly to live with relatives because family so poor. Fell in love with Herr Haferkamp whilst a teenager. She converted to Protestantism in order to marry him. Married in 1930. Her family and his always voted socialist – but she had 'not time for politics'. Her husband did join the Nazi Party though – they had a lot of children and got more money when he became a party member, and the kids got better schooling.

'But then all at once it happened. When one had ten children, well, not ten but a pile of them, one should join the Nazi Party… I already had three children and the fourth on the way. When 'Child Reich' people were in the Party, the children had a great chance to advance. Stake claims and everything. Ja, what else could my husband do?'

She didn't really think much about Hitler – too busy with her children. But she never joined the Nazi Party herself. Instead, she broke the rules and helped the slave labourers who worked nearby. She was accused of 'feeding the enemy'. She would cook a big pot of milk soup for her children and persuade the watchman to let the labourers have any that was left. The Nazis informed her husband of what she was doing and he was very cross – but it didn't stop her.

Later, 'the enemy' did something in return and rescued one of the Haferkamp children who had fallen down a deep hole.

She knew a lot of Jews – though often did not realise they were Jews until a fuss was made. She was angry and upset at the humiliation of her Jewish doctor and cross that she was not supposed to patronise certain shops. She also knew of the euthanasia programme – for example, she knew of a girl who had developed some kind of disease. She was taken away and her parents later found out she had died. She also knew a man who did no real work but who was pleasant and 'clean'. The Nazis took him away and 'gassed him too'.

Frau Haferkamp was very proud of her medals.

'Oh, ja… First I got the bronze. Then I had two more children and I received the silver one, but had to give the bronze one back. And when I had the ninth child, I got the gold one and had to give up the silver one… I was proud of it. Yes, indeed, I was proud. Was really proud of it.'

Her life centred on the family and the home. Herr Haferkamp was unusually helpful with the kids, etc. He had Jewish friends and probably would not have minded if a daughter married a Jew, though would prefer her not to overall.

She never used the greeting 'Heil Hitler'. 'Because that was too stupid.'

She didn't really want so many children – but birth control was hard to come by for Aryans.

During the war, the bombings were bad. Eventually they were evacuated to a farm in southwest Germany. Even here, she found an 'enemy' to help – a young Russian prisoner to whom she gave some of her rations. She also provided more of her famous milk soup to a French POW called Louis, but eventually she stopped because he never said thank you. At the end of the war, she gave birth for the last time and her husband returned.

4.17 Women in Nazi Germany discussion

Work in groups of four.

Each student in the group selects a different woman to read about from worksheets 4.13–4.16.

Using a highlighter pen, pick out:

- examples of how her life changed between 1933 and 1945

- her views of the Nazis at the time

- whether or not she is an example of the Nazis achieving their policies, especially their policies towards women.

Then decide on a 1–10 scale:

- was her life changed completely (1) or not at all (10)?

- was she a supporter of the Nazis at the time (1) or an opponent (10)?

- did her experiences suggest that Nazi policies were a complete success (1) or a total failure (10)?

After you have finished reading, assume the character of the woman you have read about and briefly introduce yourself to the other students in your group.

Then discuss the following statements as if the discussion was taking place just after the war:

- Women supported the Nazis until the outbreak of war.

- Women's lives changed dramatically during the Third Reich.

- The Nazis failed to achieve any of their aims regarding women.

- Women's priority was their family at this time.

- Women were unable to mount any serious opposition to the Nazis.

- Women played a role in the continuation of the Nazi regime.

Place the names of the women on the graph below. The graph shows to what extent each woman was a supporter or an opponent of the Nazi regime, and to what extent Nazi policies towards women were successful in each case. This is not a black-and-white issue – where do you think the women fit on the graph? Write on the graph brief justifications for your decisions.

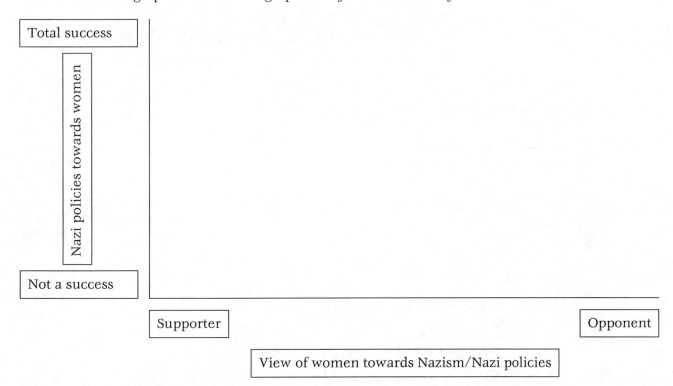

4.18 Grade Studio: 1923 exam questions and mark schemes

a Explain why 1923 was a difficult year for the Weimar Republic. **[6 marks]**

Level 1:	**General answer. Answers lack specific contextual knowledge.** e.g. 'There were lots of problems in that year.'	**[1 mark]**
Level 2:	**Identifies problem(s) OR describes.** One reason **[2 marks]**, two or more reasons **[3 marks]**. Allow: Hyperinflation, Munich Putsch, French occupation of the Ruhr.	**[2–3 marks]**
Level 3:	**Explains reason(s).** One reason **[3–4 marks]**, two or more reasons **[4–6 marks]**. e.g. '1923 was a difficult year for Germany because this was the year of the Munich Putsch. This was an attempt by Hitler to overthrow the Weimar government. He tried to take over the government of Bavaria and Nazis took over official buildings in Munich. However, he and his storm troopers were defeated. The people did not rise up and support him. But for a few moments there was a real threat to the Weimar Republic.'	**[3–6 marks]**

b These events threatened the Weimar Republic in 1923:
- **i** the French invasion of the Ruhr;
- **ii** hyperinflation;
- **iii** the Munich (Beer-Hall) Putsch.

Which do you think was the greatest threat? Explain your answer referring only to **i**, **ii** and **iii**.

[10 marks]

Level 1:	**General assertion. Answers lack specific contextual knowledge.** e.g. 'The three factors mentioned all threatened the Weimar Republic in 1923.'	**[1 mark]**
Level 2:	**Description of the threat(s) to the Weimar Republic in 1923 without explaining their contribution.** e.g. Describes 'the threat of the French invasion of the Ruhr.' Describes 'the threat of the inflation of the mark.'.	**[2–4 marks]**
Level 3:	**Explanation of the contribution of one threat.** e.g. Explains why 'hyperinflation threatened the Weimar Republic in 1923.'	**[3–5 marks]**
Level 4:	**Explanation of the contribution of threats.** e.g. Explains why 'the French invasion of the Ruhr; hyperinflation; the Munich Putsch threatened the Weimar Republic in 1923.'	**[6–8 marks]**
Level 5:	**Explanation of why these threats acted together OR comparative of importance of threats.** e.g. 'These factors together threatened the whole stability of the Weimar Republic in 1923, as the French invasion of the Ruhr destabilised the German economy and led directly to hyperinflation which caused great hardship among the German people. They blamed the government for these problems. Political groups such as the Nazis felt that the government was showing signs of weakness and used the invasion as an excuse to launch the Munich Putsch in an attempt to gain political power.' (fully explained)	**[9–10 marks]**

Explain why the period from 1924 to 1929 was successful for the Weimar Republic. **[6 marks]**

Level 0:	**No evidence submitted or response does not address the question.**	**[0 mark]**
Level 1:	**General answer lacking specific contextual knowledge.** e.g. 'It was a period of success because everyone was doing well.'	**[1 mark]**
Level 2:	**Identifies AND/OR describes reason(s).** e.g. 'The Munich Putsch had been defeated.' 'Germany was again accepted internationally.' 'There was greater political stability.' 'The Dawes Plan had been agreed.' 'Stresemann was improving things.'	**[2–3 marks]** **[1 mark for each]**
Level 3:	**Explains reason(s).** (1 explained reason **3–4 marks**; two or more explained reasons **4–6 marks**.) e.g. 'One success was the reform of the currency. A new currency called the Rentenmark was introduced. People had more confidence in this compared to the old currency which had lost its value because of hyperinflation. This helped the government to defeat inflation.' 'In 1925 Stresemann signed the Locarno Treaties guaranteeing not to change Germany's western borders with France and Belgium. As a result, in 1926, Germany was accepted into the League of Nations.'	**[3–6 marks]**

4.19 Grade Studio: Weimar Republic sample answers

a What were the main features of the Weimar Constitution?   [4 marks]

Answer A

The Weimar constitution stated that all adults over 20 could vote for members of the Reichstag, the main legislative body of the new republic. The constitution introduced a system of proportional representation which was designed to ensure that no one party gained too much power.

Answer B

The Weimar constitution introduced proportional representation, which was a problem. The issue was that often one party was not the clear winner in an election. This meant that often parties which did not agree with each other were forced to work together to try to run the country. People began to see that the different parties spent more time arguing among themselves than actually focusing on improving the lives of the German people.

---

b Explain why the period from 1924 to 1929 was successful for the Weimar Republic.   [6 marks]

Answer A

The Weimar Republic was successful in this period because it defeated the Munich Putsch, made agreements with America, Stresemann was a better leader and there was less opposition. There were also problems, however. Germany still had to pay reparations, there was still opposition to the Weimar Republic, some people did not like some aspects of German culture, and Hitler was trying to attract support.

Answer B

One success was the reform of the currency. A new currency called the Rentenmark was introduced. People had more confidence in this compared with the old currency, which had lost its value because of hyperinflation. This helped the government to defeat inflation. In addition to this, in 1925 Stresemann signed the Locarno Treaty, guaranteeing not to change Germany's western borders with France and Belgium. As a result, in 1926 Germany was accepted into the League of Nations. Stresemann also negotiated the Dawes Plan, which helped Germany to pay off reparations and start to rebuild the economy.

4.20 Grade Studio: Weimar Republic mark scheme

TEACHER MARK SCHEME

a What were the main features of the Weimar Constitution?   **[4 marks]**

Target: AO1

One mark for each relevant point; additional mark for supporting detail.
e.g. 'All adult (20 and over) Germans could vote.'
'It used a system of proportional representation.'
'Aimed at preventing any one party gaining too much power.'
'It set up a system of proportional representation where a party gaining 20% of the votes gained 20% of the seats.'   **[2 marks]**

b Explain why the period from 1924 to 1929 was successful for the Weimar Republic.   **[6 marks]**

Target: AO1, AO2

Level 0:	No evidence submitted or response does not address the question.	[0 marks]
Level 1:	General answer lacking specific contextual knowledge. e.g. 'It was a period of success because everyone was doing well.'	[1–2 marks]
Level 2:	Identifies AND/OR describes reason(s). e.g. 'The Munich Putsch had been defeated.' 'Germany was again accepted internationally.' 'There was greater political stability.' 'The Dawes Plan had been agreed.' 'Stresemann was improving things.'	[2–4 marks] [1 mark for each]
Level 3:	Explains reason(s). (One explained reason **4–5 marks**; two or more explained reasons **5–6 marks**) e.g. 'One success was the reform of the currency. A new currency called the Rentenmark was introduced. People had more confidence in this compared to the old currency which had lost its value because of hyperinflation. This helped the government to defeat inflation.' 'In 1925 Stresemann signed the Locarno Treaties guaranteeing not to change Germany's western borders with France and Belgium. As a result, in 1926, Germany was accepted into the League of Nations.'	[4–6 marks]

5 Study in Depth: Russia, 1905–41

Introduction

This topic forms the second of seven depth studies. The content focuses on Russia at the start of the 20th century and the causes of the revolutions of 1917. The topic moves on to examine Bolshevik rule and then the regime of Stalin.

Much of the supporting material concentrates on strategies to ensure students know how to approach different types of exam question, recognise the skills they are required to demonstrate, and understand the best way to deploy their knowledge. The material in this section focuses on the core content, but there are other areas that it is appropriate for higher attainers in particular to study in order to deepen their understanding of the topic, particularly in terms of complex political ideology.

Ideas for starters and plenaries

COUNTDOWN

Worksheet 5.1 provides a quick revision exercise for this topic, which can be used as either a starter or a plenary. It is a list of anagrams that need to be unscrambled. Students can be awarded a point for each one they identify, with extra points if they give an accurate definition of the keyword in the third column.

ODD ONE OUT

Another starter or plenary involves giving students lists of three or four keywords at a time and asking them which is the odd one out. A simple example for this topic could be:

- Rasputin
- Stalin
- Lenin
- Trotsky

(obviously the odd one out is Rasputin).

A less obvious list could be:

- the First World War
- Rasputin
- Bloody Sunday
- Civil War

(all are causes of the 1917 revolution apart from the last one, which is a consequence).

GUESS WHO?

Give one fact that describes someone students have studied. See if they can guess who you are talking about. Continue giving facts until students can identify the individual in question: points can be awarded according to how quickly students reach the correct answer. An example for this topic could be:

- was not originally a Bolshevik
- wore glasses
- was eventually assassinated
- played an active role in the 1917 revolution
- was responsible for organising the Red Army
- fought Stalin for leadership after the death of Lenin and lost

(Leon Trotsky).

Grabbing attention

PROPAGANDA

Students probably know a great deal less about Russia than they do about either America, Germany or China. It is helpful before beginning this depth study to try to make some connection between what happened in Russia in 1905–41 and more recent events. Students could look at all sorts of examples of more recent Cold War propaganda (popular songs, speeches by Ronald Reagan, anti-Communist headlines) and discuss why it might be that such fear and paranoia has been associated with Russia. This topic aims to explain why much of the rest of the world came to view Russia with such hostility for the majority of the 20th century.

THE MOVIES

There are several film sources that can be used to engage interest, for example Sergei Eisenstein's classic film *The Battleship Potemkin* (1925). A clip from the film can be used to grab attention at the start of the course. In addition, given that it was a deliberately produced piece of revolutionary propaganda, a more extended treatment could assess its value as a source and how successful it is in terms of its purpose. Eisenstein was an experimental film maker, and in this work he sought to edit the film to produce the greatest possible emotional response, intending to elicit sympathy for the crew of the battleship and hatred for their masters. Time permitting, students could do some useful work on both the nature of the film as a piece of source material and the propaganda/media techniques used within it. Students could then be questioned on how the events portrayed in the film could be interpreted differently.

The film *Rasputin* (dir. Uli Edel, 1996; available on DVD) is also an interesting example of how historical interpretations are manipulated in the media for various purposes, and can prompt discussions on whether such works have any value to historians. Russel Tarr, on the Active History website (membership required), provides a detailed framework to analyse the last 35 minutes of this film.

SONGS

Music can also be used: there is a copy of the lyrics to *The Internationale* in worksheet 2.3. Playing a recording of the Red Army Choir singing this (accompanied by images if possible) and looking in detail at a translation of the song should help demonstrate to students why the ideas of Marxism were so appealing to many Russians, and why many others felt very threatened and hostile towards these ideas.

The lyrics to Boney M's *Ra Ra Rasputin* are surprisingly historically detailed, and as a starter can provide a little light relief during this topic (go to www.heinemann.co.uk/hotlinks, insert the express code 0206T, and click on 'Boney M').

Activities

This depth study has four key questions, which are then subdivided into focus points. The following activities are designed to address a key question or focus point, or to communicate an area of the specified content. There are also activities designed to assist specifically in developing exam technique.

KEY QUESTION 1: WHY DID THE TSARIST REGIME COLLAPSE IN 1917?

Specified content:

- main features of Russian society and Tsarist rule in the early 20th century
- the 1905 Revolution and its aftermath

- attempts at reform
- the First World War and its impact on the Russian people
- the Tsar's running of the war
- the role of Rasputin
- the March Revolution of 1917.

Focus point: How did the Tsar survive the 1905 revolution?

Activity 5.1: The carrot and the stick

Students can organise their notes in answer to this question into two sections. The Tsar used a combination of persuasion/making small concessions and terror to ensure his regime survived the events of 1905. Students can be introduced (if they haven't already come across it) to the term 'using the carrot and the stick', and complete a table like the one below, adding details for each method using the prompts provided. Stolypin used a mixture of both methods, so students should record information about him under both headings.

Carrot	Stick
October Manifesto	Treatment of Soviets
Duma	Okhrana
Abolition of emergency powers	Stolypin
Octobrists	
Stolypin	

Students can then discuss which method they think would have been the most effective. It might be helpful to give examples of when these techniques might be used on students themselves, for example questioning them about whether they behave better for a teacher who threatens and punishes a lot, or for one who takes a different approach. Obviously there is a big difference between treatment in the classroom and in Russia in the early 20th century, but such discussions can at least get students starting to think about why and how different techniques might work.

Focus point: How well did the Tsarist regime deal with the difficulties of ruling Russia up to 1914?

Focus point: How far was the Tsar weakened by the First World War?

Activity 5.2: Answering a source question about Rasputin

Rasputin was an important factor in why some people in Russia became increasingly angry with the Tsar, especially at the start of the First World War. Worksheet 5.2 gives an example of a famous cartoon of Rasputin with the Tsar and Tsarina, which students can annotate with surface features, hidden meaning and relevant context. Structuring responses in this way should ensure all students are able access the cartoon at some level. Worksheet 5.8 contains a teacher and student mark scheme for an exam question relating to this cartoon, and worksheet 5.9 gives some answers for students to mark. Answer A is a level 3 response as although it analyses the cartoon, it does not demonstrate explicit contextual knowledge. Answer B is a level 2 response as it contains little relevant information, and Answer C reaches level 4 because it contains specific use of source details as well as contextual knowledge.

Focus point: Why was the revolution of March 1917 successful?

Activity 5.3: Card sort – causes of the March revolution

Students need to have a clear understanding of the specific events that led up to the March 1917 revolution, and be able to explain why the revolution was successful. Sometimes exam questions require students to have a good understanding of causation as it relates specifically to the March revolution. Such questions may ask for an evaluation of short- or long-term causes, or both, to explain why the rule of the Tsar came to an end. Worksheet 5.3 provides a 'diamond nine' card sort to help students order the information relating to this question. This can be used in several ways – all these can be done individually, but it helps if students are able to talk through the reasons for their prioritisations in pairs or groups to clarify their ideas.

- Students can simply divide the cards (which should be given to them already cut out) into short- and long-term causes. They will need some definitions of these terms: you could tell them that anything which has been taking place for over 20 years is a long-term cause.

- This could be made more complex by introducing 'trigger' causes – events which happened immediately before the revolution – so the cards would now be divided into long-term causes (e.g. conditions of the workers and peasants); short-term causes (e.g. the First World War); and trigger causes (e.g. mutiny of the military in Petrograd). Students can arrange the cards to make a big diamond with the most long-term causes at the bottom, building up to the trigger cause(s) at the top.

- Students can divide the causes into other types of category (e.g. political, social and economic). Higher attainers could suggest their own categories.

- Students can be given different examples of exam questions and select which causes they would need to discuss in response to the question.

- Students can order the cards to form a big diamond with the causes they consider to be least important at the bottom, building up to what they consider to be the most important cause at the top.

To achieve the highest levels in causation questions, students usually need to evaluate which causes they think were the most important or explain how causes are linked together. A useful activity is to leave space between the cards and draw lines joining connected causes, which can then be annotated with explanations of how and why the causes are connected.

Activity 5.4: Card sort – causes of the Bolshevik revolution

Students also need to understand the difference between the March revolution and the overthrow of the Provisional Government by the Bolsheviks in November: often they become confused, and describing causes of the events of November 1917 in answer to a question about the March revolution is a big problem. Worksheet 5.4 gives another diamond nine causation card sort, this time relating to the Bolshevik revolution of November.

Hopefully using both of these will help students to see the difference between the events and practise the selection of information that is relevant to the question they are being asked.

This second card sort can be used in exactly the same ways as the first, but additionally the card sorts could be mixed up and students asked to divide out the cards into the two separate events to which they relate. Again, giving students exam questions and both card sorts, then asking them to select which cards they would use to answer which questions, is very helpful in terms of developing their skills in selecting relevant information. Students can then also be asked to read out the cards they have selected and add one relevant point or piece of evidence to each one, again encouraging them to explain rather than simply list/describe/identify.

It is possible to complete this task as an ICT activity, where pupils move the diamonds around in a Word document and then print out their results. This could be useful if you have a class that is difficult to manage and you don't want to give them lots of pieces of paper or have them working in groups. The advantage of using this method is also that students can colour-code the diamonds depending on what categorisation they are using.

KEY QUESTION 2: HOW DID THE BOLSHEVIKS GAIN POWER, AND HOW DID THEY CONSOLIDATE THEIR RULE?

Specified content:

- the Provisional Government and the Soviets
- the growing power of revolutionary groups
- reasons for the failure of the Provisional Government
- the Bolshevik seizure of power
- the role of Lenin
- the main features of Bolshevik rule
- the Civil War and War Communism
- reasons for the Bolshevik victory
- the Kronstadt Rising and the establishment of the New Economic Policy.

Focus point: How effectively did the Provisional Government rule Russia in 1917?

Focus point: Why were the Bolsheviks able to seize power in November 1917?

Activity 5.5: Point, explanation, example/ evidence

A problem with many examination answers is that they lack detail and address the question with general points, or are just written in the form of a list. Questions such as 'Why were the Bolsheviks able to seize power in November 1917' (or variations on this theme as either a 6- or 10-mark question) require students not just to

identify/describe a list of reasons, but to explain those reasons.

Worksheet 5.5 provides a framework with an example already completed to encourage students to demonstrate the difference between identification/description and explanation. The first column is already completed with a simple list of reasons in answer to the question. Students can add any further relevant reasons to the list from the student book. The second column requires an explanation of why each identified reason helped bring the Bolsheviks to power. The third column requires a specific example to back up what has been written in column two. This could be in the form of a quotation from a source, if relevant.

Focus point: Why did the Bolsheviks win the Civil War?

Focus point: How far was the New Economic Policy a success?

KEY QUESTION 3: HOW DID STALIN GAIN AND HOLD ON TO POWER?

Specified content:

- Lenin's death and the struggle for power
- reasons for Stalin's emergence as leader by 1928
- Stalin's dictatorship
- use of terror and labour camps
- the purges
- Stalin's use of propaganda, official culture and the cult of personality.

Focus point: Why did Stalin, and not Trotsky, emerge as Lenin's successor?

Activity 5.6: Stalin versus Trotsky

Students could prepare to hold an election to help them understand this focus point. Some students could write a 'hustings' speech from the point of view of Trotsky and some from the point of view of Stalin. They should include:

- background of the candidate
- why they feel they would make a good leader
- support they already have
- why the other person would not make such a good leader.

This activity could be expanded so that you select two students to represent Stalin and Trotsky, give their speeches and then respond to questions from the class about why they feel they should be leader. You could then hold a vote to see who would win if the class were deciding. Before doing this, you should discuss what the priorities were for the Bolsheviks, what problems they faced, and what sort of qualities they would be looking for in a leader.

You can then move on to examine the actual events that took place following the death of Lenin, and discuss with students why it was Stalin who emerged as the victor.

Focus point: Why did Stalin launch the purges?

Focus point: What methods did Stalin use to control the Soviet Union?

Activity 5.7: Khrushchev on Stalin

Worksheet 5.6 gives a source by Khrushchev for students to analyse and annotate. They should use it to help them understand what type of leader Stalin was and how he used terror to control opponents within the Soviet Union. After annotating the source, students can discuss what effect this type of leadership would have on Russia as a whole, and whether they think this kind of repression would be enough to control the population. Higher attainers can be given some information about Khrushchev in order to help them assess the reliability of the source: of course Khrushchev had a vested interest in painting Stalin in a negative light, and this speech is part of his policy of 'de-Stalinisation'. Students should consider whether the source fits in with their prior knowledge and what other evidence they would need to fully evaluate its validity.

Activity 5.8: Stalin's methods of control

Worksheet 5.7 gives three different sources' views on Stalin and his regime. Ask students to match the three sources to the method of control they correspond to, as described in the student book (pages 223–24): informers, labour camps, propaganda and the cult of personality.

Focus point: How complete was Stalin's control over the Soviet Union by 1941?

KEY QUESTION 4: WHAT WAS THE IMPACT OF STALIN'S ECONOMIC POLICIES?

Specified content:
- Stalin's economic policies and their impact
- the modernisation of Soviet industry

- the five-year plans
- collectivisation in agriculture and the kulaks
- life in the Soviet Union and the differing experiences of social groups, ethnic minorities and women.

Focus point: Why did Stalin introduce the Five-Year Plans?

Focus point: Why did Stalin introduce collectivisation?

Focus point: How successful were Stalin's economic changes?

Focus point: How were the Soviet people affected by these changes?

Activity 5.10: Evaluating Stalin's leadership

An appropriate way to round off this topic is to look at an exam question which requires students to evaluate Stalin's leadership. This will by necessity involve a close focus on his economic policies and their effects. It can also involve some discussion of what is morally justified in order to achieve certain ends: it is certainly true that Stalin enjoyed some successes and in many ways transformed Russia, but obviously students need to consider the cost of these successes and their effects both positive and negative on ordinary Russian people.

Worksheets 5.10–5.12 contain a teacher and student mark scheme, a model answer and a writing frame for an example of this type of question (see Grade Studio on page 116). You may well not want students to look at the model answer before they attempt the question, in which case it would be helpful to look at the mark scheme and discuss explicitly what students need to do to move up the levels, asking them to explain in their own words what they would need to do to achieve each level. The writing frame (worksheet 5.12) gives starter sentences for each paragraph, but also gives students the opportunity to come up with alternative topic sentences: it is important that throughout the course they develop the skills required to answer a question in a clear and structured manner. The writing frame is obviously most appropriate for lower attainers. However, higher attainers can also benefit from looking at how to structure answers even at a basic level.

Grade Studio

USING EXAM QUESTIONS, MARK SCHEMES AND PEER ASSESSMENT TO IMPROVE ATTAINMENT

Grade Studio has been designed to help both students and teachers interpret GCSE history mark schemes.

Grade Studio has a clear and explicit focus on levels. It is the point at which the teaching and practice in the student book becomes focused on moving between levels, and therefore the learning becomes increasingly personalised and improves students' chances of achieving better grades.

The activities in the student book and on the CD-ROM should help students to improve their understanding of how to answer different types of exam question.

Worksheet 5.8 contains a teacher and student mark scheme for an exam question, and worksheet 5.9 gives some answers for students to mark. Answer A is a level 3 response as, although it analyses the cartoon, it does not demonstrate explicit contextual knowledge. Answer B is a level 2 response as it contains little relevant information, and answer C reaches level 4.

Worksheet 5.10 contains a teacher and student mark scheme for an example of an exam question that requires students to evaluate (in this case, Stalin's dictatorship). Worksheet 5.11 contains a model answer which reaches the highest level on the mark scheme (see page 127). It is annotated with comments explaining why it is a top-level answer. This worksheet can be edited to delete the annotations, and instead students can use it to highlight where the answer meets different criteria. For example, they could use one colour to underline where the answer refers to the benefits of Stalin's rule, another to underline where it refers to negative aspects of his dictatorship, and another to highlight where the answer evaluates and reaches a conclusion. They could also try and add comments (e.g. 'Refers to specific factual information to support arguments').

Worksheet 5.12 provides a writing frame to help students construct their own response to an exam question. Students with a great deal of ability can often lose many marks by not focusing sufficiently on the question, or not giving a coherent argument in their responses, particularly to 10-mark part c questions. However, higher attainers who you know are capable of understanding a mark scheme, answering specific questions and structuring their work can be encouraged to experiment with different, less restrictive ways of responding to a question than that given in a rigid writing frame.

5.1 Russian Revolution anagrams

Anagram	Keyword	Definition
ERG UPS		
KHAN OAR		
A STRAIN		
A PIN RUST		
VIOLENT OUR		
STOVE IS		
REGARD TOP		
SKY TORT		
KERN KEYS		
A SKULK		

5.2 The Russian Tsars at home cartoon

Surface feature:

Hidden meaning:

Surface feature:

Hidden meaning:

Surface feature:

Hidden meaning:

Surface feature:

Hidden meaning:

Surface feature:

Hidden meaning:

The words on the cartoon say 'The Russian Tsars at home'.

Now write down at least four pieces of contextual information you would need to have in order to understand this cartoon:

1

2

3

4

Overall, what do you think the message and purpose of the cartoon are?

5.3 Russian Revolution card sort 1

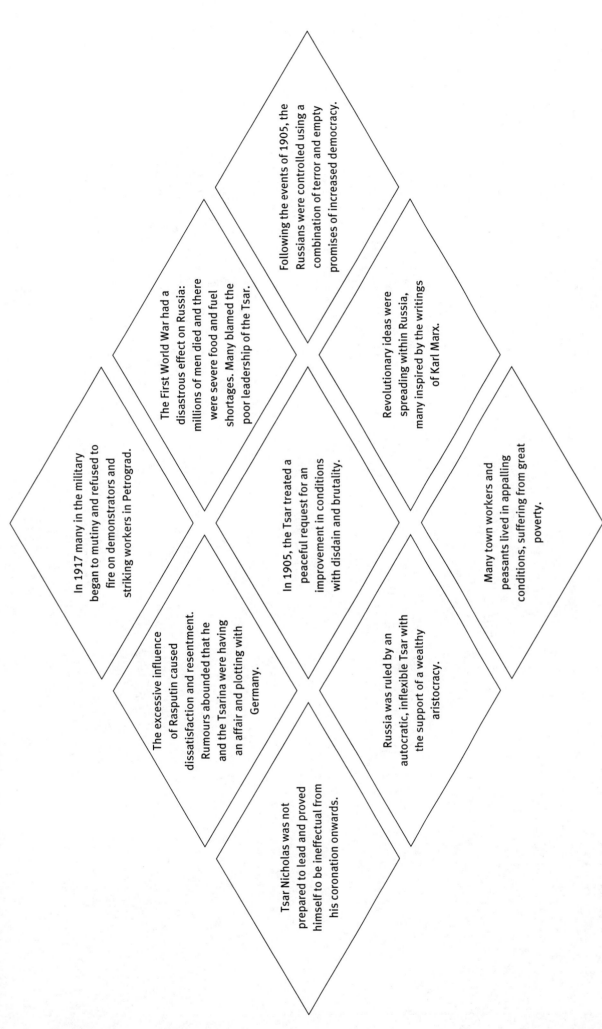

Following the events of 1905, the Russians were controlled using a combination of terror and empty promises of increased democracy.

The First World War had a disastrous effect on Russia: millions of men died and there were severe food and fuel shortages. Many blamed the poor leadership of the Tsar.

Revolutionary ideas were spreading within Russia, many inspired by the writings of Karl Marx.

In 1917 many in the military began to mutiny and refused to fire on demonstrators and striking workers in Petrograd.

In 1905, the Tsar treated a peaceful request for an improvement in conditions with disdain and brutality.

Many town workers and peasants lived in appalling conditions, suffering from great poverty.

The excessive influence of Rasputin caused dissatisfaction and resentment. Rumours abounded that he and the Tsarina were having an affair and plotting with Germany.

Russia was ruled by an autocratic, inflexible Tsar with the support of a wealthy aristocracy.

Tsar Nicholas was not prepared to lead and proved himself to be ineffectual from his coronation onwards.

5.4 Russian Revolution card sort 2

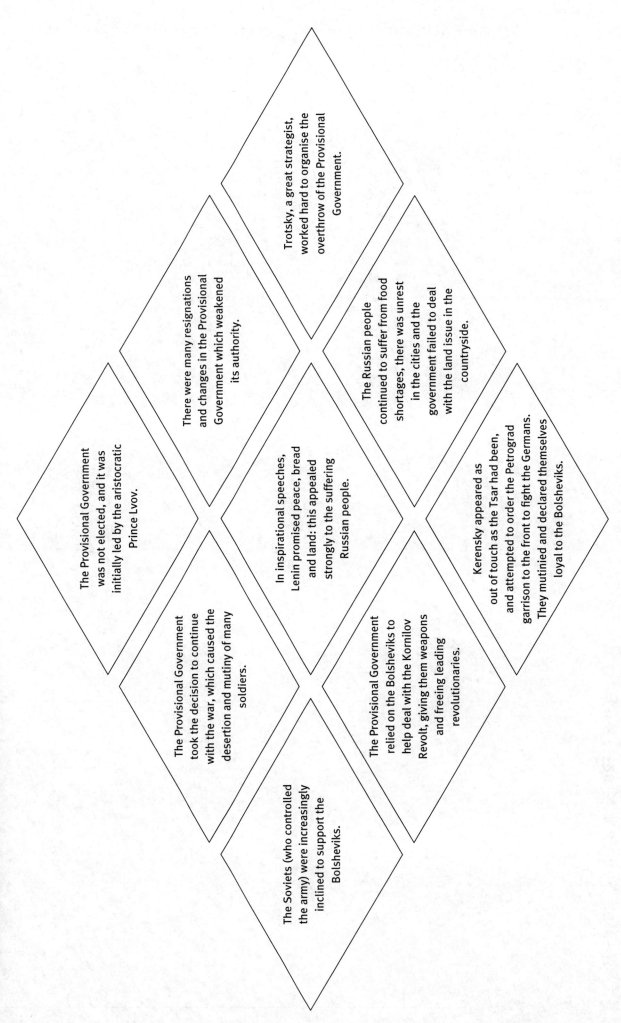

Trotsky, a great strategist, worked hard to organise the overthrow of the Provisional Government.

There were many resignations and changes in the Provisional Government which weakened its authority.

The Russian people continued to suffer from food shortages, there was unrest in the cities and the government failed to deal with the land issue in the countryside.

The Provisional Government was not elected, and it was initially led by the aristocratic Prince Lvov.

In inspirational speeches, Lenin promised peace, bread and land: this appealed strongly to the suffering Russian people.

Kerensky appeared as out of touch as the Tsar had been, and attempted to order the Petrograd garrison to the front to fight the Germans. They mutinied and declared themselves loyal to the Bolsheviks.

The Provisional Government took the decision to continue with the war, which caused the desertion and mutiny of many soldiers.

The Provisional Government relied on the Bolsheviks to help deal with the Kornilov Revolt, giving them weapons and freeing leading revolutionaries.

The Soviets (who controlled the army) were increasingly inclined to support the Bolsheviks.

5.5 Why were the Bolsheviks able to seize power in 1917?

Point	Explanation	Evidence/example
The Provisional Government was weak from the start.	It was divided, made up from several different parties. Resignations and constant changes weakened its authority and made it unable to make decisions effectively.	The one decision the government did take was disastrous. It decided to continue fighting in the First World War: this caused desertion and mutiny in the army.
The Kornilov Affair helped the Bolsheviks.		
Kerensky's leadership weakened the Provisional Government.		
Lenin had strengths as a leader.		
Bolshevik promises and propaganda appealed to many Russians.		

5.6 Khrushchev speech

1 What does Khrushchev mean by 'moral and physical annihilation'?

2 What does Khrushchev suggest you had to do to fall victim to Stalin?

3 What does Khrushchev believe the use of this term allowed Stalin to do?

5 Use pages 219–34 of the student book to find examples of individuals' experiences that Khrushchev might have used to back up what he says here.

Nikita Khrushchev, speech, 20th Party Congress (February 1956)

Stalin acted not through persuasion, explanation and patient cooperation with people, but by imposing his concepts and demanding absolute submission to his opinion. Whoever opposed this concept or tried to prove his viewpoint, and the correctness of his position, was doomed to removal from the leading collective and to subsequent moral and physical annihilation. This was especially true during the period following the 17th Party Congress, when many prominent Party leaders and rank-and-file Party workers, honest and dedicated to the cause of communism, fell victim to Stalin's despotism.

Stalin originated the concept 'enemy of the people'. This term automatically rendered it unnecessary that the ideological errors of a man or men engaged in a controversy be proven; this term made possible the usage of the most cruel repression, violating all norms of revolutionary legality, against anyone who in any way disagreed with Stalin, against those who were only suspected of hostile intent, against those who had bad reputations.

4 Why do you think Stalin used the term 'enemy of the people'?

5.7 What methods did Stalin use to control the Soviet Union?

SOURCE A

We receive our sun from Stalin,
We receive our prosperous life from Stalin
Even the good life in the tundras filled with snow-storms
We made together with him,
With the son of Lenin,
With Stalin the wise.
Thou, bright sun of the nations, the unsinking sun of our times,
And more than the sun, for the sun has no wisdom.

Song about Stalin by Alexis Tolstoy, 1937.

SOURCE B

He had to have the press extol him extravagantly every day, publish his portraits, refer to him on the slightest pretext, print his name in large type.

Stalin by Leon Trotsky (from *Stalin* by J. Simpkin).

SOURCE C

Following an operation, I am lying in the surgical ward of a camp hospital. I cannot move. I am hot and feverish, but nonetheless my thoughts do not dissolve into delirium, and I am grateful to Dr. Boris Nikolayevich Kornfeld, who is sitting beside my cot and talking to me all evening. The light has been turned out, so it will not hurt my eyes. There is no one else in the ward.

Fervently he tells me the long story of his conversion from Judaism to Christianity. I am astonished at the conviction of the new convert, at the ardor of his words.

We know each other very slightly, and he was not the one responsible for my treatment, but there was simply no one here with whom he could share his feelings. He was a gentle and well-mannered person. I could see nothing bad in him, nor did I know anything bad about him. However, I was on guard because Kornfeld had now been living for two months inside the hospital barracks, without going outside. He had shut himself up in here, at his place of work, and avoided moving around camp at all.

This meant that he was afraid of having his throat cut. In our camp it had recently become fashionable to cut the throats of stool pigeons. This has an effect. But who could guarantee that only stoolies were getting their throats cut? One prisoner had had his throat cut in a clear case of settling a sordid grudge. Therefore the self-imprisonment of Kornfeld in the hospital did not necessarily prove that he was a stool pigeon.

It is already late. The whole hospital is asleep. Kornfeld is finishing his story:

'And on the whole, do you know, I have become convinced that there is no punishment that comes to us in this life on earth which is undeserved. Superficially it can have nothing to do with what we are guilty of in actual fact, but if you go over your life with a fine-tooth comb and ponder it deeply, you will always be able to hunt down that transgression of yours for which you have now received this blow.'

I cannot see his face. Through the window come only the scattered reflections of the lights of the perimeter outside. The door from the corridor gleams in a yellow electrical glow. But there is such mystical knowledge in his voice that I shudder.

Those were the last words of Boris Kornfeld. Noiselessly he went into one of the nearby wards and there lay down to sleep. Everyone slept. There was no one with whom he could speak. I went off to sleep myself.

I was wakened in the morning by running about and tramping in the corridor; the orderlies were carrying Kornfeld's body to the operating room. He had been dealt eight blows on the skull with a plasterer's mallet while he slept. He died on the operating table, without regaining consciousness.

From *The Gulag Archipelago* by Alexander Solzhenitsyn.

5.8 Grade Studio: Rasputin mark schemes

TEACHER MARK SCHEME

Study Source C. Do you think this cartoon was published by supporters or opponents of Rasputin? Use the source and your knowledge to explain your answer. **[6 marks]**

Target: AO1 [2 marks] and AO3 (ability to understand an interpretation and explain who produced it, [4 marks])

Level 1:	**General answer** e.g. 'I think it was published by opponents of Rasputin.'	[1 mark]
Level 2:	**Identifies opponents because they hated Rasputin – no explanation** e.g. 'Opponents published this cartoon because they hated Rasputin.'	[2 marks]
Level 3:	**Explains cartoon, but no explicit contextual knowledge demonstrated** e.g. 'It shows Rasputin controlling the Tsar and Tsarina, and suggests that because the opponents hated Rasputin they would publish a cartoon showing this.'	[3–4 marks]
Level 4:	**Additional contextual knowledge used to explain why this must have been an opponents' cartoon** e.g. 'This must be a cartoon published by the aristocracy because it is criticising Rasputin's evil power. The aristocracy were against him. They believed that Rasputin's influence over the Tsar and Tsarina was destroying Russia.'	[5–6 marks]

STUDENT MARK SCHEME

Study Source C. Do you think this cartoon was published by supporters or opponents of Rasputin? Use the source and your knowledge to explain your answer. **[6 marks]**

Level 1:	General answer containing no details.	[1 mark]
Level 2:	Identifies that the cartoon was published by opponents of Rasputin but no explanation given.	[2 marks]
Level 3:	Explains cartoon, but does not demonstrate contextual knowledge (just refers to details of the cartoon).	[3–4 marks]
Level 4:	Explains cartoon, but gives extra contextual knowledge to explain why this must have been an opponents' cartoon.	[5–6 marks]

5.9 Rasputin sample answers

Study the cartoon on worksheet 5.2. Do you think this cartoon was published by supporters or opponents of Rasputin? Use the source and your knowledge to explain your answer.   **[6 marks]**

Answer A

This cartoon is published by opponents of Rasputin. I know this because Rasputin is shown in a negative light: his hair is long and straggly and he has large, staring eyes which gives him a sinister appearance. He has his hand round the Tsarina which shows he is in control of her. He dominates both the Tsar and Tsarina in this cartoon as he overshadows them in terms of size. The caption says that the cartoon shows the Russian Tsars at home. Again this suggests publication by opponents of Rasputin because it implies that he is one of the Tsars, or at least has as much if not more power than them.

Answer B

Everybody in Russia hated Rasputin and so this cartoon must have been published by opponents of him. People hated him because they thought he had too much power and influence and took advantage of his position. Rasputin claimed he could heal the Tsar and Tsarina's son, who had haemophilia. Some of the aristocrats in Russia listened to him and he allegedly had affairs with several aristocratic women. When some aristocrats became tired of the amount of power he had, Rasputin was murdered.

Answer C

This cartoon was clearly published by opponents of Rasputin. He is shown in an unfavourable light and looks like a sinister figure who overshadows the Tsar and Tsarina. This fact, along with Rasputin's hand around the Tsarina, suggests that he had control over the people who were supposed to be ruling Russia. The caption supports this, implying that all three of them are the 'Russian Tsars' with Rasputin the most influential. While the Tsar was away at the front during the First World War, Rasputin was given a great deal of power. Many Russian aristocrats were extremely angry about this and rumours also spread that he was having an affair with the Tsarina. This cartoon was probably published by those who wanted to criticise what they saw as Rasputin's evil influence over the Tsar and Tsarina and prevent him from ruining Russia.

GradeStudio

5.10 Grade Studio: Stalin mark schemes

TEACHER MARK SCHEME

How far did the Soviet people benefit from Stalin's dictatorship? Explain your answer. **[10 marks]**

Level 1:	General assertion of success or failure. Answers lack specific contextual knowledge. e.g. 'People had a terrible time under Stalin's dictatorship.'	[1 marks]
Level 2:	*Identifies* those who benefited or/and did not benefit. e.g. 'The Five Year Plans turned USSR into a modern state.' **OR** 'Stalin's purges wasted millions of human lives.'	[2–4 marks]
Level 3:	*Explains* those who benefited **OR** those who did not benefit. e.g. 'Stalin's dictatorship can be viewed as a success because it modernised the USSR's industry and agriculture, leading to huge increases in production.' **OR** 'Stalin's dictatorship can be viewed as a failure because it had a huge human cost, involving harsh discipline, persecution and millions of deaths.' (N.B. If one element is explained and the other identified allow top of level 3.)	[4–6 marks]
Level 4:	Explains those who benefited **AND** those who did not benefit. e.g. Uses *both* of the level 3 examples.	[7–9 marks]
Level 5:	**Reaches a judgement on 'how far' based on those who benefited and those who did not benefit (both explained).** e.g. 'In general, Stalin's dictatorship benefited people in that it modernised the USSR's industry and agriculture; each ran on strict Communist lines. However, there was a great human cost attached to this success, involving harsh discipline, persecution and millions of deaths. There was also much waste and inefficiency during the dictatorship caused by Stalin's purges and ill-conceived economic policies, but in later years there were real signs of improvement. Stalin's dictatorship survived the German onslaught during the Second World War and allowed the USSR to emerge in 1945 as a super power' (fully explained).	[9–10 marks]

STUDENT MARK SCHEME

How far did the Soviet people benefit from Stalin's dictatorship? Explain your answer. **[10 marks]**

Level 1:	General comment on whether Stalin was successful or not, no contextual knowledge demonstrated.	[1 mark]
Level 2:	*Identifies* (lists) ways in which people did benefit and/or did not benefit from Stalin's dictatorship.	[2–4 marks]
Level 3:	*Explains* ways in which people either benefited **OR** did not benefit from Stalin's dictatorship.	[4–6 marks]
Level 4:	*Explains* ways in which different people did **AND** did not benefit from Stalin's dictatorship (explains both sides of the argument).	[7–9 marks]
Level 5:	Same as level 4, but also evaluates 'how far' people benefited from Stalin's dictatorship (reaches a conclusion).	[10 marks]

126

© Pearson Education Ltd 2009

5.11 Grade Studio: Stalin sample answer

Stalin's leadership certainly brought some benefits to the Russian population. The first five year plan achieved a massive increase in production and the second five year plan built on this achievement. The rapid modernisation of the USSR as a whole enabled it to survive the invasion of Hitler in 1941. By the late 1930s, unemployment was virtually non-existent, there were more doctors to serve the population than there were in Britain, and education was free for all.

However, these benefits came with a considerable cost. Stalin's regime was a dictatorship and dissent was not tolerated. Countless opponents were killed. Workers were treated harshly: if they did not meet their strict targets they were fined. The workers responsible for the massive engineering projects that were completed in the USSR were often political prisoners who had been condemned to hard labour. Wages actually fell between 1928 and 1937 and consumer goods were scarce as all resources were poured into heavy industry. In addition to this, the collectivisation of agriculture, although eventually successful, created chaos in the countryside which resulted in a famine during which millions died in 1932–33.

It is clear, therefore, that Stalin brought some benefits but also great misery to the people of the USSR. Stalin created a modern industrial nation, but at an unacceptably high cost.

Topic sentences clearly signpost what each paragraph is about.

In both paragraphs examples are explained using specific factual details.

The final paragraph reaches a conclusion, stating that although Stalin's dictatorship did bring benefits, the cost outweighed them.

Paragraph one gives several examples of ways in which Stalin's dictatorship benefitted the USSR.

Paragraph two gives several examples of ways in which Stalin's dictatorship benefitted the people of the USSR.

The answer refers to the important areas of industry and agriculture as well as other areas such as education.

5.12 Grade Studio: Stalin writing frame

How far did the Soviet people benefit from Stalin's dictatorship? Explain your answer.   **[10 marks]**

(Remember: to gain the highest marks you must fully explain both sides of the argument and reach a conclusion).

Stalin's leadership certainly brought some benefits to the population of the USSR. For example... *(now give examples of some positive aspects of Stalin's leadership and explain them using details)*

Alternative topic sentence:

....

....

....

However, there was a very negative side to his leadership. For example... *(now give examples of the negative effects Stalin's leadership had on the people of the USSR. Make sure your examples are fully explained.)*

Alternative topic sentence:

....

....

....

It is clear that Stalin brought benefits but also great misery to some of the population. Overall, I believe that... *(now explain how far people in the USSR benefited from Stalin's leadership, e.g. explain whether the positives were more important that the negatives. Give your opinion on Stalin's leadership.)*

Alternative topic sentence:

....

....

....

6 Study in Depth: The USA, 1919–41

Introduction

This topic forms the third of the seven depth studies. The content is based on the economic boom that America experienced in the 1920s, its effects on different groups, and its causes and consequences. The topic then examines the Wall Street Crash, the Great Depression, and the New Deal and opinions on whether or not it was effective.

Much of the supporting material concentrates on strategies to ensure students know how to approach different types of exam question, recognise the skills they are required to demonstrate, and understand the best way to deploy their knowledge. The material in this section focuses on the core content, but there are other areas that it is appropriate for higher attainers in particular to study in order to deepen their understanding of the period.

Ideas for starters and plenaries

JEOPARDY

A quick starter and plenary can involve giving students an answer rather than a question, and asking them to work out what the question might be. For example, remind students of the specific topic they are studying, then give them a word or phrase such as 'new deal' and ask them to suggest what the question might be (one reponse could be 'What did Roosevelt introduce to tackle problems caused by the depression?')

JUST A MINUTE

Give students a topic (such as 'the economic boom in the 1920s') and tell them that they must speak to the class about that topic for one minute without repeating themselves or pausing for any length of time. Students can challenge if they hear a repetition, and if you accept their challenge, they continue to talk for the remaining time.

PICTURE PERFECT

Give students a picture or cartoon from the period and let them examine it for one minute. Students must then hide the picture, and attempt to recreate through either drawing or written description what was in the original.

They should then see how much of the picture they managed to recall. Alternatively, students could have different pictures, and could attempt to understand what each other's picture showed from their descriptions/drawings. This is a good way of encouraging students to look at a cartoon/picture source in detail and make sure they notice all the surface features.

Grabbing attention

AMERICANISATION

Students should be very familiar with certain aspects of modern American culture. It may be interesting to begin this unit by discussing what students know about America and what perceptions or misconceptions they have already. They can be questioned about the extent to which America influences the UK now, and in what ways (from the war in Iraq to the shows that are on TV). You can then explain to students that the period they are going to study was a formative one in the creation of the modern America which has so much influence over their lives.

A SOCIETY OF EXTREMES

Just as it is now, the USA of the 1920s and 1930s was a country of widely differing extremes in terms of both experiences and attitudes. One way of stimulating interest in what type of society America was then is to show a series of images that capture these extremes (such as massive building work in prosperous areas of New York compared with poverty in rural areas). Students can discuss (or write down) what they think each image suggests about the society of which they formed a part. It is helpful, if students are not already familiar with it, to explain the word 'infer' – students may not actually know much about the period, but they can infer a great deal from the images you show them. Students should be encouraged to look at the specific details of the images they are shown: for example, what type of clothes the women in the pictures are wearing and what this might suggest about the roles of women and attitudes towards them.

An alternative approach to this task is to show two sets of resources, one of which shows the positive side of America in the 1920s and the other the negative. Half the class can be given the positive images while the other half examine the other. The resulting feedback should prove interesting as students realise that they have come to completely different conclusions about the nature of American society during this period. Students can then be questioned about why their conclusions were so different, and how it could be that two such different interpretations could coexist. Depending on the ability of the group, speculation can be encouraged as to why these differences may have existed and what possible problems they could cause in society.

Activities

This depth study has four key questions, which are then subdivided into focus points. These activities are designed to address a key question or focus point, or to communicate an area of the specified content. There are also activities designed to specifically assist in developing exam technique.

KEY QUESTION 1: HOW FAR DID THE US ECONOMY BOOM IN THE 1920S?

Specified content:

- the impact of the First World War on the American economy

- the expansion of the US economy during the 1920s

- mass production in the car and consumer durables industries

- the fortunes of older industries

- the development and impact of credit, hire purchase and advertising

- increase in standard of living and consumerism

- the decline of agriculture

- weakness in the economy by the late 1920s.

Focus point: On what was the economic boom based?

Activity 6.1: Explaining the boom

Ask students to work in groups of three to discuss each of the five factors in the economic boom detailed in the student book (pages 240–41): the USA's wealth; new industries; rising wages

and stable prices; government policies; hire purchase.

- Student 1 assumes one side of the argument.

- Student 2 assumes the other side, aiming to point out the flaws in the first argument.

- Student 3 remains objective at first, but based on the statements and any further questions they want to ask, must make a judgement in private.

All three then write down the answer according to their perspective. The group should then have two arguments exclusively representing either side and a judgement that is informed by the best bits of both.

Activity 6.2: Explaining the boom and developing exam technique

Students need to consider a variety of reasons why the American economy boomed in the 1920s. Worksheet 6.9 contains a question relating to this issue and both a copy of the OCR mark scheme and a student-friendly version which can be used to help students learn how to answer this type of question.

One problem that both higher and lower attainers often have in examinations is that they do not focus on the specific demands of the question. For example, this question asks them to consider whether Republican policies were the real reason the boom occurred. What students need to avoid is either offering a simplistic answer ('yes I agree with the statement because Republican policies helped businesses make greater profits), or merely listing all the things that contributed to the boom. If they merely identify a list of causes, then they cannot achieve more than four marks. Therefore they need to practise explaining causes; for example, 'New technology contributed to the boom. For example…This meant that…'

Then they need to think about how to structure a response to a question like this. Providing a simple structure will help, and students can practise adapting this structure in order to answer different types of question about the same topic. Worksheet 6.10 gives a structure, along with some other questions, which students can adapt in order to answer. The suggested structure for this question also encourages students to use topic sentences to clearly signpost what each paragraph of their answer is about (to avoid confused lists of everything they know about a topic). Students are asked to suggest alternative ways of phrasing the topic sentences to develop this skill of structuring work, and can then use the worksheet to write up a full answer to the question. When this is done, peer assessment grids can be used for students to mark each other's work. Higher attainers should complete all sections of the structure, whereas it may be appropriate for lower attainers to complete just the first two.

Focus point: Why did some industries prosper while some did not?

Activity 6.3: Impact of the motor vehicle industry

Students can use the example of the car industry to demonstrate how wide-ranging the effects of development in some industries could be. The source on worksheet 6.1 forms the starting point of this activity. Students should be questioned about what such a big increase in motor vehicle production might mean for American society in the 1920s. They will probably come up with several relevant suggestions, but may not anticipate the extent of the impact. Students should then stick the source down in the centre of a big piece of sugar paper.

They can then be given worksheet 6.2, which contains a list of words that can be connected to the growth of the car industry. They should cut these words out and use them to create a mind map on the sugar paper. They should connect as many words as they can to the main source and to each other. In groups, they can use board markers to annotate their connections with explanations, and draw arrows to show in what direction effects were happening. Students can use the student book (page 244) to help them make the connections if necessary, although it can be interesting to let them complete the task first, then use the student book to see if their ideas remain the same and add the connections they have been unable to make. Everything should eventually be connected, and students will hopefully see how what initially appears to be an individual, discrete example of increased production in one particular industry actually had a big effect on society as a whole.

Worksheet 6.3 contains a completed version of this mind map, which can be adapted to give lower attainers a copy with as many examples as you choose for modelling purposes. Students can also add any examples they can think of that are not included (possibly some negative effects such as pollution, road accidents, etc.)

Focus point: Why did agriculture not share in the prosperity?

Activity 6.4: Farmers complain to the president

Using the student book (pages 244–48), students can write a letter to Roosevelt explaining why they are dissatisfied with his leadership. Worksheet 6.4 contains a writing frame that lower attainers can use to complete this task.

'Explain why American farmers faced problems during the 1920s' is a possible candidate for a six-mark exam question: students should ensure they have at least three reasons, with explanations, to enable them to answer this question. General questions about groups who did not benefit from the economic boom of the 1920s will also require students to refer to farmers.

Focus point: Did all Americans benefit from the boom?

KEY QUESTION 2: HOW FAR DID US SOCIETY CHANGE IN THE 1920S?

Specified content:

- society in the 1920s
- the 'Roaring Twenties'
- film and other media
- changing attitudes
- the Red scare
- the case of Sacco and Vanzetti
- race relations and discrimination against black Americans
- the Ku Klux Klan
- prohibition and gangsterism
- the changing roles of women.

Focus point: What were the 'Roaring Twenties'?

Students can begin an examination of this focus point by discussing what the phrase 'Roaring Twenties' suggests. The question gives students an opportunity to conduct some research on areas that particularly interest them. As a homework task, students could select a topic to research and report back to the class at the start of the next lesson. Suggested areas, along with some specific examples, could be:

- growth of cities/architecture
- New York
- Chicago
- art deco
- radio
- music
- dance crazes
- Louis Armstrong
- Duke Ellington
- jazz/blues clubs
- flappers
- sport
- boxing
- baseball
- cinema
- Hollywood
- Charlie Chaplin
- Buster Keaton
- Douglas Fairbanks.

Together with the student book (pages 249–50), this should cover the more positive aspects of the 1920s, following which students can examine the less pleasant side of the decade addressed in the following focus points.

Focus point: How widespread was intolerance in US society?

Links should be made here between this unit and others that students may have studied (international relations units or even work at KS3). Students should be asked to recall what happened in Russia in 1917 and what the attitude of the USA was towards communism. They should make links between this and what was happening in the USA in the 1920s, and they should understand how opposed communist ideology was to what was happening in this period in the USA (massive profits being made by some and rising living standards for many while other groups were left behind; promotion

of the entrepreneurial ideal). They should also understand why communist ideology threatened those who benefited most from the boom of the 1920s, and the consequent persecution of those who showed sympathy with such ideals of equality. This can lead on to an examination of the Sacco and Vanzetti case.

Students also need to examine the treatment of black Americans during this period. They should be encouraged to recall and deploy the knowledge they have gained at KS3, where they will probably have examined the existence of segregation, the Ku Klux Klan, etc.

Activity 6.5: Discrimination on grounds of race

Students could complete the exercise in worksheet 6.5 to gain knowledge on how black people experienced the 1920s.

The Scopes trial is also an interesting example of how, in some ways, American society has not changed a great deal: the absurdity of putting a man on trial for teaching evolution should illustrate to students how attitudes in some parts of America in particular were extremely old-fashioned and strongly influenced by dogmatic religious opinion.

Focus point: Why was prohibition introduced, and then later repealed?

Some useful citizenship links can be made here. Students can be asked to consider the different attitudes held regarding the status of illegal drugs: they may well have discussed this in PHSE/tutorial sessions in school already. They should discuss what arguments some people put forwards for maintaining the *status quo* (keeping drugs illegal) and arguments for legalising some/all illegal drugs. Comparisons can be drawn now, or after having examined the prohibition issue to determine what arguments surrounding prohibition were similar to/different from the arguments surrounding illegal drugs today (for example, religious arguments perhaps influenced the prohibition debate more than the illegal drugs debate today, whereas the issue of public safety and removing opportunities for criminal elements in society to prosper is still an argument for legalising some substances).

Activity 6.6: The sources of prohibition

Students could discuss the following organisations or contexts that contributed to the prohibition and its effects – how important was each one?

- Anti-Saloon League.

- Can't control or enforce the law.

- Volstead Act – any drink more than five per cent proof was deemed to be 'alcoholic' – by 1929, 50 million litres had been destroyed.

- Extreme religious views.

- Al Capone – mob leader with an army of over 700 mobsters, murdered more than 200 opponents.

- Rip-offs and bootleggers – moonshine and speakeasies (over 200,000).

- Christian Temperance Union.

- Rural Americans shocked by flappers and speakeasies.

- Isolationists hated German beer.

- Madness, crime, poverty and illness were apparently caused by alcohol.

- *Easy Street* – a comedy by Charlie Chaplin – made it clear how drink can be damaging.

Focus point: How far did the role of women change during the 1920s?

Activity 6.7: How did life change for women during the 1920s?

You could begin to address this question by discussing what the roles of women are now. Students can discuss whether they think women now have the freedom to do whatever they want, whether restrictive attitudes still exist, and what other pressures there may be on women to conform to certain expectations in terms of appearance, behaviour, jobs, etc. Students can be questioned on what kind of behaviour from women results in moral outrage now ('bad' mothers, female binge drinking), and then compare this with what shocked some people in the 1920s. They should notice some similarities as well as obvious differences.

To answer this question, it is necessary for students to have some sort of understanding of what the roles of women were before the 1920s. This does not need to be massively detailed, but they need to understand basic attitudes towards women's work, morality and 'appropriate' behaviour.

Students can then move on to examine the information in the student book (pages 257–58) and the supporting worksheet 6.6, which contains several sources relating to the roles of women in the 1920s. Students can use these resources to gather evidence in answer to the question. They can then either write a response to the question, debate it from two opposing points of view, or write a dialogue between two women at the end of the 1920s looking back over the decade and disagreeing about whether roles for women have really changed or not. One suggestion could involve a mother talking to her daughter: students could develop the characters, suggesting how their experiences of youth, marriage and work might have differed. They could then write a script between the women after being given an outline structure such as:

- each woman must describe her experiences of youth, education, work and marriage, mentioning similarities/differences between mother and daughter

- each woman must explain what she thinks the positive and negative aspects of her life have been, and what she would change if she had the chance

- the women should reflect on whether or not they think changes have been significant, and whether they have been positive or negative.

KEY QUESTION 3: WHAT WERE THE CAUSES AND CONSEQUENCES OF THE WALL STREET CRASH?

Specified content:

- the Wall Street Crash and its financial effects

- the economic and social effects for Americans in urban areas and in the countryside

- the reaction of President Hoover to the Crash and the Depression

- the Bonus Marchers and 'Hoovervilles'

- the Presidential election of 1932

- Hoover's and Roosevelt's programmes.

Focus point: How far was speculation responsible for the Wall Street Crash?

Students can carry out the exercise in worksheet 6.7. This exercise asks them to create a flow chart and explain their charts to one another.

Focus point: What impact did the Crash have on the economy?

Focus point: What were the social consequences of the Crash?

Focus point: Why did Roosevelt win the election of 1932?

Activity 6.8: Election campaigning

A starter for this topic could be to discuss modern elections with students. They could be shown a sample of modern election materials and identify the different techniques that are used. From this they should realise that election materials often make very vague promises about what the party in question will do if it achieves power, and that much material focuses on negative aspects of the opposition, rather than on explaining what the party seeking votes would do to make things better (a famous example would be the Conservatives' 'New Labour – New Danger' campaign in the 1997 UK election).

Students should then use the student book (pages 267–68) to read about the election campaign of 1932 and the reasons why Roosevelt won. They can use this information to produce some election materials of their own, on behalf of Roosevelt in the 1932 campaign. Worksheet 6.8 gives a structure for lower attainers to use; higher attainers should be able to compile their own evidence and materials to suggest what Roosevelt might want to include. This task will help students understand not only why Roosevelt won the election of 1932, but also how selection of information and images depends on the purpose of a source – they must bear in mind the purpose of, and audience for, their materials. For example, encourage students to think about what types of images and captions could be included to help make their points.

Roosevelt's plans for America were vague – students can practise making promises that don't actually say very much that is concrete (perhaps using quotations from Roosevelt's speeches).

Activity 6.9: The election of 1932

Following on from the activity on page 268 of the student book, students should split from their pairs and meet up with fellow Democrat and Republican candidates, and pull out the key points from the speeches. The class can elect speakers to play the roles of Roosevelt and Hoover, and hold a presidential debate, taking a vote on who is the most persuasive. Discuss how easy it would be to be persuaded for or against change in such a fragile time as the Depression.

KEY QUESTION 4: HOW SUCCESSFUL WAS THE NEW DEAL?

Specified content:

- Roosevelt's Hundred Days

- the New Deal legislation

- the 'alphabet' agencies, their work, and the economic and social changes they caused

- the Second New Deal

- the election of 1936

- opposition to the New Deal from the Republicans, the rich, business interests, the Supreme Court, radical critics such as Huey Long

- the strengths and weaknesses of the New Deal programme in dealing with unemployment and the Depression

- the impact of the New Deal on people's lives.

Focus point: What was the New Deal as introduced in 1933?

Focus point: How far did the character of the New Deal change after 1933?

Focus point: Why did the New Deal encounter opposition?

Activity 6.10: Opposition from left and right

How far you want to go into left- and right-wing opinions will depend on your students' level of attainment. If you want to stretch high attainers, you could use this key question to help explain why historians themselves differ ideologically. A stock response to source-based questions is often that primary sources are 'better' because they were written 'at the time'. This kind of simplistic response seems to be lessening, but students (even high attainers) often take the opposite (and still simplistic) perspective that historians can't be biased because they have no reason to be, as they weren't actually involved in events 'at the time' and have access to 'all the evidence.'

To stretch high attainers, you could give them the following examples of two modern historians and question them about why they might have different (biased) perspectives on the New Deal, and how this might affect their arguments and selection of evidence. Students needed to be reminded that just because an argument is biased, it is not necessarily wrong or not useful.

Historian A
A relatively left-wing historian who believes that governments should take responsibility for looking after vulnerable citizens. Holds the opinion that poverty is usually not the fault of the individual concerned, but rather the fault of the circumstances with which they are faced. Is worried that 21st-century American government is not providing enough welfare services for the population. Believes business needs to be controlled or it will exploit people.

Historian B
A right-wing historian who believes that businesses and individuals should be allowed to get on with things without government interference. Believes that if welfare provision is generous, people will rely on it and not make the effort to look after themselves. Believes that 21st-century American government still spends too much money on setting up programmes to intervene in the lives of ordinary citizens, and that the economy will always be stronger if business is allowed as much freedom as possible.

Focus point: Did all Americans benefit from the New Deal?

Focus point: Did the fact that the New Deal did not solve unemployment mean that it was a failure?

Activity 6.11: How successful was the New Deal?

This type of question is a useful way of rounding off the unit. Worksheets 6.11–6.12 provide a teacher mark scheme, student-friendly mark scheme and some model answers to this question. Students can use the peer assessment grids (page 146) to mark these questions and/or attempt their own answer (see Grade Studio section, above right). After looking at these answers, students can see if they can put some of the content together to improve the answers and add sections that would be necessary to move the answer up the levels (e.g. overall evaluation).

Grade Studio

USING EXAM QUESTIONS, MARK SCHEMES AND PEER ASSESSMENT TO IMPROVE ATTAINMENT

Grade Studio has been designed to help both students and teachers interpret GCSE history mark schemes.

Grade Studio has a clear and explicit focus on levels. It is the point at which the teaching and practice in the student book becomes focused on moving between levels, and therefore the learning becomes increasingly personalised and improves students' chances of achieving better grades.

The activities in the student book and on the CD-ROM should help students to improve their understanding of how to answer different types of exam question.

Worksheet 6.9 contains an exam question and both a copy of the OCR mark scheme and a student-friendly version, which can be used to help students learn how to answer this type of question. Worksheet 6.10 gives a structure, along with some other questions, which students can adapt in order to answer.

Worksheets 6.11–6.12 provide a teacher mark scheme, student-friendly mark scheme and some model answers:

- Answer A: Level 3 (low) as it explains one aspect of the New Deal's failure.
- Answer B: Level 2 as it gives successes and failures but does not explain them; it is essentially just a list.
- Answer C: Level 3 (high – 6 marks) as it explains some successes but just identifies failure.

Worksheets 6.13 and 6.14 provide a cartoon for analysis, teacher mark scheme and some model answers to help familiarise students with what is required at the different levels.

6.1 US production of motor vehicles 1921–29

Figures from US Department of Commerce

1921	1,682,000
1922	2,646,000
1923	4,180,000
1924	3,738,000
1925	4,428,000
1926	4,506,000
1927	3,580,000
1928	4,601,000
1929	5,622,000

6.2 Mind map labels

Mass production	Factories
Towns	Suburbs
Roads	Employment
Railways	Free time
Small businesses	Advertising
Raw materials	Henry Ford
Rural communities	Billboards
Hire purchase	Other industries
House building	Assembly line
Lower prices	

6.3 Vehicle production mind map

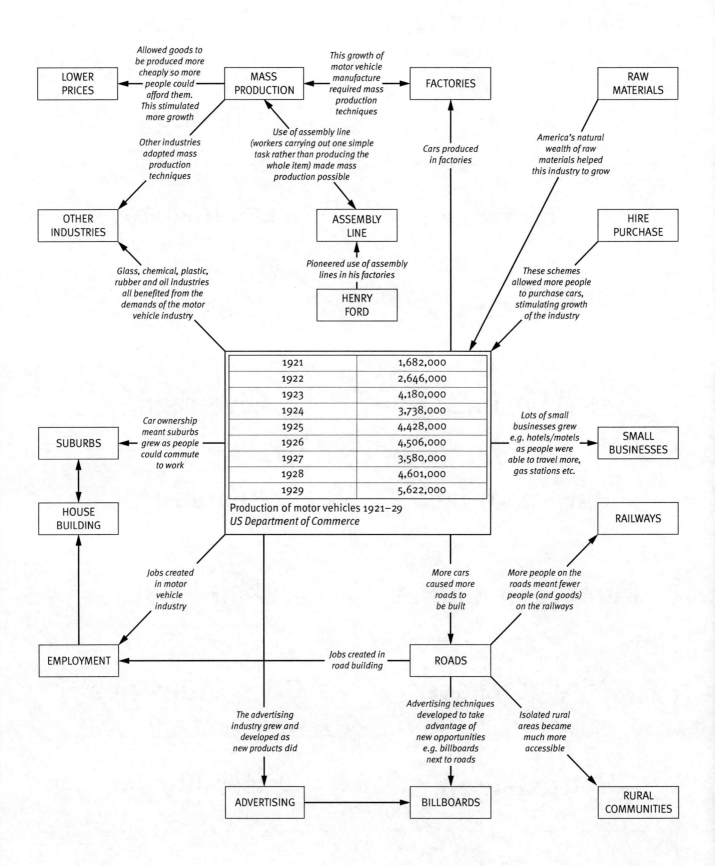

LOWER PRICES

Allowed goods to be produced more cheaply so more people could afford them. This stimulated more growth

MASS PRODUCTION

This growth of motor vehicle manufacture required mass production techniques

FACTORIES

RAW MATERIALS

Use of assembly line (workers carrying out one simple task rather than producing the whole item) made mass production possible

Other industries adopted mass production techniques

Cars produced in factories

America's natural wealth of raw materials helped this industry to grow

OTHER INDUSTRIES

ASSEMBLY LINE

HIRE PURCHASE

Glass, chemical, plastic, rubber and oil industries all benefited from the demands of the motor vehicle industry

Pioneered use of assembly lines in his factories

These schemes allowed more people to purchase cars, stimulating growth of the industry

HENRY FORD

1921	1,682,000
1922	2,646,000
1923	4,180,000
1924	3,738,000
1925	4,428,000
1926	4,506,000
1927	3,580,000
1928	4,601,000
1929	5,622,000

Production of motor vehicles 1921–29
US Department of Commerce

SUBURBS

Car ownership meant suburbs grew as people could commute to work

Lots of small businesses grew e.g. hotels/motels as people were able to travel more, gas stations etc.

SMALL BUSINESSES

HOUSE BUILDING

RAILWAYS

Jobs created in motor vehicle industry

More cars caused more roads to be built

More people on the roads meant fewer people (and goods) on the railways

EMPLOYMENT

Jobs created in road building

ROADS

The advertising industry grew and developed as new products did

Advertising techniques developed to take advantage of new opportunities e.g. billboards next to roads

Isolated rural areas became much more accessible

ADVERTISING

BILLBOARDS

RURAL COMMUNITIES

6.4 Farmers' complaints

Dear Mr President,

We farmers feel that we have been left out. The conditions we live in are very poor. *(Now give some examples of the poor conditions you suffer.)*

....

....

....

....

....

Agriculture in this country is in a crisis. *(Describe the main problems facing agriculture.)*

....

....

....

....

....

Your policies may benefit big businessmen and people who work in new industries. However, they are not helping us. We have a particular problem with… *(Explain how tariffs in particular have had a negative effect on you.)*

....

....

....

....

....

I hope that you will believe what I'm telling you, but in case you don't here are some facts and figures to help convince you. *(Now use some sources to support what you have said.)*

....

....

....

....

....

It would help if you could… *(Now suggest some things the president could do to help your situation.)*

....

....

....

....

....

Yours truly,

....

6.5 Discrimination against black people

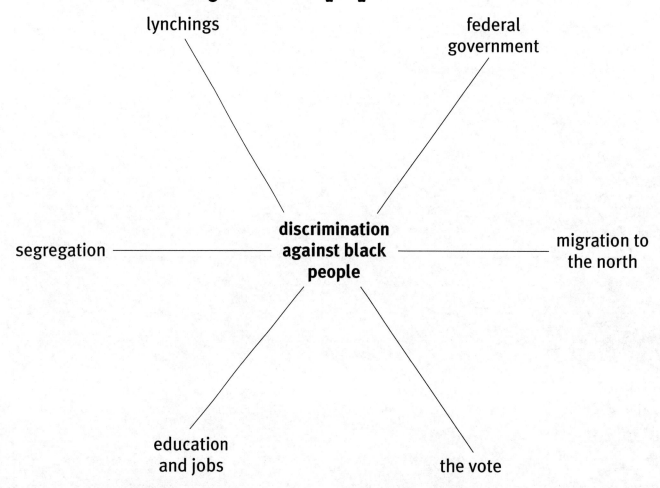

Cut out the following information and arrange it around the spider diagram.

In the south, mobs of white people regularly took the law into their own hands – they would find, try and hang black people. The authorities did nothing to prevent this.	The government held back on supporting minorities for fear of upsetting the southern states and politicians.
'Jim Crow' laws kept white and black people separate, everywhere from buses to schools, and even water fountains, restaurants and toilets.	The post-war boom encouraged thousands of black people to leave and look for work in the north.
Black people had the lowest education standards and therefore the poorest paid jobs.	They were usually the first to be laid off and still faced discrimination.
The law enforced a language exam and a fee to entitle someone to vote – a subtle but effective way of blocking black voters without affecting the constitution.	

6.6 Women in the 1920s sources

Women who live on farms – and they form the largest group in the United States – do a great deal of work besides the labour of caring for their children, washing the clothes, caring for the home and cooking... thousands still labour in the fields... help milk the cows... The other largest group of American women comprise the families of the labourers... of the miners, the steel workers... the vast army of unskilled, semi-skilled and skilled workers. The wages of these men are on the whole so small (that) wives must do double duty – that is, caring for the children and the home and toil on the outside as wage earners.

(Doris E. Fleischman, 1932)

Though a few young upper-middle-class women in the cities talked about throwing off the older conventions – they were the flappers – most women stuck to more traditional attitudes concerning 'their place'... most middle-class women concentrated on managing the home... Their daughters, far from taking to the streets against sexual discrimination, were more likely to prepare for careers as mothers and housewives. Millions of immigrant women and their daughters... also clung to traditions that placed men firmly in control of the family... Most American women concentrated on making ends meet or setting aside money to purchase the new gadgets that offered some release from household drudgery.

J. T. Patterson, *America in the 20th Century* (1999)

In 1920 women composed 23.6 per cent of the labor force, and 8.3 million women older than the age of fifteen worked outside the home. By 1930 the percentage of women in the work force rose to 27, and their numbers increased to 11 million. The First World War had expanded women's employment in new sectors of the economy, and by 1920, 25.6 per cent of employed women worked in white-collar office-staff jobs, 23.8 per cent in manufacturing, 18.2 per cent in domestic service, and 12.9 per cent in agriculture. While the first generation of college-educated women entered professions in the 1920s, they found opportunities only in nurturing 'women's professions', such as nursing, teaching, social work, and, within medicine, pediatrics.

Go to www.heinemann.co.uk/ hotlinks, insert the express code 0206T, and click on 'women-go-to-work'.

Do they ever think, these beautiful young girls? Do they ever ask whence they have come, whither they are going? It would seem not. Their aim appears to be to allure men, and to secure money. What can a man with a mind find to hold him in one of these lovely, brainless, unbalanced, cigarette-smoking morsels of undisciplined sex whom he meets continually? Has the American girl no modesty, no self-respect, no reserve, no dignity?

Extract from an article in *Cosmopolitan* magazine, written by a female English journalist in 1921.

6.7 How far was speculation responsible for the Wall Street Crash?

Discuss the following statements with a partner and complete the tasks below.

- For companies, falling demand and falling prices meant lower profits.
- Between 1924 and 1929, the value of shares rose by five times.
- Lower profits eventually had to mean a lower share price.
- Share prices were driven up by the number of people wishing to invest in order to make what appeared to be a guaranteed profit.
- Share prices rose to higher than was justified – once investors realised this, they would have to sell.
- Overproduction was encouraged by the government.
- Underconsumption was an inevitable consequence of a capitalist society.
- Many people who did not have the cash to buy shares bought them 'on the margin'.
- Tariffs made American companies strong, but made the economy fragile and reliant on US customers.
- When investors realised that their shares were overpriced, they began to sell to ensure they got their money back.
- Those who bought on the margin soon realised, as share prices slowly fell, that the loan they had taken to get them was more expensive than their supposedly profitable shares.
- The rush to sell forced shareholders to panic, and the spiral of depression struck quickly.

TASKS

1 First take out the three biggest causes, then look for the three least important.

2 Expand on your discussions to see if you can reduce your two piles down to one reason each. Note down the statement and your reasons for picking it.

3 Now try to place the statements in chronological order.

4 Compose a short paragraph to try to justify your choices, then check your answer with your teacher.

5 Now try to lay your information out in a more memorable and constructive way:
   - using the statements and/or your own thoughts, create a flow diagram to show how the crash happened – the most important thing to remember is that the diagram should be memorable to you
   - you may want to add colour to make your work stand out, or even some pictures to make it more memorable.

6 The final stage is to talk through your diagram with a partner. This is more important than you might expect. A crucial area in building your understanding is to try to share it verbally. Take turns to read through your diagrams aloud – do this carefully, you may want to use a stopwatch and aim to talk for a set time, say three minutes.
   - The role of the listener is not passive – when it is your turn to take this role, you should encourage the speaker to expand on particular points, challenge their judgements or ask them to be clearer.
   - The role of the speaker is equally important – you must carefully direct the listener round your diagram, and take time to make sure they understand what you are trying to explain. A good policy here is to keep your finger on the page you are talking about and move it when you change topics or digress.

   After your discussions, comment on how well you performed in each role – were you a better speaker or listener?

   Take time to revise your diagram and add or change any parts that you expanded on or found more difficult to explain.

6.8 Roosevelt election poster

Give your poster an eye-catching, snappy title here.

Use this section to explain briefly what has happened in America following the Wall Street Crash.

Use this section to explain why people should not vote for Roosevelt's opponent Hoover.

Give some background here about Roosevelt that you think might help convince people to vote for him (e.g. previous experience)

Include an image here which sums up why people should not vote for Hoover, along with a caption.

Use this section to tell people what Roosevelt plans to do for America.

6.9 Grade Studio: Republican policies mark scheme

TEACHER MARK SCHEME

'American industry boomed in the 1920s because of Republican policies.' How far do you agree with this statement? Explain your answer. **[10 marks]**

Level 0:	No evidence submitted or response does not address the question.	[0 marks]
Level 1:	General answer lacking specific contextual knowledge. e.g. 'There was a boom because America was the richest country in the world.'	[1–2 marks]
Level 2:	Identifies AND/OR describes reasons for the industrial boom. e.g. 'Government policies encouraged a laissez-faire attitude towards businesses.' 'Low taxation was applied to industry.' 'Industry was protected by tariffs.' 'America had taken advantage of the First World War.' 'New technology was introduced.' 'Credit facilities were introduced.' 'The impact of the motor industry through mass production.'	[2–4 marks]
Level 3:	Explanation of the contribution of one reason.	[4–6 marks]
Level 4:	Explanation of the contribution of at least two reasons. Developed explanation to be given two marks. (Three reasons to be dealt with for maximum mark.) e.g. 'The Republicans believed in a policy of non-interference with the economy. Instead they encouraged the growth of industry by low taxation. This encouraged industrial growth and sales which were protected by the introduction of tariffs to prevent foreign competition.' New technology brought a great demand for radios following the introduction of broadcasting in 1921. The widespread availability of electrical supplies created a demand for household, labour-saving devices such as vacuum cleaners. The chemical industry created cheap materials such as rayon, bakelite and cellophane. If you didn't have the cash to pay for goods you could borrow the money needed on hire purchase. Many people began to live on credit, buying the goods they wanted and repaying a loan weekly together with interest.'	[6–9 marks]
Level 5:	Explains with evaluation.	[9–10 marks]

STUDENT MARK SCHEME

'American industry boomed in the 1920s because of Republican policies.' How far do you agree with this statement? Explain your answer. **[10 marks]**

Level 0:	Answer does not relate to the question.	
Level 1:	General, vague answer with no supporting detail.	[1–2 marks]
Level 2:	*Identifies* AND/OR *describes* reasons for the industrial boom. (more reasons = more marks within this level)	[2–4 marks]
Level 3:	*Explains* the contribution of one reason for the boom.	[4–6 marks]
Level 4:	*Explains* the contribution of two or more reasons for the boom (three reasons for maximum mark).	[6–9 marks]
Level 5:	*Explains* the contribution of two or more reasons for the boom AND evaluates (weighs up) how far the student agrees with the statement in the question.	[9–10 marks]

6.10 Grade Studio: Republican policies writing frame

'American industry boomed in the 1920s because of Republican policies.' How far do you agree with this statement? Explain your answer. **[10 marks]**

1 Explain how Republican policies contributed to the boom.
(*Remember to* **explain** *how each policy helped the economy to boom, not just say what the policies were.*)

Suggested topic sentence: Republican policies certainly made a contribution to the boom of the 1920s. For example...

Alternative topic sentence:

....

....

2 Explain at least two other factors which contributed to the boom.
(*Again, remember to explain each factor rather than just describe it: you could include new technology, hire purchase schemes, natural resources, etc.*)
Suggested topic sentence: However, Republican policies were not solely responsible for the growth of the American economy. Other factors which played a part included...

Alternative topic sentence:

....

....

3 Evaluate whether you agree with the statement in the question.
(*In other words, do you agree that the boom was essentially down to Republican policies? Was this the most important factor? How were different factors connected?*)

Suggested topic sentence: In my opinion, the statement 'American industry boomed in the 1920s because of Republican policies' is... (correct, incorrect, partially true) because...

Alternative topic sentence:

....

....

Now try suggesting a structure for these questions. They are about exactly the same topic, but require a slightly different focus:

1 'The most important factor enabling American industry to boom during the 1920s was the development of mass production.' Do you agree with this statement? Explain your answer.
[10 marks]

2 The following were reasons why American industry boomed in the 1920s:

i   the effects of the First World War;
ii   Republican policies;
iii new methods of production.

Which of these reasons do you think was the most important? Explain your answer, referring only to **i**, **ii** and **iii**.
[10 marks]

GradeStudio

6.11 Grade Studio: New Deal mark schemes

TEACHER MARK SCHEME

How successful was the New Deal? Explain your answer. **[10 marks]**

Target: AO1. (Written communication to be assessed in this question – see examiner instructions)

Level 1:	**General answer lacking specific contextual knowledge.** e.g. 'I think it was very successful. It helped lots of people and made sure that they had better lives.'	**[1–2 marks]**
Level 2:	**Identifies examples of success or failure.** e.g. Success – unemployment reduced, building of schools, sewage plants, hospitals, restored confidence and hope, GNP increased. Failure – millions still unemployed, another depression in 1937, Second World War responsible for recovery, agricultural workers and black Americans not helped much.	**[2–4 marks]**
Level 3:	**Explains examples of success OR failure.** e.g. 'I think the New Deal was a failure. There was still a lot of unemployment and there was another depression in 1937. The real reason for the recovery of the American economy was the Second World War. American industry had to produce lots of military equipment and this created lots of jobs and solved unemployment. The war was more important than the New Deal in achieving this.' **OR** 'The New Deal set up the CCC, with the government providing work for unemployed young men on a whole range of environmental projects in the countryside. Many useful projects were carried out to help prevent soil erosion, with the CCC providing the first taste of work for many young men under the age of 25.' N.B. If one element is explained and the other identified, allow top of level 3.	**[4–6 marks]**
Level 4:	**Explains examples of success AND failure.**	**[6–9 marks]**
Level 5:	**As for level 4 but also reaches, and supports, judgement about how successful.**	**[9–10 marks]**

STUDENT MARK SCHEME

How successful was the New Deal? Explain your answer. **[10 marks]**

Level 1:	General answer with no specific details.	**[1–2 marks]**
Level 2:	*Identifies* but does not explain examples of success or failure.	**[2–4 marks]**
Level 3:	*Explains* examples of success *or* failure. If one side of the argument is explained and the other just identified, give 6 marks.	**[4–6 marks]**
Level 4:	*Explains* examples of success *and* failure.	**[6–9 marks]**
Level 5:	As for level 4 but also *reaches and supports a judgement* about how successful the New Deal was.	**[9–10 marks]**

146

© Pearson Education Ltd 2009

GradeStudio

6.12 Grade Studio: New Deal sample answers

Answer A

I think the New Deal was a failure. There was still a lot of unemployment and there was another depression in 1937. The real reason for the recovery of the American economy was the Second World War. American industry had to produce lots of military equipment and this created lots of jobs and solved unemployment. The war was more important than the New Deal in achieving this.

Answer B

The New Deal was a mixture of successes and failures. In terms of successes, the New Deal did reduce unemployment. Schools were built and benefits provided for citizens. Grants were given to provide for the unemployed. Home owners were helped as were very poor areas. Prohibition was ended.

However, there were also failures. Some groups were not helped as much, for example black Americans and farmers. There was another depression in 1937 and millions of Americans were still unemployed. It was actually the Second World War that really caused America to recover.

Answer C

The New Deal set up the CCC, with the government providing work for unemployed young men on a whole range of environmental projects in the countryside. Many useful projects were carried out to help prevent soil erosion, with the CCC providing the first taste of work for many young men under the age of 25.

The PWA was also created which aimed to use unemployed, skilled industrial workers on large-scale public construction projects, such as building roads and bridges. Over the next few years, PWA workers would construct many of the USA's public buildings, including schools, hospitals, city halls and court houses.

There were some failures in addition to this such as continuing unemployment and a lack of help for some groups.

6.13 Grade Studio: Hoover vs Roosevelt mark scheme

TEACHER MARK SCHEME

Study the source.

What is the message of this cartoon? Use the source and your knowledge to explain your answer.

[6 marks]

An American cartoon published in 1933. The two men are Roosevelt and Hoover.

Level 0:	No evidence submitted or response does not address the question.	[0 marks]
Level 1:	Uses surface features of cartoon only. e.g. 'Rubbish is being thrown out.' 'FDR is holding a rubbish bin.'	[1 mark]
Level 2:	Sees message as one of factual information. e.g. 'Hoover is leaving and Roosevelt is taking over.'	[2 marks]
Level 3:	Interpretation only. e.g. 'Roosevelt is throwing out all of Hoover's failed policies.'	[3 marks]
Level 4:	Interpretation supported by details of the cartoon OR by contextual knowledge. e.g. 'Roosevelt is throwing out Hoover's old policies and these policies can be seen in the dustbin. The policies included "rugged individualism".' **OR** 'Hoover's policies had failed to deal with the worst effects of the Depression.' 'Roosevelt was elected to replace Hoover and he promised new policies.' 'His main policy was a New Deal.'	[4–5 marks]
Level 5:	Interpretation supported by details of the cartoon AND by contextual knowledge	[6 marks]

6.14 Grade Studio: Hoover vs Roosevelt sample answers

Study the source.

What is the message of this cartoon? Use the source and your knowledge to explain your answer.

[6 marks]

Answer A

Hoover had, by the time this cartoon was published, become very unpopular. Following the Wall Street Crash, Hoover's policies had proved ineffectual. Millions of people were unemployed, there was a great deal of homelessness and the people of America wanted a change. They compared their lives under the leadership of Hoover during the early 1930s with the prosperity many had enjoyed in the previous decade.

Hoover believed that the government should intervene as little as possible in the lives of its citizens. This may have seemed to work well when the country was in a good economic position, but increasingly people saw the need for government assistance.

Therefore Roosevelt won the election with a landslide majority.

Answer B

This cartoon refers to the fact that Hoover was replaced by Roosevelt as president of the USA. Hoover lost an election against Roosevelt because people believed he had not done enough to address the problems caused by the depression. Therefore in the cartoon the man labelled FDR represents Roosevelt. He is throwing out what the cartoonist clearly believes is the 'trash' of the Hoover years, and we can see the figure of Hoover leaving in the background. Hoover had increasingly absurdly insisted that 'prosperity is just around the corner' and that the government should encourage 'rugged individualism' in its people, despite the fact they desperately needed help. For this reason you can see these ideas in the trash can Roosevelt is carrying, along with other failed policies.

---

7 British Depth Study: How was British society changed, 1890–1918?

Introduction

Unit A972 involves historical enquiry into a period of British history. Students are expected to investigate specific historical questions, problems and issues, use a range of historical sources and reach reasoned conclusions, and analyse and evaluate how the past has been interpreted and represented in different ways. Students are expected to use their contextual knowledge to help them comprehend, interpret, evaluate and use sources and historical interpretations and representations. This British Depth Study focuses on the key question: How was British society changed, 1890–1918?

Much of this supporting material concentrates on strategies to ensure students know how to approach different types of exam question, recognise the skills they are required to demonstrate, and understand the best way to deploy their knowledge. The material in this section focuses on the core content, but there are other areas that it is appropriate for higher attainers in particular to study in order to deepen their understanding of the period.

Ideas for starters and plenaries

MARKING PEERS

As a starter reflecting on the previous lesson, or as a plenary, you can ask one student to volunteer to answer ten questions on the topic in question. As the student answers the questions you ask them verbally, other members of the group should decide whether or not they think the answer was correct, recording this in their book with a cross or a tick. This can be followed by a discussion about who agreed with which response and why, and an explanation of the correct answers.

RESOURCES

An effective starter is to provide students with some resources. This could be photographs, written sources or video clips. Students use the resources to formulate a list of questions which each resource raises about the topic they are studying. They should identify the most

significant key question they want to ask about each resource and explain why they have selected this question. The resources and questions can then be discussed straight away, or they can be returned to at the end of the lesson to see if the questions have been answered. Students can make notes around their own questions as the lesson progresses.

SPOT THE DELIBERATE MISTAKE

Accounts of an event can be given (either in written form or verbally) which include some deliberate mistakes (incorrect dates, inaccurate chronology, etc.) for students to identify.

JEOPARDY!

Students can be given an answer to an exam question. They then have to decide what they think the question was. This can be particularly useful for Unit A972 as it will help students to become more used to identifying the different generic types of question that often come up (e.g. 'How useful is this source?' or 'Which source do you think is more reliable?').

Grabbing attention

This unit is usually taught as three separate strands:

- the Liberal reforms
- votes for women
- Britain during the First World War.

It is important to maintain connections between them, as this depth study should be an examination of the ways in which British society changed during this period. It is therefore important for students to have an overview of the strand and period: if the three strands are taught as separate entities, many students will see them as such, which does not allow for a sophisticated understanding of the period.

POVERTY TODAY

Regarding the Liberal reforms, it is interesting to begin by addressing modern attitudes towards poverty. First, students can be asked to consider what constitutes poverty: depending on your school, the definitions may be very different. Students are often shocked by the *laissez-faire* attitude of many 19th-century politicians, but by showing them different images of poverty today (single mothers on tough estates, gang members in deprived areas, beggars with alcohol) it is reasonably easy to draw out the idea that today we still have notions of 'deserving' and 'undeserving' poor, and many people still take the attitude that people are poor because of their own failings and should help themselves, rather than relying on the government. Over-excited newspaper headlines about 'benefit scroungers' serve to make the point as well. Students can then consider what the government today does do to help those in poverty, and what students believe the responsibility of government should be.

This can lead to an examination of the state of Britain in the late 19th century: it is important that students realise the severity of the conditions in which many lived. Sources describing the appalling state of many towns and cities, workplaces, housing, sanitation, etc. are plentiful. Students generally seem fascinated by the gruesome details of such sources, so they can provide a good 'hook' into the topic.

WOMEN TODAY

In terms of the suffragettes, useful citizenship links can be made by discussing the roles of women in society today, and attitudes towards them. Students will hopefully give a range of opinions, from the idea that women are completely equal to men to the notion that although they have gained rights (such as the right to vote, divorce, etc.) they are still oppressed in many ways. This again is a good connection to make when looking at sources that are critical of militant suffragettes: it is possible to see comparisons with the derogatory attitude that still exists in many areas towards women who do not conform to traditional norms of femininity or expectations of female behaviour.

Activities

This depth study focuses on a single key question, which is subdivided into focus points. The following activities are designed to address a key focus point, or to communicate an area of the specified content. There are also activities designed to specifically assist in developing exam technique.

KEY QUESTION 1: HOW WAS BRITISH SOCIETY CHANGED, 1890–1918?

Specified content:

- poverty and distress in the 1890s, the work and impact of Charles Booth and Seebohm Rowntree

- reasons for the liberal victory in the 1906 election

- reasons for liberal reforms, e.g. the extent of poverty, new liberalism, the roles of Lloyd George and Churchill, the threat from the recently formed Labour Party

- children's charter – compulsory medical inspections in schools, free medical treatment and free school meals for the poor, the establishment of juvenile courts and borstals

- old age pensions 1909, labour exchange 1909, National Insurance Act 1911

- attempts to reform the poor law

- the social, economic and political position of women in the 1890s

- the campaign to win women the vote

- Millicent Fawcett and the founding of the National Union of Women's Suffrage Societies (NUWSS) in 1897

- the Pankhursts and the founding of the Women's Social and Political Union (WSPU) in 1903

- the leaders' tactics and activities of the two groups, including the use of violence

- the effectiveness of the different tactics and the reactions of the authorities including Lloyd George and Asquith

- attempts to get a bill for women's suffrage through parliament

- the situation regarding votes for women in 1914

- the contribution of women during the First World War, including women in employment

- what happened to the issue of votes for women during the war? The 1918 Representation of the People Act

- recruiting in the early years of the war

- new government powers: the Defence of the Realm Act 1914, conscription, rationing, use of propaganda and their impact on civilian life

- the mood of the British people at the end of the war and the different attitudes about what should happen to Germany.

Focus point: What were the working and living conditions of the poor like in the 1890s?

Students will have studied the industrial revolution at KS3 and should be encouraged to recall key issues from the period, such as working and living conditions in the growing towns and cities. There is a wealth of descriptive source material that can be used to interest students and make the poverty in which many lived more real.

Alternatively, studying pictorial sources of London in the 1890s and/or the work of social reformers like Charles Booth can prove an interesting starting point.

The Spartacus website (go to www.heinemann. co.uk/hotlinks, enter express code 0206T and click on 'Spartacus Educational industry') contains a wealth of source material about various aspects of Britain in the nineteenth century.

Focus Point: How were social reformers reacting to the social problems of the 1890s?

Worksheet 7.1 contains a table which students can use to record research about social reformers in the late nineteenth/early twentieth century. The work of these reformers gives an insight into not only the living conditions of the poor but also changing attitudes towards them. Again, the Spartacus Educational website (go to www.heinemann.co.uk/hotlinks, enter express code 0206T and click on 'Spartacus Educational poverty') has some original source material on Booth and Rowntree, and gives examples of other reformers that students can select to fill in the final row of the table.

Worksheet 7.2 provides a writing frame which can be used to consolidate understanding of poverty in the nineteenth century and attitudes towards it. In the first paragraph, students should summarise the research of people like Booth and Rowntree, giving actual statistics if possible. In the second, they should write about the traditional attitude of laissez-faire that prevailed in British politics and how this affected the situation. They should then outline a possible different approach to poverty and the dangers that might be faced if things do not change.

Higher attainers in particular could suggest dangers of rebellion/protest/revolution, possibly also mentioning the emergent Labour Party.

Focus point: Why did the Liberal government introduce reforms to help the young, old and unemployed?

Following on from the student book activity (page 291) to prepare party political broadcasts, students' broadcasts could be presented to the class to share ideas about why the reforms needed to take place. A mark sheet could be distributed to allow students to identify the most persuasive/informative presentation.

Individually, students should write a reflective sentence in each area, with examples of evidence to support their belief where possible. Students should reflect on the difficulties facing the government in situations like this.

Focus point: How effective were these reforms?

Activity 7.1: Evaluating the Liberal reforms

Worksheet 7.3 provides a table for students to record information about the Liberal reforms as they relate to key groups. They should think about how and why the reforms were regarded in different ways by different people. They need to be able to explain why some people were so positive, whereas others opposed the reforms with such vehemence. This can be related to modern attitudes about the supposed possibility of too much government support creating a 'culture of dependency'.

Activity 7.2: Party politics

Ask students to work in groups of three, each one choosing one of the three major political parties to represent. Using worksheet 7.4 they should consider the opinions of the three parties on what reforms should have occurred, and compare them with what did occur.

Once they have completed the worksheet, this can be opened up to the class, holding a final class vote and comparing opinions.

Activity 7.3: One-liners

A good activity to engage concise and controlled thought after lively activities like this would be for students to try to come up with one line to evaluate the reforms from their perspective. Like a car bumper sticker, it should be short, memorable and catchy. Perhaps it might rhyme or be an acrostic. This activity serves as a good review of achievement within the lesson, and as a great starting point for revision/review in subsequent lesson.

Activity 7.4: Liberal reforms – exam questions

Worksheet 7.13 contains an exam question about the liberal reforms, with mark schemes. Worksheet 7.14 provides sample answers to this question at different levels, which students can try to assess using the mark scheme. It is perfectly sufficient for students to place answers within a level, although higher attainers may be able to award a specific mark.

Focus point: What was the social, political and legal position of women in the 1890s?

Focus point: What were the arguments for and against female suffrage?

Sometimes students write impassioned and well argued passages in exam questions describing their own arguments for female suffrage. But in this source-based exam, students need to understand opinions from the time in context, rather than explain and justify their own opinion on the matter. Students should be encouraged to think about why opinions were different *at the time*.

An understanding of beliefs about the 'nature' of women is therefore important (see worksheet 7.5). Some literature can provide a revealing insight into the notion of women as irrational creatures who were too emotional to vote. Higher attainers, in particular, may well be able to make connections between the portrayal of women in literature from this period and arguments against female suffrage. Queen Victoria argued that it would better if women stayed out of politics and concentrated on their role at home – can students identify any sympathy for this argument?

Again, interesting citizenship links can be made with modern notions about the 'nature' of women and different attitudes about the aptitudes of men and women.

Focus point: How effective were the activities of the suffragists and the suffragettes?

Activity 7.5: Arguments for and against militancy

One of the key historiographical debates surrounding this period is whether the actions of militant suffragettes damaged or furthered the cause of women's suffrage. Worksheet 7.6 contains a card sort which students can divide into arguments for and against militant action. The card sort also includes some quotations from sources which can be placed with the arguments they support. This can also provide a useful opportunity to consider the reliability of sources: students should assess what they can learn from the sources, but also what problems there may be with taking what they say at face value. A useful prompt question can be 'What different reasons might student A have for expressing the opinions he/she has given?'

Activity 7.6: Suffragists versus suffragettes

Display the following two statements, one at each side of the room.

A: The Suffragists did much to maintain the moral high ground, but their efforts were in vain because of the rash headline-snatching of the short-sighted Suffragettes.

B: We should not blame the Suffragettes for being violent – it was men who drove them to act in this way. The Suffragists could have campaigned for 100 years and still had their letters returned to sender.

Ask each member of the class to find a place on the line between the two statements that suits their opinion. Ask students at various points along the line to explain their choice – do they have enough passion to make other students change their minds?

Focus point: How did women contribute to the war effort?

Focus point: How were civilians affected by the war?

Using the cartoon in worksheet 7.7 and the timeline of the events of the war abroad in the student CD (pages 62–73), ask students to draw links between the problems in the trenches and the government's response. How effective do they think the government was in responding to need?

Focus point: How effective was government propaganda during the war?

Activity 7.7: Analysing propaganda

If the home front during the First World War is the topic of Unit A972, then students will probably face some examples of propaganda within the source material provided. Worksheet 7.8 contains an example of wartime propaganda with questions attached: this can either be done in lessons or completed as a self-contained homework task. Students should be encouraged to consider the different aims and target audiences of the examples, and the techniques used. The cartoon on worksheet 7.7, as well as other pieces of wartime propaganda are also useful when considering attitudes to women during the period.

Activity 7.8: What are sources useful for?

Even higher attainers can be simplistic in their approach to source analysis. They can confuse reliability with usefulness, often claiming in some fashion that if a source is not reliable, then it cannot be useful. This is particularly important when related to the skills students need to demonstrate in their Unit A972 answers. Here they may face several types of question that ask them to evaluate or compare the usefulness of one or more sources. It should be emphasised to students that sources are often more useful in terms of telling us something that the author/artist did not intend, particularly about themselves (e.g. their purposes, attitudes or methods).

Worksheet 7.9 provides a table which students can use to evaluate a set of sources and relate them back to some of the key focus point questions they will address in this depth study. Students should go through the sources and record under each of the focus points whether, and if so how, each source can help to answer the question. You could ask students to award the source a 'usefulness' score for each question (1 being not useful at all and 5 very useful) and to give at least one reason for the score. Students can use the final box to record any 'warnings' they want to make about the source, focusing here on its provenance, reliability and purpose. This should hopefully help students to see that however biased or unreliable a source may be, it is usually useful for something, depending on the question which is being posed. Worksheet 7.10 contains some sources taken from OCR's new sample assessment material to use in conjunction with the table.

Ask students to design their own piece of propaganda – this could be in the form of a traditional poster, or if time permits it could be a short radio broadcast or a patriotic poem. Whatever format they decide to work in, their piece should be snappy and in line with the existing type of propaganda the government issued in the period. This should demonstrate to students that each piece of propaganda may look simple, but is actually very carefully constructed – it has an emotional focus and a specific target audience. Students should be clear about their own focus before they start.

Focus point: Why were some women given the vote in 1918?

Worksheet 7.11 provides a graph on which students can plot the events of the early part of the 20th century and evaluate how likely it was that women would be given the vote at each stage. This can be used to help them begin to consider what the key turning points in the campaign for women's suffrage were.

Focus point: What was the attitude of the British people at the end of the war towards Germany and the Paris Peace Conference?

Activity 7.9: Making connections between units

Useful synoptic links can be made here to several other possible options in the Modern World History syllabus. Students often see units as discrete entities, and fail to make connections between what they have studied at different stages of the course. It is important to make these links explicit: using timelines with dates of key events from different topics overlaid on it can be helpful. Students should be encouraged where appropriate to connect this focus point with International Relations Unit 1 (Chapter 1 in this Teacher's Guide) and with the Germany depth study (Chapter 4 in this Teacher's Guide), especially when examining Lloyd George's motivations and pressures at Versailles.

Activity 7.10: Steps to success

Worksheet 7.12 contains some key tips to help students with Unit A972. The Liberal reforms questions can be used in conjunction with this, as they provide examples relating to different types of questions.

Grade Studio

USING EXAM QUESTIONS, MARK SCHEMES AND PEER ASSESSMENT TO IMPROVE ATTAINMENT

Grade Studio has been designed to help both students and teachers interpret GCSE history mark schemes.

Grade Studio has a clear and explicit focus on levels. It is the point at which the teaching and practice in the student book becomes focused on moving between levels, and therefore the learning becomes increasingly personalised and improves students' chances of achieving better grades.

The activities in the student book and on the CD-ROM should help students to improve their understanding of how to answer different types of exam question.

Worksheets 7.13–7.14 provide sample answers to exam questions about the liberal reforms at different levels, which students can try to assess using the mark scheme.

7.1 Social reformers

Group/individual concerned with poverty	Attitudes towards people living in poverty	Research completed/key findings	Beliefs about what should be done
The Salvation Army	Divided the poor into categories: the honest poor, those who live by vice, and those who live by crime. Believed most people fell into the first category.		
Charles Booth		Published 'Life and Labour of the People in London' in 1889 and 1903. Calculated that 31% of Londoners were living below the poverty line and 85% of poverty was caused by unemployment and low wages.	
Seebohm Rowntree			
Choice			

7.2 Letter to the Prime Minister about poverty

Dear Prime Minister,

Conditions in this country are very bad for ordinary people. Concerned citizens have researched this subject and discovered some appalling facts and figures. For example...

....
....
....
....
....
....

The problem is made worse by the attitude of the government...

....
....
....
....
....
....

Many people now believe that the government should take a different approach. We believe that...

....
....
....
....
....
....

There are dangers in ignoring the needs of the people...

....
....
....
....
....

Yours truly,

....

7.3 Liberal reforms

Group	How they were helped before the reforms	Reforms introduced by the Liberals to help this group	Problems/limitations of the reforms
The elderly	It was expected that they would be cared for by family. If this was not possible, then they had to rely on charity or enter the workhouse.	The Pensions Act (1908). This gave weekly pension contributions from government funds to the elderly. Pensions were non-contributory, so you could receive one without having previously paid into a fund.	People with an income over £31 per year did not qualify for a state pension. Only people who had lived in Britain for the previous 20 years could receive a pension.
People suffering from illness			
Children			
The unemployed			

7.4 Attitudes to the Liberal reforms

Labour Party concerns	Conservative (Tory) Party concerns	Liberal Party strengths
• You are the party of the 'working classes'. • You feel that the Liberal reforms have not gone far enough. • You also feel that the reforms are ideas that the Liberals have taken from you. • You need to make sure that you find any flaws in the new acts that will not help the poor! • You are a new political party and not 'tainted' with the old politics of *laissez-faire* from the 19th century.	• You are concerned with the protection of the Empire and the businesses that trade in it. • Anything you feel will not help Britain needs to be used in your comments. • The Liberals have used threats to the House of Lords and have only done so cynically to win votes. • You need to find any of the flaws in the new laws that will affect the business and economy of Britain. • You do not believe Booth and Rowntree: you regard them as 'interfering busybodies'.	• As Lloyd George said: 'These are the first steps towards greater welfare for all classes: they aren't perfect but we've done more than any other party to help the poor'. • Booth and Rowntree are right! • Labour are too new and inexperienced a party to know what is best for the country. • *Laissez-faire* does not work: the Tories would have done nothing to help. • Winston Churchill left the Conservatives in order to work with the Liberals: because he knew it was the right thing to do!

How far did the reforms upset or satisfy each side? Work in threes, each of you holding a different point of view: one Labour, one Conservative and one Liberal. Each of you should complete the following table of reforms from your own viewpoint.

Year	Reform	Description	Benefits	Failures
1906	School Meals Act			
1907	Compulsory medical inspections in schools			
1908	Children's Charter			
1909	Old Age Pensions			
1909	Labour Exchanges			
1911	National Insurance Act			

Place the reforms between 1906 and 1911 in the diamond below. Most would probably be in the middle area – but place them where you think.

You could complete the diamond differently from different perspectives;

- the poor
- the opposition parties
- the social reformers.

Areas where the liberals exceeded expectation

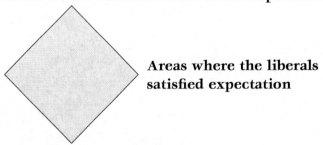

Areas where the liberals satisfied expectation

Areas where the liberals failed to deliver

Keeping in character, debate whether each reform worked/didn't work until you reach a consensus.

Then as a group, pick the best arguments, making adjustments where necessary, and compile an answer that considers all three perspectives and offers an overall evaluation of the reforms.

7.5 Victorian women

A Victorian woman was expected to be:

- angelic – a wife provided a safe and loving home for her children and husband

- obedient – a wife obeyed her husband

- a possession – when a woman married, her money, her possessions and even the woman herself legally became her husband's property

- separate – Victorians spoke about men and women having separate 'spheres'

- pale and delicate – a wife was expected to look slim and sensitive

- silent – a woman was not expected to attend public meetings or speak about politics.

If you are a female student, for each point, consider how you match up (or are likely in the future to match up) to the Victorian ideal. If you are a male student, carry out the same exercise on behalf of a female well known to you – e.g. your mother, sister or friend.

....
....
....
....
....
....
....
....
....
....
....
....
....
....
....
....
....

7.6 Arguments for and against direct action

Such actions brought the issue to the front page and made sure nobody could ignore it.	Violence gave the government an excuse to refuse demands for female suffrage.
Violent tactics lost the support of moderate men and MPs.	Violence confirmed the stereotype of women as too hysterical and emotional to be given the vote.
Women had been peacefully asking for the right to vote for many years. Nothing had been achieved.	Asquith was firmly against votes for women. He was never going to be in favour of female suffrage, so violence did not ruin the chance of gaining his support.
The government seemed at times as if they might agree to giving women the vote, but they did not want to be seen as responding to violence.	Sometimes fighting for rights that are denied you requires violence. Things do not change unless people are willing to take militant/extreme action.
In 1913 and 1914, the NUWSS was growing in popularity wheras the WSPU was not.	The government treated suffragettes with contempt and violence: they deserved the same treatment.
People took the idea of women's suffrage more seriously when they saw what lengths some women were willing to go to to get it.	'Haven't the Suffragettes the sense to see that the very worst kind of campaigning for the vote is to try to blackmail or intimidate a man into giving them what he would otherwise gladly give?' *David Lloyd George, 1913.*
'We are not destroying Orchid Houses, breaking windows, cutting telegraph wires, injuring golf courses, in order to win the approval of the people who were attacked... We don't intend that you should be pleased.' *Emmeline Pankhurst in 1913*	'A deed of this kind, we need hardly say, is not likely to increase the popularity of any cause with the ordinary public... Persons who destroy property and endanger innocent lives must be either desperately wicked or entirely unbalanced.' *From* The Times *1913, following the death of Emily Davison*

7.7 Attitudes during the First World War

- Do you think this cartoon is an accurate view of the attitudes and actions of British people during the war?

- Explain your answer fully: don't forget to look at how the source looks, why it was produced, and what the cartoon was for.

7.8 First World War propaganda

What is the message of this piece of propaganda?

....

....

....

....

What is it supposed to achieve?

....

....

....

....

What techniques are used?

....

....

....

....

7.9 Focus point table

Source	Focus point: How did women contribute to the war effort?	Focus point: How were civilians affected by the war?	Focus point: How effective was government propaganda during the war?	Focus point: Why were some women given the vote in 1918?	Source warning!
A					
B					
C					
D					

7.10 First World War Home Front sources

SOURCE A

You see, us being an island hardly any food could get through, because of what the Germans were doing. My family lived on black bread and on bones from the butcher made into soups. When some food did get delivered to the shops everyone for miles around gathered, but if you were old, sickly or a child you stood no chance. If the police kept control a queue would form and stretch for miles. Many people, especially children, died of starvation. Food riots were very common.

A Londoner, speaking in 1984, about his experiences in the war.

SOURCE B

The women at a London aircraft works painted aeroplane wings with poisonous varnish. They worked from 8am to 6.30pm, but often until 8pm. Meals were taken in the horrid atmosphere of the workshop. So terrible were the varnish fumes that it was common for six or more of the 30 women to be lying ill on the stone floor outside the workshop for half an hour, unconscious for part of the time.

Sylvia Pankhurst describing the war work of women, 1932.

SOURCE C

In 1915 I decided to make a contribution to the war effort and volunteered to make shells in a London munitions factory. I don't think any worker can have enjoyed their work more than I did. Other women developed much more skill than me and they did far more important work, but they would never have known the enjoyment I experienced. When I was on an interesting job it was nothing to leap out of bed at 5.15 on a frosty morning and I almost danced down Queen's Road under the stars, thinking of the day's work before me.

An extract from the memoirs of an upper-class woman, published in 1970.

SOURCE D

My staff officer went outside the hotel and saw a Zeppelin overhead, very distinct against a clear sky, at a height estimated by him as 3000 feet. It was reported that a Zeppelin had passed over at 12.15am and had dropped 32 bombs on Hull. All arrangements for collecting wounded and extinguishing fires worked very well. Great credit is due to the splendid troops and fire brigade for saving Holy Trinity Church from destruction by the Hun. The casualties up to date are 19 killed (five men, nine women and five children), 24 seriously wounded, and 40 cases dealt with at dressing stations and sent home.

Report by Major General Ferrier, Commander of East Coast Defences, June 1915.

7.11 Suffrage graph

More likely

Less likely

Likelihood of women gaining the right to vote

	1906	1907	1908	1909	1910	1911	1912	1913	1914

7.12 Unit A972: five steps to success

STEP 1

- Choose one of the three topics: Liberal reforms, Suffrage, the First World War.

- Read the instructions.

- All questions are compulsory.

- Answer them in order.

- 90 per cent of the marks available are based on the sources.

STEP 2

- Read the background information first.

- This will tell you which topic it is.

- Read the first question and look at the source (A).

- Look at the marks available; this should give you an idea how many points to include. (6 = 3 points minimum explained).

STEP 3

- Answer 'useful' questions by pointing out what a source is useful for – and what it is not useful for. Remember, sources are *always* useful for something. They often tell us something that the author/artist did not intend, particularly about themselves (e.g. their purpose, attitudes or methods).

- Always reach a conclusion at the end of your answer.

- You *must* include details from the source to support your answer.

STEP 4

- Answer questions contrasting two sources by explaining the purpose of the sources. Who has produced the sources and why? What message do they want to get across to people?

- Support your explanation of the purpose by giving examples of details from the sources. What are they actually saying?

- Refer to the tone/language used in the source. Give examples of emotive or exaggerated use of language. Pick out some of these words and put them in speech marks.

- Give examples of your own knowledge about the period to support your answer AND/OR cross-reference with other relevant sources on the paper, which are not mentioned in the question.

STEP 5

- Use every source in your final answer (6).

- Plan your answer. The final question will often give you a statement – you have to reach a conclusion about to what extent you agree with the statement on the basis of the sources and your own knowledge. A good way to start is to draw a simple table to divide up the sources into those that support the statement and those that don't.

- Evaluate the sources. (Do you trust them?)

- Reach a conclusion.

7.13 Grade Studio: Liberal reforms mark scheme

SOURCE A

It was shameful that the old were bleeding and footsore as they struggled through the thorns and brambles of poverty. We cut a new way for them – an easier way, a pleasanter way. We are raising money to pay for the new way and to widen it, so that hundreds of thousands of the poor can benefit.

Lloyd George making a public speech at Limehouse, London, in July 1909.

SOURCE B

For the whole of England, 12 per cent of newborn babies die before they are one year old. In the East End of London and the industrial areas of England, twice as many babies die before their first birthday. The reason for this great evil in the East End is that children are so very badly neglected. Their mothers go out to work, shutting the children up in a room for the whole day with just a loaf of bread and a jug of milk.

Mrs Green, Secretary of the National Society of Day Nurseries, writing in 1910.

Study both these sources. Why do they give different views of how far the Liberals helped the poor? Use details of the sources and your own knowledge.   **[9 marks]**

STUDENT MARK SCHEME

Level 1:	Describes differences rather than explains them.	[1–2 marks]
Level 2:	Explains reasons for differences without any supporting evidence from the sources.	[2–3 marks]
Level 3:	Explains reasons for differences with supporting evidence from the sources.	[4–6 marks]
Level 4:	Evaluates ONE source explaining its message supported by evidence from the source, commenting on tone/language/purpose and including own knowledge and/or cross referencing with other relevant sources.	[6–8 marks]
Level 5:	As for level 4 but for BOTH sources.	[8–9 marks]

GradeStudio

7.14 Grade Studio: Liberal reforms sample answers

Mark these sample answers using the mark scheme and exam question on worksheet 7.13.

Answer A

Source A is written to show that the Liberal government have done a good job of helping the poor people. It was shameful that old people were suffering so the liberals have helped hundreds of thousands by raising money to help them out of poverty. It was written as a political speech.

Source B is written to show how bad conditions were for children. 12 per cent of babies die before they are a year old. Their mothers neglect them and shut them up in rooms while they go out to work. It was written to highlight neglect.

Answer B

They give different views because Source A is a political speech by the Liberal Chancellor Lloyd George. He will be biased because he wants his government to look good. He uses extreme language to highlight how bad things were for old people, 'shameful that the old were bleeding and footsore as they struggled through thorns and brambles'. So in 1909 the Liberals provided pensions of 7s 6d a week for a married couple over the age of 70. They did not have to pay towards this.

Source B on the other hand is written by the Secretary of the National Society of Day Nurseries, so she will not be concerned with old people. But with highlighting the problems of young people: 12 per cent of babies dying in their first year. She speaks of 'great evil', children being 'badly neglected' and having 'just a loaf of bread and a jug of milk'. She is writing in 1910 when children had free medical inspections, but treatment would have to be paid for and many parents couldn't afford this. This didn't change until 1912.

---

8 British Depth Study: How far did British society change between 1939 and the mid-1970s?

Introduction

This topic forms one of two British depth studies. The content is defined through one broad key question, which is broken down into more specific focus points. It is essentially about the changes that took place in British society from the outbreak of the Second World War until the mid-1970s. Much of the supporting material in this teaching unit concentrates on different strategies to use when trying to deliver the core content to students. These strategies take into account differentiated needs, in addition to incorporating Assessment for Learning strategies. This subject will have particular relevance for students as many will be able to relate to a great many of the issues discussed. This is an advantageous situation, and this unit, where possible, has attempted to identify some ways of capitalising on this.

Ideas for starters and plenaries

PAINTING A PICTURE

Students are given a copy of a picture to study for two minutes and are asked to remember its details. This student then passes the details on to another student in the class, who guesses what the message of the source is, based on what they hear from the first student. This type of activity can prove effective in focusing students' attention on pictorial sources, as well as with reinforcing the idea that it is important to distinguish between the details and message of a source.

POINTS OF VIEW

Students are given three or four different sources which are concerned with a similar theme. They are asked to point out the two sources that are the most and least reliable. They then compare these sources with each other. This is an important skill – the nine-mark questions in the exam require this same skill. Students must recognise that a source's reliability can be determined by:

- what it says – is it believable?

- who produced it – are they biased?

- when it was produced – was it too long after the event for the person to remember the details?

- the nature of the source – a poster, for example, normally produces an exaggerated rather than a balanced point of view.

JUST A MINUTE

At the beginning of the lesson, students can be given a topic to research, for example immigration in Britain in 1945. After a given period of time, they are hot-seated at the front of the class and have to talk on that topic for one minute without hesitation, deviation or repetition. Students can challenge the content of what the speaker says by shouting 'challenge'. This will build up the students' knowledge of the facts of the different topics. In addition, the 'challenge' aspect encourages a pressurised (although still friendly) atmosphere, which can be useful when preparing to sit an examination.

WHAT'S NEW?

At the end of each lesson, one student is asked to explain something new they learned that day to another member of the class. The second student must then explain where this bit of knowledge fits into the overall scheme (see worksheet 8.1). This encourages greater attentiveness during class and also helps students get into the habit of seeing the study of history through the lens of an enquiry question.

OPINIONS

Another idea for a plenary could consist of students writing their own opinion about a topic they have learned that day. For instance, they could write their own opinion about whether music was the most important factor in a teenager's life. This reinforces the important skill of coming to an opinion about a historical event, yet it also demonstrates that opinions can differ – it is important that this is reflected in their answers to exam questions.

SLOGANS

Students can take control of their learning by coming up with a useful or memorable slogan to help remember key historical events learned that lesson. For instance, 'The Welfare State Was Well Fair'. Students could collect these slogans as they go through the lessons. The more artistic among them might be able to put them together in some visual way; for example, as a series of posters.

Grabbing attention

Films are a useful way of demonstrating the extent to which British society had changed by the 1960s. One way to do this is by showing carefully selected and suitable scenes from iconic films of the time, such as *Billy Liar* (dir. John Schlesinger, 1963), *Blowup* (dir. Michelangelo Antonioni, 1966) and *Alfie* (dir. Lewis Gilbert, 1966), all available on DVD.

There are many opportunities to use music to illustrate ways in which young people were influenced by bands such as the Beatles and the Rolling Stones. Songs such as 'I Wanna Hold Your Hand', 'Lucy in the Sky with Diamonds' and 'Brown Sugar' all carry potent messages. It is possible to use them in an activity where the students have to analyse the content of the lyrics and spot any links between these words and the behaviour of teenagers.

Newspaper cartoons are also an effective way of provoking debate – not only do they provide some information and opinion about historical events, but they also show the views of society on issues such as immigration and teenagers. It is a good way of getting the students to focus not just on the message of the source, but also on its provenance.

Activities

KEY QUESTION 1: HOW FAR DID BRITISH SOCIETY CHANGE, 1939–75?

Specified content:

- immigrants in Britain in 1939; experiences and impact of groups such as Italian and German prisoners of war, GIs and Commonwealth soldiers; immigration from the Caribbean, India, Pakistan and Uganda, their experiences and British attitudes towards them; their contribution to British society; the riots in 1958 and the activities of the British National Party (National Front); legislation relating to immigration and race in the 1960s and early 1970s; Enoch Powell in 1968; emergence of a multicultural society by the mid-1970s

- the changing role and contribution of women during the Second World War (civil defence, land army, factory work, joining the armed forces and looking after families); the impact of these changes after the war; women in the 1950s; discrimination in the 1960s and early 1970s; impact of the introduction of the pill, the women's lib movement; abortion; the 1969 Divorce Law Reform Act, the 1975 Sex Discrimination Act; the extent of progress made by 1975

- the experiences of children during the Second World War: the Blitz, evacuation, rationing, diet, children's health and education, the absence of fathers; increasing awareness of the condition of working-class children

- the Beveridge report; the creation and impact of the National Health Service

- the lives of teenagers in the 1950s: increased affluence; impact of American culture; introduction of comprehensive education and university expansion; student protests in the 1960s; youth culture, e.g. mods and rockers, growing popularity and impact of rock music, clothes and fashion; teenagers as consumers; reactions of the authorities to these changes; how much the lives of all teenagers were changed by the mid-1970s.

Activity 8.1

Before students tackle this key question, they need a framework in which to record examples of change as they progress with the topic. They can do this using a table in which they record the level of change in the three main areas (immigration, women and teenage culture), and also in other areas (worksheet 8.1). This will help students to remain aware of the overall key question as they go through the course. It will probably be necessary to direct them to fill in the worksheet as they go along, but for some higher-ability students this should not be necessary.

Activity 8.2

Students need to be aware at the beginning that the upcoming lessons are all going to link to the idea of change between the 1950s and the mid-1970s. They first need to be made aware of what is meant by 'British society'. For some students, this activity could be done in the form of a brainstorm, perhaps putting together a spider diagram about what areas this key question will be looking at. This could be differentiated by providing worksheet 8.2, which lists different areas of the British political system, British economy and British society, and asks students to circle the areas they think concern British society. Following on from this, students could work on constructing an agreed definition of what 'British society' means.

Focus point: What impact did the Second World War have on the British people?

Activity 8.3

An effective starter activity could be for students to listen to four separate clips from the Second World War, and then make notes on life during the war for the British people. For four useful audio clips, go to www.heinemann.co.uk/hotlinks, insert the express code 0206T, and click on 'Announcement of war', Public health issues', 'Evacuation of British children', and 'Air raid'.

Following on from this, hold a discussion aimed at helping students understand how the war brought people closer together, and how people became more aware of the different problems others had to face.

Activity 8.4

This should take students to the main activity, which concerns the Beveridge Report. Students are asked to organise 15 listed items into three categories (giant evils, proposed solutions and practical solutions), then link them together (worksheet 8.3). For lower-level students you could put the five giant evils already in place and ask students to find the two solutions that fit each one (worksheet 8.4).

You could then bring this subject to a close by linking this topic back to the table in worksheet 8.1, as it is an example of other events of change. Higher-ability students should be able to consider how the Beveridge Report might indirectly give rise to changes for women, teenagers and immigrants.

Focus point: What immigrants were living in Britain in 1945?

Activity 8.5

A quick starter should concentrate on the idea that immigration to Britain did not begin in 1945. Students are asked to do a card sort on immigration to Britain up to 1945 (worksheet 8.5). For lower-level students, the card sort could be partially completed (worksheet 8.6). Alternatively, students could arrange a timeline in the classroom. Students could be allocated roles as representatives of the different groups of immigrants, then asked to select a card with the appropriate reason from those available, and finally then arrange themselves on the timeline in the correct order.

Activity 8.6

One of the key ingredients for successful exam performance is the ability to answer questions in an appropriate amount of time. Students can practise this skill by using the information from the student book to answer the following questions, giving themselves exactly five minutes for each one.

Describe the following patterns of immigration:

* Jewish immigration
* German and Italian prisoners of war
* GIs and Commonwealth soldiers.

Students can review their own performance by using self-assessment sheets to track whether they feel they were able to describe the points in sufficient detail in that amount of time (worksheet 8.7).

You could then return to the focus point and ask students to write notes about how this lesson has shown some of the immigration patterns at the start of the period. It is important also to discuss which immigrant groups eventually did settle in Britain – but not at this time.

Focus point: Why did different groups migrate to Britain between 1948 and 1972?

Activity 8.7

A useful entry into this focus point could be to launch the 'Population history of Britain' animation on the BBC history website (go to www.heinemann.co.uk/hotlinks, insert the express code 0206T, and click on 'Population history of Britain'). This interactive diagram will help to reinforce students' understanding that immigration has been a constant feature of British history. The animation ends with a reference to immigration from the Caribbean and the Indian subcontinent, which has formed the bulk of the new arrivals since 1945.

Students should then start to focus on the causes of this immigration (and therefore the causes of change). Ask them to use the student book (pages 332–33) to make notes on the various different causes of migration to Britain. For lower-level students, you could use worksheet 8.8, which contains the relevant headings.

Next, students can form small groups and discuss which factor was the most important cause of immigration to Britain. Each group should then present their findings to the rest of the class. Higher-ability students should be encouraged to focus not just on the strength of one particular factor, but on the weaknesses of the other factors.

You could use a plenary to address the issue of causation and also the fact that the students in this lesson arrived at a judgement on a particular question. It is vital to explain to students that in the exam, particularly in the nine-mark questions, students will have to come to a judgement after weighing up different arguments.

Focus point: What were the experiences of immigrants in Britain?

Activity 8.8

A useful way to enter into this topic could be to discuss the various different experiences that immigrants face now. Ask students whether they know of any first-hand experiences of immigrants today. You could compare their experiences and views with those of children interviewed in the national press; go to www.heinemann.co.uk/hotlinks, insert the express code 0206T, and click on 'Nice place you've got here'). In the ensuing discussion, highlight key themes such as racial tensions, protection from the government, and employment patterns. This is a useful way for students to realise that experiences do vary, and that they are not always positive.

Activity 8.9

Lead a discussion about the changing experiences of immigrants, and how there

was no single experience shared by all groups throughout the entire period. As a main activity, students could match up the headings of the different stages to the various descriptions. In addition, they have to think of explanations to show why immigrants went from one experience to another (worksheet 8.9). Lower-ability students could use worksheet 8.10 to match up the headings to the different descriptions of each experience, and then think of three bullet points to summarise that particular experience.

To summarise some of the work that has been done, give students the cartoon in worksheet 8.11, which was published in the 1960s, and see if they can understand its message, the context in which it was written, and what it tells the historian about British society's attitudes towards immigration. To help explain the context, you could briefly explain that Cyril Osborne was a Conservative MP and a member of the Monday Club, who preceded Enoch Powell in arguing against immigration from the new Commonwealth countries, and promoted a Bill to introduce 'periodic and precise limits on immigration' (although the Bill did not become law).

Focus point: What contribution had immigrants made to British society by the early 1970s?

The lesson could start with the playing of Bob Marley's hit record 'Jamming', which could then be used as a basis for a discussion on the contribution of immigrants to British society. It is important to stress that despite the negative experiences of many immigrants during this period of history, they still made an important contribution. This can be quite challenging, as sometimes students do not gravitate towards looking at things from a balanced perspective. But it should be stressed that the content of this lesson reveals a different side to the story of immigration during this period.

Activity 8.10

Working in groups, students could prepare a poster or ICT presentation about the contribution immigrants have made in one particular area. Suggested areas include:

- permanent communities
- economy

- festivals and celebrations

- music

- or one or more groups could choose their own subject area.

They could get their information from the student book (pages 338–39) and focus on presenting a clear message to the rest of the class. Higher-ability students could describe the overall contribution immigrants have made, and focus on reaching a judgement based on the different presentations they see.

In addition, students could have the extra incentive of being marked by their peers as they do their presentation according to the following criteria:

- did it mention the key points?

- did it have a clear message?

- did the group come to an overall judgement?

As a plenary, you could return to worksheet 8.1 and take students through the process of filling in the boxes that concern immigration.

Students could begin by brainstorming what impact the National Health Service (NHS) has made on their own lives. Do they use the NHS? Do they know of anyone else who has used it? What service have they received? Did it help? This will help them recognise that if the NHS is able to make an impact on people's lives nowadays, it is likely to have had even more of an impact in the 1940s.

Activity 8.11

Using the student book for information (pages 344–45), students should write a report for a local newspaper on the day after the NHS came into operation. In their article they should include a bit of background about what healthcare was like before the Second World War, some details about the National Health Service Act, and, finally, a warning of the potential problems that might arise.

The end of this lesson could focus on the decision by Aneurin Bevan to resign. Engage the class in a debate about whether or not this was the right thing to do. You could enliven the debate by asking for volunteers to speak as Aneurin Bevan and Hugh Gaitskell, and ask the class to vote on who they support in light of the arguments they have heard. Encourage students,

once they have made their choice, to follow it up with an explanation. Finally, students could be directed back again to worksheet 8.1 and represent this change in the appropriate category.

Focus point: What was the impact of the National Health Service on people's lives

Most students ought to have some knowledge and understanding of the NHS. It is important for the teacher to explore the students' own experiences of the NHS so that the class can gain an insight into the type of work it does. The discussion could then be extended by asking questions about the management of the NHS, the cost of using the NHS, and how it is possible to provide a service which is free.

For this unit, the most important aspect of the NHS which students need to be aware of relates to the significance of its creation. Students can form working groups to look at the different ways in which the National Health Service Act was significant. These could include: its impact on the health of the nation; how it established the principle of equal opportunity; the way its existence demonstrates that government felt it had a large role to play in the health of the nation; the degree to which it raised expectations about what the population could expect from the state; and, finally, its effect in making Britain more attractive to people from other countries.

Focus point: What was life like for most women in the 1950s?

It is important for the students to be aware of what the situation was really like for women in the 1950s in order to judge properly the scale of the change that had taken place by the 1970s. Students could do this in several ways:

- Looking at images of women from the 1950s and images of women today to compare the way they looked and dressed.

- Investigating key statistics such as how many women were MPs in the 1950s compared with today.

- Analysing cartoons about the role of women from the national newspapers of the 1950s to understand the general view of society towards women at the time.

Focus point: How were women discriminated against in the 1960s and early 1970s?

This lesson could begin with students looking at a cartoon from the *Daily Mail* on 3 February 1960 ('Every morning when my husband goes to work I hate him…'). Discuss with students what this newspaper cartoon says about what life was like for women in the 1950s and early 1960s. With higher-ability students, try to take the discussion forward by asking why women felt that they could and should do more than what they were already doing.

Activity 8.12

Using the student book (pages 346–47), students should provide answers to the following questions:

- Is it fair to say that the Second World War did not produce much change for women? (Show both points of view.)

- Were there any changes in education? (If so, explain your answer.)

- Were there any changes in employment? (If so, explain your answer.)

This could then be supplemented by students considering the different options open at this time to women who wanted to change their status and lives, and the advantages and disadvantages of each one. Lower-ability students could be given some examples of different options and write down the likely advantages and disadvantages of each one (worksheet 8.12).

Complete the lesson by asking students to guess which option was eventually chosen for women, and whether or not they are surprised by this.

Focus point: How much change had taken place for women by 1975?

It is worth proceeding with this focus point next, as it will help to have some contextual understanding of the type of change that occurred for women before investigating the causes of this change. To start this lesson, students could write down what they think are women's most important rights. They should try to put this into some kind of order, starting with what they consider the most important. Their list will hopefully be similar to the demands made by the feminist movement in the 1960s, and should help them understand the extent of change that occurred for women during this time.

Activity 8.13

After these ideas have been discussed, students should then analyse what changes actually took place (worksheet 8.13). Encourage them to think about more than simply the details of each change – they need to consider the effects these events had on women's lives. Students should then be expected to come to an overall judgement about the level of change which had taken place for women by 1975.

Finally, this lesson can conclude with a quick discussion about which was the most significant Act or event. Encourage each student to follow up their judgement with an explanation. Make clear to them the importance of coming up with an overall judgement at the end of each answer to a nine-mark question.

Focus point: What factors led to changes in the roles of women?

Students can recap what has been covered in the previous two lessons and fill in worksheet 8.1. As part of this process, ask them which area of the worksheet they have not filled in fully for women. Hopefully, the answer 'What caused the change?' should emerge, which should instil further enthusiasm for the coming lesson.

Activity 8.14

For the main activity, students divide into groups and concentrate on one of the four main causes of change in the roles and lives of women. Their task is to prepare a presentation which describes what the situation was like for women at the start of the period, the end of the period, and the role of their particular factor in bringing about this change. The students could then be marked by their peers as they do their presentation according to the following criteria (worksheet 8.14).

- Did they mention the situation for women at both the beginning and end of the period?

- Did they present the case for the importance of their factor in a clear way?

- Did the group show why their factor was important compared with the other factors?

Finally, students should bring their study of changes to women's lives to a close by filling in the remainder of worksheet 8.1.

This lesson is about whether or not students feel the judgement of Harold Macmillan – 'You never had it so good' – was an accurate description of life in the 1950s. First reinforce the concept in students' minds that any question such as this must show *both* points of view, and be followed by an overall judgement which is supported by the evidence. While higher-ability students might reasonably be expected to answer this question without any assistance, some differentiation in the form of a writing frame will probably be needed (worksheet 8.15).

Activity 8.15

Using the student book, students should complete worksheet 8.16 where they are asked to explain the effects of certain changes on people's lives. This could be differentiated by including some keywords to help with this explanation.

Next, students need to think abut the other side of the argument, which will require them to refer back to the experiences of immigrants and women. They should factor in the key points which will help them to present an alternative view. Following on from this, they should come up with an overall judgement about whether they think Macmillan's quote is an accurate description.

To finish off this lesson, some of the students could read their answers out. As they do so, emphasise the different stages of the answer. The new information acquired in the lesson should be added to the relevant box in worksheet 8.1.

Focus point: What was it like growing up in the 1950s?

One possible starter activity for this lesson is to ask the students to engage in a hypothetical scenario which involves them choosing to have only one of the following (TV, radio and magazines) for the remainder of their lives. After some discussion, the teacher can then explain that the 1950s saw the birth of the consumer society, which allowed many people to experience these three things for the very first time.

However, it is also worth stressing the comparisons between society during the 1950s and today (see worksheet 8.17) to make the point that although the 1950s represented a sizeable change from what had taken place

before, it was also the precursor to even more change throughout the next five decades.

Focus point: Why were there changes in the lives of teenagers in the 1960s?

Students will probably find the idea of 'a history of teenagers' slightly strange. It is important to make the point that the concept of teenagers did not develop until the 1950s.

A useful starter would be to show a short clip of Harry Enfield's 'Kevin the teenager' for today's stereotypical view of teenagers. For one example go to www.heinemann.co.uk/hotlinks, insert the express code 0206T, and click on 'Kevin'.

Then discuss with students what influences they think have an effect on their lives. You could do this in the form a spider diagram. Following on from this, students should use the information in the student book (pages 352–53) to complete worksheet 8.18 about the influences on teenagers' lives in the 1950s.

Then ask students to compare the types of things that influence their lives today with those that affected the teenagers in the 1950s.

Focus point: How did teenagers and students behave in the 1960s?

To start this lesson, students could analyse a historical cartoon of the 1960s which depicts mods and rockers. Afterwards, the teacher should direct a discussion on the following themes:

- what were the characteristics of teenage behaviour?
- what were the consequences of teenage behaviour?
- what were other people's attitudes towards it?

There are of course very many video clips of the time available. Just a few examples include:

- a clip of mods and rockers in the 1960s
- a Pathe news report on the Beatles in 1963
- a personal video of the Isle of Wight festival in 1970.

Go to www.heinemann.co.uk/hotlinks, insert the express code 0206T, and click on 'Brighton', 'Beatles' and '1970'.

Activity 8.16

Students could be asked to talk to their parents – and grandparents – about their teenage years. Using these conversations, the student book and other resources, ask them to focus on a particular teenage subculture of the 1960s or early 1970s, and produce a 'mood board' displaying images, texts, cartoons or any other media that convey the spirit of the time. Song lyrics such as 'Lucy in the sky with diamonds' (Beatles, 1967), or many others, could be useful here.

After this has been done, students then display their mood boards to the rest of the class and explain why this choice inspired them. The aim is that, by the end of the lesson, students do not just have an idea of *how* students behaved in the 1960s and early 1970s – but also an idea about *why* they behaved in such a way.

Focus point: How far did the lives of teenagers change in the 1960s and early 1970s?

As seen in the previous lesson, 'teenage behaviour' covered a wide range of views and ideologies. At the same time, many had more opportunities available to them than ever before, particularly in education.

Activity 8.17

For the main activity, students can organise different statements into an order which makes sense (worksheet 8.19). This should lead into a discussion about the expansion of university education.

To conclude, students should complete worksheet 8.1. A useful revision task for students would be to formulate all the information in this worksheet into points for an essay, so that they can make sense of how all that they have learned fits into the key question. Lower-level students may need some prompts (worksheet 8.20).

Grade Studio

USING EXAM QUESTIONS, MARK SCHEMES AND PEER ASSESSMENT TO IMPROVE ATTAINMENT

Grade Studio has been designed to help both students and teachers interpret GCSE history mark schemes.

Grade Studio has a clear and explicit focus on levels. It is the point at which the teaching and practice in the student book becomes focused on moving between levels, and therefore the learning becomes increasingly personalised and improves students' chances of achieving better grades.

The activities in the student book and on the CD-ROM should help students to improve their understanding of how to answer different types of exam questions. Activity 8.14 is based on students' peer review of one another's work, which will help them to understand what is required to obtain marks at the different levels.

Worksheet 8.20 provides a source for analysis and a mark scheme to help familiarise students with what is required at different levels.

8.1 Overview of change in Britain

	Immigration	Women	Teenage culture
1 Situation in 1939			
2 Causes of change			
3 Situation by the mid-1970s			
Other examples of change in this period			

8.2 What is meant by British society?

This chapter is about the changes in **British society**. You need to be clear about what is meant by **British society**.

The 12 themes listed below are concerned with either British society, the British economy, or the British political system.

Circle the four themes that are concerned with **British society**.

Health of the nation	Immigration	Teenage culture
Women's rights	Labour–Conservative rivalry	Winston Churchill
Decolonisation of the Empire	Relationship between the UK and the USA	Nationalisation (state ownership)
Wages	Inflation	Price

8.3 Solutions to society's giant evils 1

The issues listed below can be divided into three categories:

- giant evils of British society
- proposed solutions
- practical solutions (government laws).

Your task is to match each giant evil with both a proposed and a practical solution and put them in the table below.

	Giant evil	Proposed solution	Practical solution
1			
2			
3			
4			
5			

1944 Education Act; free primary and secondary education for all; tripartite system

1946 National Insurance Act; benefits for the sick, disabled and unemployed; maternity pay; pensions; national assistance

1946 National Insurance Act; benefits for the sick, disabled, and unemployed; maternity pay; pensions; national assistance

1946 New Towns Act (Milton Keynes, Telford, Stevenage)

A new health service for all citizens

A wider National Insurance scheme

Disease

Full employment

Idleness

Ignorance

More and better housing

More and better schools

Pre-fab housing; 157,000 pre-fabs built

Squalor

Want

8.4 Solutions to society's giant evils 2

The solutions listed below can be divided into two categories:

- proposed solutions
- practical solutions (government laws)

Your task is to match each giant evil with both a proposed and a practical solution and put them in the table below.

	Giant evil	Proposed solution	Practical solution
1	Disease		
2	Idleness		
3	Ignorance		
4	Squalor		
5	Want		

Proposed solutions

A new health service for all citizens

A wider National Insurance scheme

Full employment

More and better housing

More and better schools

Practical solutions

1944 Education Act; free primary and secondary education for all; tripartite system

1946 National Insurance Act; benefits for the sick, disabled and unemployed; maternity pay; pensions; national assistance

1946 National Insurance Act; benefits for the sick, disabled, and unemployed; maternity pay; pensions; national assistance.

1946 New Towns Act (Milton Keynes, Telford, Stevenage)

Pre-fab housing; 157,000 pre-fabs built

8.5 Different reasons for British immigration 1

The table shows a list of key dates when different groups of immigrants came to Britain. Sort out the cards to decide which group came at which time, and why.

Era	Newcomers	Reason
Pre-1066		
1066		
1500s		
1680s		
1840s		
1880s		
1914–18		
1939–45		
1946		

8.5 Different reasons for British immigration 1

Newcomers:

Dutch Protestants	Eastern Europeans	French Protestants
Irish	Jews	Normans
Refugees	Refugees	Romans, Saxons, Vikings

Reasons:

Invasion force	To escape from communism	Religious persecution
Potato famine in Ireland	To escape the fighting in mainland Europe	To escape Nazi rule
Pogroms in Russia	Invasion force	Religious persecution

8.6 Different reasons for British immigration 2 (see page 184)

Reasons:

Invasion force	To escape from communism	Religious persecution
Potato famine in Ireland	To escape the fighting in mainland Europe	To escape Nazi rule
Pogroms in Russia	Invasion force	Religious persecution

8.6 Different reasons for British immigration 2

The table shows the arrival of different groups of immigrants in Britain. Sort out the cards to decide why each group came.

Era	Newcomers	Reason
Pre-1066	Romans, Saxons, Vikings	
1066	Normans	
1500s	Dutch Protestants	
1680s	French Protestants	
1840s	Irish	
1880s	Jews	
1914–18	Refugees	
1939–45	Refugees	
1946	Eastern Europeans	

8.7 Describing patterns of immigration

	Key points	Did you get all the key points?	Did you need more time?	What could you do to make sure you answer questions in time – without compromising quality?
Jewish immigration	10,000 Jewish children Kindertransport Nazi persecution			
German and Italian prisoners of war	300,000 PoWs Displaced persons Work-permit schemes Aliens			
GIs and Commonwealth soldiers	Dominions 100,000 marriages			

8.8 Reasons for British immigration, 1948–72

Why did different groups migrate to Britain between 1948 and 1972?

1 The 1948 British Nationality Act

....

....

....

....

....

2 Likelihood of finding work

....

....

....

....

3 Romantic vision of Britain

....

....

....

....

4 Economic problems at home

....

....

....

....

5 Violence at home

....

....

....

....

6 Other factors

....

....

....

....

8.9 Explaining the treatment of British immigrants

List of headings:

- Conservative government gets tougher on immigration laws (Commonwealth Immigrants Act 1962)

- Enoch Powell draws attention to racial tensions ('Rivers of blood' speech, 1968)

- Increased tension (riots in 1958)

- Anti-immigrant political party (establishment of the National Front in 1967)

- A gradual, uneasy welcome

- Labour government attempts to protect immigrants (Race Relations Act 1965 and 1968)

Heading 1: ....

Experience 1

On arrival, immigrants usually settled in a relatively small number of towns and cities, because they preferred to live in communities of people with the same background. They were often discriminated against in housing. At this time, it was perfectly lawful for landlords to stipulate 'No Coloureds' or 'No Blacks'. Some landlords, like the notorious Peter Rachman, took advantage of the situation by charging very high rents for overcrowded accommodation. In addition to this specific discrimination, many black immigrants encountered a generally racist response to their arrival.

Reasons for Experience 1: ....

....

....

....

....

Heading 2: ....

Experience 2

In 1958, white youths attacked a group of West Indians. On the night of Saturday 30 August in Notting Hill, a mob of 300–400 white people, many of them Teddy Boys, were seen on Bramley Road attacking the houses of West Indian residents. The disturbances, rioting and attacks continued every night until they finally petered out by 5 September. The Metropolitan Police arrested over 140 people during the two weeks of the disturbance, mostly white youths, but also many black people who were found carrying weapons. Although the Notting Hill Carnival was started in January 1959 as a positive response to the riots, the overall effect was that tension increased between the black community and the Metropolitan Police, which was accused by the black community of not taking their reports of racial attacks seriously.

Reasons for Experience 2: ....

....

....

....

....

Heading 3: ....

Experience 3:
In 1962, the Commonwealth Immigrants Act imposed restrictions on immigration into Britain from the Commonwealth for the first time. Whereas previously citizens of the Commonwealth of Nations had extensive rights to migrate to the UK, now the government permitted only those with government-issued employment vouchers to settle. This was a response from Harold Macmillan's government to the many complaints made against the new arrivals, such as they would not work, or that they would work for lower wages which undercut other workers, or that they were responsible for crime, and finally that they were unwilling to mix with local communities. This trend of restricting immigration increased as time went on, and by 1972 only holders of work permits, or people with parents or grandparents born in the UK, could gain entry.

Reasons for Experience 3: ....

....

....

....

Heading 4: ....

Experience 4
Many politicians, were appalled by the level of prejudice the immigrants had to endure. The 1965 Race Relations Act made it illegal to discriminate on grounds of race in public places. As well as this, the Race Relations Board and the National Committee for Commonwealth Immigrants were set up to handle racial complaints and to promote contacts between the different races in Britain, respectively. The 1968 Race Relations Act went further than the 1965 Act, as it outlawed discrimination in housing, employment, the provision of goods and services, trade unions and advertising. The legislation did not succeed in changing many people's attitudes.

Reasons for Experience 4: ....

....

....

....

Heading 5: ....

Experience 5
Enoch Powell was a Conservative MP who held strong views about immigration and used speeches to warn Britain of its dangers. On 20 April 1968 in Birmingham, Powell said that he could see storm clouds brewing for Britain because of the admission of immigrants. He pointed to the growing numbers of immigrants and their unwillingness to integrate and famously said, referring to a quotation from ancient Rome, 'I seem to see the River Tiber foaming with much blood'. The speech produced intense interest and anger. Many immigrants felt insulted and believed their time here might be limited. Although the press condemned his speech, Powell received thousands of letters of support, which showed that anti-immigration feeling certainly existed in Britain.

Reasons for Experience 5: ....

....

....

....

8.10 Explaining the treatment of British immigrants 2

List of headings:

- Conservative government gets tougher on immigration laws (Commonwealth Immigrants Act 1962)

- Enoch Powell exploits racial tensions ('Rivers of blood' speech, 1968)

- Increased tension (riots in 1958)

- Anti-immigrant political party (establishment of the National Front in 1967)

- A gradual, uneasy welcome

- Labour government attempts to protect immigrants (Race Relations Act 1965 and 1968)

Heading 1: ....

Experience 1
On arrival, immigrants usually settled in a relatively small number of towns and cities because they preferred to live in communities of people with the same background. They were discriminated against in housing. At this time, it was perfectly lawful for landlords to stipulate 'No Coloureds' or 'No Blacks'. Some landlords, like the notorious Peter Rachman, took advantage of the situation by charging very high rents for overcrowded accommodation. In addition to this specific discrimination, many black immigrants encountered a generally racist response to their arrival.

Summary of Experience 1:

- ....
- ....
- ....

Heading 2: ....

Experience 2
In 1958, white youths attacked a group of West Indians. On the night of Saturday 30 August in Notting Hill, a mob of 300–400 white people, many of them Teddy Boys, were seen on Bramley Road attacking the houses of West Indian residents. The disturbances, rioting and attacks continued every night until they finally petered out by 5 September. The Metropolitan Police arrested over 140 people during the two weeks of the disturbance, mostly white youths, but also many black people who were found carrying weapons. Although the Notting Hill Carnival was started in January 1959 as a positive response to the riots, the overall effect was that tension increased between the black community and the Metropolitan Police, which was accused by the black community of not taking their reports of racial attacks seriously.

Summary of Experience 2:

- ....
- ....
- ....

Heading 3: ....

Experience 3:
In 1962, the Commonwealth Immigrants Act imposed restrictions on immigration into Britain from the Commonwealth for the first time. Whereas previously citizens of the Commonwealth of Nations had extensive rights to migrate to the UK, now the government permitted only those with government-issued employment vouchers to settle. This was a response from Harold Macmillan's government to the many complaints made against the new arrivals, such as they would not work, or that they would work for lower wages which undercut other workers, or that they were responsible for crime, and finally that they were unwilling to mix with local communities. This trend of restricting immigration increased as time went on, and by 1972 only holders of work permits, or people with parents or grandparents born in the UK, could gain entry.

Summary of Experience 3:

- ....
- ....
- ....

Heading 4: ....

Experience 4
Many politicians were appalled by the level of prejudice the immigrants had to endure. The 1965 Race Relations Act made it illegal to discriminate on grounds of race in public places. As well as this, the Race Relations Board and the National Committee for Commonwealth Immigrants were set up to handle racial complaints and to promote contacts between the different races in Britain, respectively. The 1968 Race Relations Act went further than the 1965 Act, as it outlawed discrimination in housing, employment, the provision of goods and services, trade unions and advertising. However, the legislation did not succeed in changing many people's attitudes.

Summary of Experience 4:

- ....
- ....
- ....

Heading 5: ....

Experience 5
Enoch Powell was a Conservative MP who held strong views about immigration and used speeches to warn Britain of its dangers. On 20 April 1968 in Birmingham, Powell said that he could see storm clouds brewing for Britain because of the admission of immigrants. He pointed to the growing numbers of immigrants and their unwillingness to integrate and famously said, referring to a quotation from ancient Rome, 'I seem to see the River Tiber foaming with much blood'. The speech produced intense interest and anger. Many immigrants felt insulted and believed their time here might be limited. Although the press condemned his speech, Powell received thousands of letters of support, showed that anti-immigration feeling certainly existed in Britain.

Summary of Experience 5:

- ....
- ....
- ....

8.11 Source analysis

What does this source say about British attitudes towards immigration?

What is the context in which it was written?

What is the message of this source?

Maybe Cyril Osborne is right—the fewer immigrants we have, the better off we'll be

8.12 Evaluating the options for bringing about change for women

We are in the 1950s. At this time, women do not have anywhere near the same rights as men – but women who want change are not sure what they should do about it. Below are some of their potential options. Write down at least one advantage and one disadvantage of each option.

Option 1: Do nothing and hope the British government soon sees sense.

Advantages: ....

....

....

....

Disadvantages: ....

....

....

....

Option 2: Copy the example of the suffragettes and behave violently (destroying property, kidnapping politicians) to put pressure on the government.

Advantages: ....

....

....

....

Disadvantages: ....

....

....

....

Option 3: Launch an active movement that campaigns solely for women to have more rights.

Advantages: ....

....

....

....

Disadvantages: ....

....

....

....

8.13 Legislation for women during this period

Legislation or change	Area with which the Act or change was concerned	How was it passed/ agreed?	Why was there a need for it?	What were its effects?
Oral contraceptive pill made available on the NHS (1961)				
Abortion Act (1967)				
Divorce Reform Act (1969)				
Equal Pay Act (1970)				
Sex Discrimination Act (1975)				

8.14 Causes of change in the lives and role of women

	Did they mention the situation for women at both the beginning and end of the period?	Did they present the case for the importance of their factor in a clear way?	Did the group show why their factor was important compared with the other factors?
Group 1 – Women's Liberation Movement			
Group 2 – European influence			
Group 3 – attitude of the Labour government			
Group 4 – Private Members' Bills			

8.15 Was Harold Macmillan right?

'You've never had it so good!'

Is this an accurate description of life in Britain during the 1950s?

In 1957, Harold Macmillan made a speech to his fellow Conservatives in which he celebrated the success of Britain's post-war economy, while at the same time urging wage restraint and warning against inflation. His most memorable line came when he said: *'Let us be frank about it: most of our people have never had it so good'*. However, while there is some evidence to back up his comments, there is also evidence to the contrary.

Evidence which backs up his statement includes:

- rationing
- the consumer society
- housing.

Firstly...

....

....

....

Secondly...

....

....

....

Thirdly...

....

....

....

On the other hand, the experiences of women and immigrants do not necessarily support Macmillan's view.

In the case of women's lives...

....

....

....

Regarding the experiences of immigrants...

....

....

....

Overall, it is evident from the information gathered that...

....

....

....

8.16 Effect of 1950s society

Feature of the 1950s	Effect it had on people at the time
End of rationing	
Consumer society	
More housing	

Which one was the most beneficial to people's lives?

....

....

....

....

Why did these benefits occur in the 1950s and not at the end of the 1940s?

....

....

....

8.17 Comparing the 1950s with today

Put the following words from the list below into either the '1950s', 'Today' or 'Both' column:

Elvis Presley   **Festival of Britain**   **Reality TV shows**

James Dean   **TV**   *Grease*   **David Beckham**

Foreign holidays   **Musical chairs**   **Laptop**   **Harry Potter**

Rock'n'roll   **Movies**   **Attendance at football games**

1950s	Both	Today
1.	1.	1.
2.	2.	2.
3.	3.	3.
4.	4.	4.
5.	5.	5.
6.	6.	6.

8.18 How did teenagers live in the 1950s?

There were three main influences on teenagers in the 1950s:

Cultural influnces:

....

....

....

....

....

....

Consumer goods:

....

....

....

....

....

....

Financial power:

....

....

....

....

....

....

Extension questions:

Which one was likely to have been the most important?

....

....

....

....

Why were these influences able to have such an effect on teenagers?

....

....

....

....

8.19 Comprehensive education

Put the following events into an order that makes sense.

The main consequence of the new comprehensive schools was that they allowed many children to gain access to further and higher education and prevented many children from feeling like second-class citizens on failing the 11-plus.
This new free education was managed under the tripartite system, which consisted of grammar schools, secondary technical schools (very few were ever built) and secondary modern schools.
The new comprehensive schools provided free education from 11 to 16 and did not select children on the basis of academic ability. Following the 1964 General Election, the new Labour government instructed all local authorities to prepare plans for the creation of comprehensive schools.
Due to the lack of technical schools, there ended up being fierce competition for the available grammar school places, which put a great deal of pressure on young people at an early age. However, there was a great uproar at the perceived low standards in the secondary modern schools which, from the late 1940s onwards, paved the way for the introduction of the comprehensive school.
The 1944 Education Act ensured that secondary education in England, Wales and Northern Ireland was free to all pupils at least up until the age of 14.

Why was the growth of comprehensive education so important for students in the 1960s and 1970s?

....

....

....

....

....

....

....

What effect do you think the increase in comprehensive education had on universities?

....

....

....

....

....

....

....

8.20 How far did British society change between the 1950s and the 1970s?

These three decades saw many changes in British society, particularly with regard to immigration, women's lives and youth culture. There were also changes to the welfare state and in consumer habits. In order to answer this question, it is important to go through each area in turn.

At the start of the period, immigrants were...

....

....

....

By the end of the period...

....

....

....

At the end of the war, the role of women...

....

....

....

However, by the end of the war....

....

....

....

Throughout the 1950s, the concept of a 'teenager' hardly existed. Most young people...

....

....

....

By the 1960s, though, teenagers...

....

....

....

In addition, the Beveridge Report caused a great deal of change, particularly in the area of health. This can be shown by...

....

....

....

Overall, it is clear that British society changed a great deal during this time. This was mainly because...

....

....

....

GradeStudio

8.21 Grade Studio: Immigration mark scheme

> **SOURCE A**
>
> England was a strange place in May 1968. On the one hand, immigrants were playing more of a part in the social and economic life of Britain but on the other hand, Enoch Powell was gathering support. Some people would even graffiti the slogan, 'Powell for PM' onto walls. It was very odd that these two events should happen at the same time.
>
> An anonymous account of London in 1968.

Are you surprised that the content of this source refers to 1968? Use details of the source and your knowledge to explain your answer. **[8 marks]**

Level 1:	No attempt to answer the question but just a commentary of what is taking place. e.g. Immigrants were playing more of a part in British society.	**[1–2 marks]**
Level 2:	Comes to a judgement based on the material in the source but does not refer to the source. e.g. There was a debate about who should lead Britain.	**[2–3 marks]**
Level 3:	Gives one point of view – that it is not surprising – with reference to the source and own knowledge. e.g. No, there was much discussion about immigration and race relations. Powell was a politician who wanted to stop immigration and the source highlighted the debate – graffiti slogans of 'Powell for PM' are likely to be a direct consequence of more involvement of immigrants in British jobs.	**[4–5 marks]**
Level 4:	Gives one point of view – that it is surprising – with reference to the source and own knowledge. e.g. Yes, there was much discussion of immigration and race relations, and tension was increased by Powell's 'Rivers of Blood' speech in Birmingham in April 1968. Consequently, it is strange that the author of the source sees it as 'odd' that increasing immigration and increasing support for Powell should go together. Also, if this source was not written by a supporter of Powell, it is a strange thing to write: it unintentionally provides a great deal of publicity for Powell as it makes him out to be very popular.	**[5–6 marks]**
Level 5:	Gives both points of view and refers to the source and own knowledge. e.g. No, there was much discussion of immigration and race relations. Powell was a politician who wanted to stop immigration and the source highlights the debate and the situation at the time accurately. However, it is surprising since there was so much tension created by Powell's 'Rivers of Blood' speech in Birmingham in April 1968 that publishing a source which mentions the words 'Powell for PM', could have been insensitive. It is also strange how the writer cannot see the connection between increasing immigration and the resulting political support for Enoch Powell.	**[7–8 marks]**

Your task

Write the answer to this question in your own words and ensure that: every time you refer to the source <u>underline</u> what you write. Every time you refer to your own knowledge write in CAPITALS.